Logic with trees

Logic with trees is a new and original introduction to modern formal logic. Unlike most texts on the subject, it includes discussions of more philosophical issues such as truth, conditionals and modal logic. Preferring explanation and argument to intimidatingly rigorous development, Colin Howson presents the formal material in a clear and informal style that both beginners and those with some knowledge of formal methods will appreciate. Examples and exercises guide readers through the book, and answers to selected exercises at the end allow them to monitor their own progress. *Logic with Trees* gives students

- a complete and clear account of the truth tree system for first-order logic
- an understanding of the importance of logic and of its relevance to other disciplines
- the skills to grasp sophisticated formal reasoning techniques that are necessary to explore complex metalogic
- and the ability to contest claims that 'ordinary' reasoning is well represented by formal first-order logic

Howson's carefully planned textbook covers both truth-functional and full first-order logic, using the truth tree or semantic tableau approach; he gives completeness and soundness proofs for both truth-functional and first-order trees, and makes extensive use of induction. In addition, he discusses alternative deductive systems, transfinite numbers and categoricity, the Löwnheim–Skolem theorems and the celebrated theorems of Gödel and Church. The book concludes with an account of Kripke's attempt to solve the Liar Paradox and a discussion of the weaknesses of the truth-functional account of conditionals.

Logic with Trees will be particularly useful for those who feel wary of formal methods, since it shows how simple even quite sophisticated formal reasoning can be. It will be of interest to students of philosophy at undergraduate level and beyond, as well as to students of mathematics and computer science.

Colin Howson is Reader in Logic at the London School of Economics and Political Science.

The London School of Economics and Political Science/ Routledge

Books published under the joint imprint of LSE/Routledge are works of high academic merit approved by the Publications Committee of the London School of Economics and Political Science. These publications are drawn from the wide range of academic studies in the social sciences for which the LSE has an international reputation.

Logic with trees

An introduction to symbolic logic

Colin Howson

London and New York

First published 1997
by Routledge
11 New Fetter Lane, London EC4P 4EE

Simultaneously published in the USA and Canada
by Routledge
29 West 35th Street, New York, NY 10001

© 1997 Colin Howson

Typeset in Times Ten by Florencetype Ltd, Stoodleigh, Devon
Printed and bound in Great Britain by Mackays of Chatham PLC, Chatham, Kent

British Library Cataloguing in Publication Data
A catalogue record for this book is available from the British Library

Library of Congress Cataloguing in Publication Data
Howson, Colin.
  Logic with trees: an introduction to symbolic logic/Colin Howson.
  p. cm.
  1. Logic, Symbolic and mathematical. I. Title.
  BC135.H68 1996 96–7315
  160–dc20

ISBN   0–415–13341–6 (hbk)
        0–415–13342–4 (pbk)

To Minou, who would have enjoyed sitting on this book

Contents

Acknowledgments

I should like to express my gratitude to Tony Dale, Gustavo Fernandez and Tony Ungar for their detailed comments on earlier versions of this book. Other people who have offered very helpful advice and discussion are Rose Gibson, R. I. G. Hughes, Peter Milne, Margaret Morrison, Jan von Plato, Demetris Portides, Adam Rieger, Aldo Visintin, John Worrall, Elie Zahar, and many undergraduates and postgraduates of the London School of Economics. I should like to express my thanks also to Theresa Hunt, Pat Gardner, Cynthia Ma and Towfic Shomar for their assistance in preparing the typescript.

Introduction

Logic was one of the first scientific disciplines to be identified and studied systematically. For various reasons, which historians of ideas still disagree about, the Stoic and Aristotelian beginnings were left undeveloped, and no real advances were made until over two thousand years later. Then, in the second half of the nineteenth century, a succession of mathematicians took up the subject, and as a result of their attentions it grew rapidly into a discipline of great power; it has generated results which have transformed the way we think, at a quite fundamental level. In particular, it has given us information about the limitations of theorising that could hardly have been imagined, even if the questions could have been formulated, only a century ago. Some of these results have been interpreted in extraordinary ways. In Douglas Hofstadter's best-seller *Gödel, Escher, Bach* (1979), two celebrated theorems of Gödel have been compared to the works of Bach. Elsewhere, they have convinced some people that we are more than machines, and others that we are no more than machines.

On a more practical level, however, logic is now acknowledged to be of central importance, particularly in computer science and artificial intelligence, and anyone who wants to work in the area of software development will have to have an increasingly considerable degree of acquaintance with it. 'Logic', as the foreword to one of a rapidly increasing number of recent texts on logic oriented towards applications in computing attests, is 'the calculus of computer science'[1]. Indeed, because of its central role there, logic is now playing a similar enabling role in the information technology revolution to that which mathematics played in the scientific revolution of the seventeenth and eighteenth centuries.

Logic texts exemplify a variety of proof systems. The one used in this book is the increasingly popular, arguably the most user-friendly, and the most obviously machine-implementable system, based on the semantic tableau method pioneered by the Dutch logician Evert Beth. It has been developed and simplified since, receiving its classic exposition in Raymond Smullyan (1968). Recently Richard Jeffrey has used a simplified form of it in his marvellous *Formal Logic: Its Scope and Limits* (1994). The present book is much more elementary than Smullyan's, while I have attempted to introduce more standard material about first-order logic than Jeffrey does (including, in Chapter 3, an exposure to the crucially important role in many metatheorems played by induction), and less of the theory of computation. I have also added some 'philosophical' discussions, of truth and the Liar Paradox, categoricity, second-order logic, modal logic and conditionals.

This book can be used in various ways. Chapters 1, 2, 4 (the unstarred sections), 5 and 6 are material for an introductory course, while 1–9 would make up a comprehensive one-year course in first-order logic, and are suitable for students at both undergraduate and postgraduate level with no mathematical background who want to be able to understand the mesh of syntactic and semantic arguments that makes up modern formal logic. Chapter 11 attempts to give some idea of the depth and significance of the classic results of modern (meta)logic, while Chapter 12 outlines some of the ways in which first-order logic has been extended, and some of the principal objections brought against the representation of conditionals in first-order logic. These chapters could be used as a supplementary text in philosophy of logic, with the earlier material used as a source of reference for the main technical results of first-order logic. Proofs of soundness and completeness theorems for truth-functional and full first-order truth trees are given in Chapters 4 and 8. In Chapter 10 there is a discussion of examples of two of the main alternative proof systems, Hilbert-style and Natural Deduction. Various sections of the first eight chapters are starred, to indicate that the material is not so elementary there, and starred exercises indicate a greater level of difficulty.

I have tried to fulfil three principal aims: (i) to give a complete and clear account of the truth tree system for first-order logic, and of the important metatheorems associated with it; (ii) to show why logic is an exciting and flourishing discipline; and (iii) to show that the sorts of formal techniques exploited in proving even some 'deep' metalogical results are within the grasp of even determinedly non-mathematical students; for example, the various soundness and completeness proofs are not intrinsically difficult, and are certainly within the capacity of the non-specialist in logic to work through and understand.

There are frequent failures in the book to achieve, and sometimes to approach, the highest standards of rigour, which I hope can be pardoned as sacrifices to clarity. There is no shortage of very rigorous texts for those who want them. One particular lapse is a more or less systematic failure to make explicit the 'use–mention' distinction. Labouring that distinction with typographical devices of one sort or another both disfigures a text and makes it difficult to read. Usually context suffices to distinguish use from mention, and there are warnings where I believe that there is any danger of conflation. Those who believe that departure from the use–mention orthodoxy approaches mortal sin may be induced to take a more lenient view by noting the inclusion of a discussion of and running references to the object-language–metalanguage distinction, and a separate discussion of the Liar Paradox.

Note

1 Foreword to Garton 1990.

Part I

Truth-functional logic

Chapter 1

The basics

1 DEDUCTIVELY VALID INFERENCE

There is much more to logic than the question of what makes *inferences* deductively valid or invalid, but to most people that is what logic is all about, so that is where we shall begin. One of the most basic features of these inferences is that they seem to be composed of *declarative sentences*, that is to say sentences which make assertions capable of being true or false. 'Boris Yeltsin became President of Russia in 1993', 'All hydrogen atoms have one proton in their nucleus' and 'Michelangelo painted the ceiling of the Sistine Chapel' are declarative sentences, and (we believe) true ones at that. 'Shut that door!' and 'Is Hanoi in Scotland?' are not. Neither is Chomsky's funny example 'Colourless green ideas sleep furiously', which has the grammatical form, but only the form, of a fact-stating sentence.

So far, so good. The sentences composing an inference are its *premises* and *conclusion*, the latter usually signalled by the prefix 'therefore' (for which, for brevity, we shall often use the symbol ∴). If the inference is deductively valid the conclusion is called a *deductive* or *logical consequence*, or simply *consequence*, of the premises. What else do we know? Well, one of the most familiar facts about deductively valid inferences, and the one which probably goes farthest towards explaining the importance they have always been accorded, is that it is impossible for their conclusions to be false if their premises are true: if anything is basic to the notion of deduction, that surely is. Consider this example, known as a *disjunctive syllogism*:

> It's raining or it's snowing.
> It's not raining.
> ∴ It's snowing.

Clearly, you don't have to know whether it's actually raining or not, or snowing or not, to know that if the premises are true, so too is the conclusion. Not only is the conclusion true if the premises are. The conclusion *must* be true if the premises are true; there is no possibility of its being false.

Not only is this the most important property of deductively valid inferences; it is difficult to think of any other that has that same generality. This being so, we might as well take it as the defining property, and accordingly frame the following

Provisional definition: a valid deductive inference is one whose premises cannot all be true and conclusion false.

The definition is provisional because the word 'cannot' itself rather obviously needs a definition, and providing an adequate one is not trivial: most of this book will be occupied in the task. But one thing we do know is that 'cannot' here has nothing at all to do with empirical fact, as it does in the statement that water cannot unaided run uphill. 'Cannot' in this context refers to a *logical* impossibility. It is a logical, not merely a physical, impossibility that 'It's snowing' is false if both 'It's either raining or it's snowing' and 'It's not raining' are true (assuming sameness of spatio-temporal reference in premises and conclusion). Here are two more examples to consider.

If Lev is in Moscow then Irina is in Kiev.
Lev is in Moscow.
∴ Irina is in Kiev.

Cain was hairy and Abel was his victim.
∴ Cain was hairy.

It is intuitively clear that these remain deductively valid, in the sense of the definition above, whatever sentences are substituted for 'Cain was hairy', 'Abel was his victim', 'Lev is in Moscow', 'Irina is in Kiev' and, in the disjunctive syllogism, 'It's raining' and 'it's snowing'. Another way of putting it is to say that if we replace these sentences by the letters A, B, C, D, E and F, the respective formal representations (or *formalisations*) of these inferences

E or F
not E
∴ F

If A then B
A
∴ B

C and D
∴ C

will always generate deductively valid inferences when the letters A, B, C, D, E and F are replaced by any sentences.

An explanation of why this is so will plausibly rest on an analysis of the logical role played by the particles 'and', 'or', 'not', and 'if ...

then —'. Now, a common method of analysing some phenomenon is to construct a model of it and see whether the model behaves in a way sufficiently resembling what it is supposed to model. This will be our procedure. The model, which will be presented in a systematic form in Chapter 3, is called a *propositional language*. 'And', 'or', 'not', etc. are basic syntactical items of these languages, and in the following sections we shall describe the way they are used to form *compound truth-functional sentences*, and the rules which determine how truth and falsity should be ascribed to these. (The *syntax* of a language is the set of rules which determine its formal structure, that is to say the way its basic vocabulary is organised into well-formed expressions, among which are the sentences of the language; the rules by which the sentences are equipped with truth-conditions constitute the language's *semantics*.)

2 SYNTAX: CONNECTIVES AND THE PRINCIPLE OF COMPOSITION

'And', 'or', 'if ... then —' are structural items, called *connectives* by logicians, which articulate sentences into further sentences. 'Cain was hairy' and 'Abel was his victim' are said to be conjoined by 'and' to yield the *conjunction* 'Cain was hairy *and* Abel was his victim'; the two sentences forming the conjunction are its *conjuncts*. 'Not' operates on the sentence 'It's raining' to generate its *negation* 'It's *not* raining.' 'It's raining' and 'it's snowing' are disjoined by 'or' to form the *disjunction* 'It's raining *or* it's snowing' of those two sentences, which are called the *disjuncts*. The sentences 'Lev is in Moscow' and 'Irina is in Kiev' are combined into the *conditional* sentence '*If* Lev is in Moscow *then* Irina is in Kiev'; 'Lev is in Moscow' is the *antecedent*, and 'Irina is in Kiev' is the *consequent*.

These connectives play such a fundamental role that they have been given special symbols by logicians. The following are now standard:

Connective	Symbol
not	¬
and	∧
or	∨
if ... then	→

Because they operate on pairs of sentences to generate other sentences, ∧, ∨ and → are *binary* connectives; ¬ is *unary*, because it operates on single sentences. In what follows we shall refer, as just now, to ∧, ∨, and → directly as connectives rather than as connective symbols.

In our model the basic items out of which its sentences are built are these connectives and a stock of capital letters A, B, C, D, etc., called *sentence letters*, from the beginning of the Roman alphabet. These are intended to represent some given set of English sentences with whose internal structure we are not concerned. The sentence letters are often called the *atomic sentences* of the model, because all its other sentences are compounded from them, using the connectives. The first level of composition consists of the negations, disjunctions, conjunctions of sentence letters, and conditionals formed from them. Each of these compounds is represented as follows: the negation of A by ¬A (¬ is prefixed to A, in contrast to the way 'not' is ordinarily embedded within a sentence to form its negation); the conjunction of A and B by A∧B; the disjunction of A and B by A∨B; and the conditional with antecedent A and consequent B by A→B.

In a natural language there is no theoretical limit, though there are obviously practical ones, to the extent that sentences can be successively compounded together by means of connectives. Such a *principle of composition* will also operate in our model, to allow the sentences to be compounded ad infinitum using ¬, ∧, ∨ and →, generating symbol-strings like A→¬B, ¬(A→B), ((A→B)∨(B∧A))→C, etc. The brackets indicate which component sentences in each compound the various connectives connect. Denoting arbitrary sentences in the model by the letters X, Y, Z, etc., we can give a compact statement of the principle of composition in which the bracketing is automatically taken care of. The statement has two clauses, one unconditional, the other conditional: *A, B, C, etc. are sentences, and if X and Y are sentences, then so also are ¬X, ¬Y, (X∨Y), (X∧Y), (X→Y)* (in informal discussion the outer brackets will generally be dropped). In Chapter 3 we shall see that these two clauses determine for each sentence in the model a unique *ancestral tree*.

3 SEMANTICS: TRUTH-FUNCTIONALITY

There are two other important elements in our model, the *truth-values* 'true' and 'false', which will be represented by the letters T and F. We shall make the important assumption that the truth-values of compound sentences depend on the truth-values of their component sentences; in particular, it will be assumed that the truth-values of ¬X, X∧Y, X∨Y and X→Y depend on those of X and Y and *only* on those. Call this assumption that of the *truth-functionality of the connectives*.

Mostly, this assumption works quite well, though there are apparent exceptions which we shall investigate at length later in the book. It has the following consequence, on which the whole of truth-functional logic is based. Consider X∧Y. Its truth-value depends on those of X and Y; the truth-value of each of these, if it is not a sentence letter, depends on those of the sentences out of which it is immediately compounded; and so on backwards in the same way until we arrive at the sentence letters which are not compounded out of anything. In other words, *the truth-value of any compound X in the model depends only on the truth-values of the sentence letters appearing in it.* This consequence will be called the *truth table principle*, for the following reason. Let X be any compound. Suppose we arrange all the finitely many sentence letters, say A, B, C, etc., which appear in X, in a row, and write underneath all the possible distributions of truth-values to these in rows underneath A, B, C, etc. We then write X to the right of all the A, B, C, etc, giving a diagram that looks like this:

```
A B C ... X
T T T ...
T T F ...
.........
F F T ...
F F F ...
```

The truth-functionality assumption implies, as we have just seen, that each row of truth-values on the left of the diagram determines a unique truth-value for X, which we shall write beneath X opposite the relevant row of truth-values on the left. The resulting table is called the *truth table for X*.

The assignment of truth-values to sentence letters themselves is what model-builders call *exogenous*, determined outside the model. Our concern here is only with how those truth-values, whatever they might be, determine the column of Ts and Fs beneath X in its truth table. The truth table principle tells us that this problem is solved once we have determined the truth tables for ¬A, A∧B, A∨B, A→B. In the next section we shall make a start by determining the truth tables for ¬A and A∧B.

We end this section on a philosophical note. There is a long-standing debate about whether sentences are truly bearers of truth-values, or whether only *propositions* can be (the usual definition of a proposition is that it is what is expressed by a sentence). While there is considerable disagreement, however, about exactly what sorts of *things* propositions actually are, there is absolutely no doubt that in everyday life the bearers of truth-values are the sorts of structured linguistic items described above, variously called statements or sentences; logicians tend to call them sentences. At any rate, it is with modelling these things that logicians have concerned themselves. And so shall we.

4 NEGATION AND CONJUNCTION

If someone says to you that it is not the case that so and so, and you take what they say to be true, then this means that you take 'so and so' to be false. And if you take what they say to be false, this is because you take 'so and so' to be true. Putting these observations together in the model, we represent 'so and so' by the sentence letter A and construct the following truth table for ¬A:

A	¬A
T	F
F	T

In words:

¬A is true when A is false, and false when A is true.

Similarly, the truth table for A∧B, i.e. 'A and B', is obtained by the same method of identifying the conditions under which we believe a conjunction to be true and those under which we believe it to be false. If you agree that A∧B is true, you are agreeing that A and B are both true, while if you think that A∧B is false, it is because you think that at least one of A and B is false. This immediately gives the truth table for ∧:

A	B	A∧B
T	T	T
T	F	F
F	T	F
F	F	F

In words:

A∧B is true just in case A and B are both true; otherwise it is false.

Important note The truth-functionality assumption says that the truth-value of a conjunction or negation depends only on the *truth-values* of the sentences conjoined or negated, *not on those sentences themselves*. This means that, though the truth tables above are written for sentence letters A and B, they are equally valid when A and B are replaced by X and Y, i.e. by arbitrary sentences of the model language, compound or atomic. We could make this explicit by writing, as some do, the truth tables for negation and conjunction like this:

	¬		∧	T	F
T	F		T	T	F
F	T		F	F	F

However, we shall continue to use the earlier tables, because their format is straightforwardly extended to the evaluation of any compound sentence, however complex.

Exercises

1 If ¬A is true, what is the truth-value of A?
2 If A∧B is false and B is true, what is the truth-value of A? If you know merely that A∧B is false, does that tell you anything about the truth-value of A?

5 DISJUNCTION

It is often claimed that there are two types of disjunction, or use of the word 'or', in English and other natural languages, *inclusive* and *exclusive*. To assert an exclusive disjunction (i.e. to claim implicitly that it is *true*) is to assert that one or other disjunct is true, but not both, while to assert an inclusive disjunction is to assert that at least one is true, and possibly both. There is certainly an inclusive use of 'or' in English; examples abound (here is one: 'If you're old or disabled nobody bothers with you'; we would all take the 'old or disabled' here to include any who are both old and disabled). By contrast, it is actually quite difficult to find a genuine use of exclusive 'or' which is not exclusive simply because the disjuncts are themselves exclusive, for example 'He got either ten or twenty years; I can't remember which.'

At any rate, logicians regard the inclusive 'or' as primary, and ∨ is accordingly given the truth table

A	B	A∨B
T	T	T
T	F	T
F	T	T
F	F	F

In words:

A∨B is false only when A and B are both false, and otherwise true.

Nothing is lost in apparently ignoring the exclusive disjunction, because as we shall see in the next section, it is already implicit in the connectives ¬, ∧ and ∨.

Warning Words are notoriously not always what they seem. Consider the statement 'You may have tea or you may have coffee', which is not, as it appears to be, a disjunction but a conjunction: it actually says that you may have tea *and* you may have coffee (though it does not mean that you may have both).

Exercises

If A∨B is true and A is false, what is the truth-value of B?

6 TRUTH-FUNCTIONAL EQUIVALENCE

We can use the truth table principle to evaluate arbitrary truth-functional compounds built up from sentence letters using connectives from the list ¬, ∧, ∨ and →. Consider, for example, the compound (A∨B)∧¬(A∧B). We first evaluate the inner conjunction A∧B against each row of the truth table, then the negation ¬(A∧B), and finally the conjunction (A∨B)∧¬(A∧B), as below. The truth-values of this final conjunction are listed in bold type in the central column of the truth table:

A B	(A∨B)	∧	¬	(A∧B)
T T	T	**F**	F	T
T F	T	**T**	T	F
F T	T	**T**	T	F
F F	F	**F**	T	F

Not a very exciting compound, one might think. However, suppose we introduce a new binary connective *xor* (exclusive 'or'; i.e. exclusive disjunction), whose truth table is

A B	A *xor* B
T T	F
T F	T
F T	T
F F	F

Inspection of the truth table for (A∨B)∧¬(A∧B) now reveals that it depends on the truth-values of A and B *in exactly the same way* as does the truth-value of A *xor* B: for each row of the truth table the two compounds take the same truth-values. This is interesting for two reasons. First, it verifies the claim that exclusive 'or' is implicit in the connectives ¬, ∧ and ∨. So we do not need a special symbol like *xor* for exclusive disjunction: we could simply *define* the exclusive disjunction of A and B to be the compound (A∨B)∧¬(A∧B).

Second, we have a new concept: truth-functional equivalence. *A pair X, Y of compounds are said to be truth-functionally equivalent if, like A xor B and (A∨B)∧¬(A∧¬B), X and Y take the same value at each row of the truth table generated by listing all distributions of truth-values over the set of all the sentence letters that appear in each compound.* This set of sentence letters may be the same for both compounds, as it is above, but it may not. For example, A and A∧(B∨¬B) do not have the same set of sentence letters, but for all rows of the truth table generated by the four distributions of T and F over A and B, A and A∧(B∨¬B) take the same truth-values, and are therefore truth-functionally equivalent. We shall use the notation X ⇔ Y to signify that X and Y are truth-functionally equivalent. *(Note that ⇔ is not itself a connective.)* As we shall see in the following chapters, the notions of truth-functional equivalence and its extension, first-order equivalence, will turn out to be of fundamental importance.

As an exercise in the truth table evaluation of compound sentences, we shall end this section by showing that (A→C)∧(B→C) and (A∨B)→C are truth-functionally equivalent:

ABC	(A→C)∧(B→C)			(A∨B)→C	
TTT	T	**T**	T	T	**T**
TTF	F	**F**	F	T	**F**
TFT	T	**T**	T	T	**T**
FTT	T	**T**	T	T	**T**
FFT	T	**T**	T	F	**T**
FTF	T	**F**	F	T	**F**
TFF	F	**F**	T	T	**F**
FFF	T	**T**	T	F	**T**

Note There is no logical significance to the order in which the eight truth-value distributions over A, B and C are listed, though it is a good practical rule, as above, to start with all Ts, then all the ways (three) two Ts can be combined with one F, then all the ways (three) one T can be combined with two Fs, and then finish with all Fs. If a compound is built up from n distinct sentence letters, its truth table will have 2^n rows, since there are two ways of assigning T or F to the first letter, and for each of these there will be two ways of assigning T or F to the second, and for each of these there will be two ways of assigning T or F to the third, and so on, giving 2.2.2. . . ., n times, which is equal to 2^n.

Exercises

1 Construct truth tables for the following compounds:
   (i)   (B∨C)∧(C∨B)
   (ii) ¬(A∧¬C)∨B
   (iii) ¬A∧(¬C∨B)
2 Construct truth tables to show that
   (i)   A∧(B∧C)⇔(A∧B)∧C and A∨(B∨C)⇔(A∨B)∨C. This property of ∧ and ∨ is called *associativity*.
   (ii) A∧(B∨C)⇔(A∧B)∨(A∧C) and A∨(B∧C)⇔(A∨B)∧(A∨C). These are the so-called *distributivity laws*.

7 THE CONDITIONAL

It is time to look at the final connective in the list of connectives drawn up in section 2, the conditional or arrow →, intended to symbolise the

English 'if . . . then —'. Imagine that you are listening to an old-fashioned melodrama, and at one point one of the protagonists exclaims 'You will not reveal all, or I am lost!' The substance of this assertion could equally well be conveyed, albeit more prosaically, by the conditional 'If you reveal all then I am lost.' This suggests that whatever English sentences A and B might represent, ¬A∨B and A→B should be merely different formulations of the same information, and hence be truth-functionally equivalent. Supposing this to be the case, the truth table for A→B is

A B	A→B
T T	T
T F	F
F T	T
F F	T

because that, as the reader should check, is the truth table for ¬A∨B. In words:

A→B is false when A is true and B false, and true in all other cases.

(Readers who have some familiarity with logic programming will probably be more accustomed to seeing A→B written B←A, i.e. 'B if A').

However, there seem to be other types of conditional statement in everyday life that are not expressed by →. One in particular seems to demand a definitely *non*-truth-functional analysis, and this is where the antecedent is counterfactual. For example, consider the sentence 'If I had struck the match at that particular moment [t, say], a genie would have appeared', where you did not in fact strike the match at that moment. Most people would regard this sentence as false, but if it is expressed as 'I strike the match at moment t → a genie appears', and evaluated by means of the truth table for →, then, given that the antecedent is false (counterfactual), the truth table for → makes the sentence true! This goes strongly against intuition, and to make matters worse, 'If I had struck the match at that particular moment a genie would not have appeared' also comes out true on the truth-functional reading using →, because the antecedent remains false in this sentence too.

We shall postpone further discussion of counterfactuals to Chapter 12, where we shall also look at some challenges to the truth-functional reading of some *non*-counterfactual conditionals.

Exercises

1 Construct truth tables to show that the following truth-functional equivalences hold:

A→(B→C)⇔(A∧B)→C

A→B⇔¬B→¬A

A→B⇔¬(A∧¬B)

2 Let å(A, B) be false only when A is false and B true. How would one express å(A, B) using only the connective →?

3 Verify that A→B has the same truth table as ¬A∨B and ¬(A∧¬B).

8 SOME OTHER CONNECTIVES, AND THE BICONDITIONAL

Other connectives in common use in English, like 'unless', 'but' and 'only if', for example, can be more or less faithfully defined in terms of ¬, ∧, ∨ and →, and we shall deal with them in turn:

But 'I went to see the film but I didn't like it' says, from the point of view of simple truth and falsity and shorn of the nuance of regret, 'I went to see the film and I didn't like it.' Logic is concerned with the way the truth-values of sentences depend on each other, and not with one's feelings about what the sentences describe; so from the purely logical point of view, 'but' is 'and'.

Unless 'You will not reach 100 unless you first reach 99 (years of age)' plausibly means the same as 'If you do not first reach 99 you will not reach 100'; so we shall take 'A unless B' to mean the same as 'If not B then A', represented in the model by ¬B→A.

Only if 'You will reach the age of 100 only if you first reach the age of 99' means the same as 'If you don't first reach the age of 99 you won't reach the age of 100'; so we take 'A only if B' to mean the same as ¬B→¬A. Now look at the truth table for ¬B→¬A:

A B	¬B→¬A
T T	T
T F	F
F T	T
F F	T

But this is the truth table for A→B, which means that we can render 'A only if B' directly by A→B. If A→B is true then A is often called a *sufficient condition* for B, and B a *necessary condition* for A.

There is one further connective which is often distinguished by being given a special symbol, even though it too will turn out to be definable in terms of other connectives among ∧, ∨, ¬ and →. This is the so-called *biconditional* 'if and only if', and it will be symbolised by ↔. It has its own symbol because statements of the form 'A if and only if B' crop up very frequently. However, the biconditional could also be *defined* in terms of ∧ and →. 'A if B' is clearly B→A, and we have just seen that 'A only if B' has the same truth table as A→B. Hence, A↔B, 'A if and only if B', is truth-functionally equivalent to (A→B)∧(B→A), from which it follows that its truth table is evaluated as

A	B	A↔B
T	T	T
T	F	F
F	T	F
F	F	T

i.e.: A↔B is true just in case A and B have the same truth-value.

Exercises

1 You are in a country whose inhabitants randomly tell the truth or lie. You are trying to reach the capital city, which you know lies on the road you are following, but to your dismay the road forks. The capital is on one of the forks, but there is no signpost. A native of the country appears. A law of the country is that the natives are allowed only to answer 'yes' or 'no' to questions. How they will do so will depend on whether they are telling the truth or lying, but which they will do on any given occasion of course you simply don't know (but you do know that they are very good at logic). All seems hopeless until you remember that, long ago, you attended a logic course. Suddenly you realise that there is a slightly complicated question you can ask this person, such that their answer will tell you for certain which fork the capital lies on. What is the question? (There is more than one, but the following method will certainly generate one. Consider a question of the form 'Is X(A,B) true?', where X(A,B) is a truth-functional compound of A and B which you are familiar with, A is the sentence 'You are lying', and B is 'The capital lies on the left fork.' You want the native's answer to be 'yes' if and only if B is true, and working back from this will identify X(A, B) – or, similarly, you may want to correlate the native's 'yes' answer with B's falsity; either way, once the native has answered, you'll know for sure whether the capital lies on the left fork.)

2 Which connective among ∧, ∨, ¬, → and ↔ would you use to represent 'just in case' in the statement 'A∧B is true just in case A and B are both true'?

3 Display the truth-functional structure of the assertions in (i) and (ii) below using the sentence letters indicated and the appropriate connectives among ∧, ∨, ¬ and → (omit the '*Therefore*' in each case).

   (i)   If wage-settlements continue at this high level (A) or they increase (B), and nothing is done to take money out of the economy (C), then inflation will continue to rise (D) and we shall be in serious trouble (E). *Therefore* if nothing is done to take money out of the economy we shall be in serious trouble.

(ii) Tracey won't return *Also sprach Zarathustra* (A) unless Wayne gives her the £5 he owes her (B), but Wayne will not do this without Rudolf giving him some of the money (C). Amaryllis doesn't want Rudolf to do this (D), and if Amaryllis doesn't want Rudolf to then Rudolf won't. Carlos will only be able to do his homework (E) if Tracey returns *Also sprach Zarathustra*. *Therefore* Carlos won't be able to do his homework.

4 Which connective among ∧, ∨, ¬ and → would you use to represent 'whilst' in the sentence 'Whilst I believe in law and order, the actions of the police sometimes make me unhappy'?

5 Give one way of expressing the truth-functional form of 'Untidy or inaccurate work will cost you marks.' (Be careful!)

6 Is the sentence 'Jill and Siân are the opposing team' a conjunction of two sentences?

7 'If you are over 18 and married, then your name will go on the register unless you have already received benefit.' How would you formalise this statement using the propositional connectives already given?

Chapter 2

Truth trees

1 TRUTH-FUNCTIONALLY VALID INFERENCE

We now have a slightly better vantage point from which to investigate the inferences with which we started in Chapter 1:

> If Lev is in Moscow then Irina is in Kiev.
> Lev is in Moscow.
> ∴ Irina is in Kiev.

> Cain was hairy and Abel was his victim.
> ∴ Cain was hairy.

> It's raining or it's snowing.
> It's not raining.
> ∴ It's snowing.

These have the respective truth-functional representations (A and B will obviously represent different sentences in each):

(i) $A \rightarrow B$ (ii) $A \wedge B$ (iii) $A \vee B$
      A ∴ A $\neg A$
 ∴ B ∴ B

In each of (i)–(iii), consider what happens if we try to assume that the premises could be true and the conclusion false:

(i) If B were to be false and A true, then the truth table tells us that $A \rightarrow B$ would be false. Thus we could not, *on pain of contradiction*, have true premises and a false conclusion. Therefore the inference is truth-functionally valid. It is usually referred to by its classical Latin name: *modus ponens*.

(ii) is immediate. If $A \wedge B$ is true then, from the truth table for $\wedge$, both A and B are true. Hence in particular A must be true.

(iii) is the disjunctive syllogism. Suppose that B is false, and that $\neg A$ and $A \vee B$ are both true. Then we have a contradiction, for A must be false, and we have assumed that B is false, so that $A \vee B$ must be false, contrary to assumption.

(i), (ii) and (iii) are therefore deductively valid inferences. They are deductively valid, moreover, by virtue of their truth-functional structure alone, and inferences which are valid by virtue of their truth-functional structure alone are called *truth-functionally* valid. More precisely,

> A truth-functionally valid inference is one whose premises and conclusion can be represented as truth-functional compounds built up from some set of sentence letters, such that there is no distribution of truth-values over those sentence letters which makes the premises all true and the conclusion false.

Just as the conclusion of a deductively valid inference is said to be a deductive consequence of the premises, so the conclusion of a truth-functionally valid inference is said to be a *truth-functional consequence* of the premises.

If there is a distribution of truth-values making all the premises true and the conclusion false, then that distribution is called a *truth-functional counterexample* to the inference. Hence:

> An inference is truth-functionally valid just in case there is no truth-functional counterexample to it.

A very important consequence of the definition of truth-functionally valid inference is that there is an *algorithm* for deciding whether any given inference is truth-functionally valid or not (an algorithm is a 'mechanical' procedure which decides all members of a given class of problems in finite time, and is now usually regarded as a program which can be run on a suitably powerful computer). If there are n sentence letters in the sentences making up the inference, we know that there are 2^n truth-value distributions over those sentence letters, and a truth table will evaluate all the sentences for each of these distributions. Then all we have to do is see whether one or more of those 2^n distributions make all the premises true and the conclusion false.

However, for even quite moderate values of n, 2^n is a biggish number (2^{20} is about a million). That search procedure is therefore exponentially complex, and it turns out that it contains in addition a lot of redundancy. For we learn nothing about the validity of the inference from examining the truth-value distributions which make either the premises false or the conclusion true: the only relevant distributions when considering deductive validity are clearly just those which make the premises true or the conclusion false. This is where the tree diagrams for the connectives come in so useful, for as we shall see in the next sections, they can be used to systematically eliminate the uninformative paths in the search for counterexamples.

Exercises

1 Show that if X and Y are any two truth-functional compounds, then X⇔Y if and only if X and Y have exactly the same truth-functional consequences.

2 Show that X⇔Y if and only if X is a truth-functional consequence of Y and Y is a truth-functional consequence of X.

2 CONJUGATE TREE DIAGRAMS

There is another way of displaying the information given in the truth tables for ∧, ∨, → and ↔, which as we shall see shortly generates a powerful and elegant method of proving truth-functional validity. This is to represent the truth tables for binary connectives by *tree diagrams*, or more exactly by conjugate pairs of tree diagrams. Since the truth-value of, say, a conjunction depends only on the truth-values of its conjuncts, and not on the conjuncts themselves, we can write the truth table for the conjunction X∧Y of two compounds X and Y in the same way as if they were sentence letters:

X	Y	X∧Y
T	T	T
T	F	F
F	T	F
F	F	F

Now consider the following pair of diagrams:

```
TX∧Y      FX∧Y
  |        / \
 TX      FX  FY
 TY
```

For the time being, regard the boldface **T**'s and **F**'s as integral parts of each diagram (T and F are printed in bold type to distinguish them from the letters X and Y). Read upwards, the left-hand diagram can be interpreted as saying that when X and Y are both true (**T**), so is X∧Y, and the right-hand diagram can be interpreted as saying that if X is false (**F**), *whatever the truth-value of Y*, then so is X∧Y, and that if Y is false, *whatever the truth-value of X*, then so is X∧Y. So interpreted (and we shall see later that the diagrams can be read both upwards and downwards), the left-hand diagram represents the one row of the truth table for X∧Y in which X∧Y takes the value T, and the right-hand diagram represents the three rows for which X∧Y takes the value F.

In other words, the pair of diagrams contains exactly the information contained in the truth table for X∧Y. The diagrams are called *signed tree diagrams* because they are tagged (or signed) with truth-values. We can eliminate these tags in the following way. Noting that when any sentence Z is false its negation ¬Z is true, we can rewrite the second diagram as

$$\mathbf{T}\neg(X\wedge Y)$$
$$/ \quad \backslash$$
$$\mathbf{T}\neg X \quad \mathbf{T}\neg Y$$

Now both the left- and the right-hand diagrams are signed only with **T**s, and that being the case we can regard the **T**s as understood and omit explicit mention of them. So we are left with a pair of unsigned diagrams, the unsigned conjugate tree diagrams for ∧:

$$X\wedge Y \qquad\qquad \neg(X\wedge Y)$$
$$| \qquad\qquad\qquad / \quad \backslash$$
$$X \qquad\qquad\qquad \neg X \;\; \neg Y$$
$$Y$$

We could equally accurately have represented the F rows of the truth table for X∧Y by an unsigned diagram with three branches:

where each branch represents one row of the truth table for which X∧Y is F. However, the function of conjugate diagrams is not simply, or even primarily, to represent truth tables; *their principal function is to provide rules of inference*, for what will be called tree proofs, and for them to perform this role efficiently the number of branchings from any sentence is best limited to *at most* two. We shall see very shortly how these diagrams can then be put together to form elegant and virtually mechanical proofs.

The left-hand diagram in a conjugate pair will always represent the T rows of the truth table for the relevant connective, and the right-hand diagram the F rows. With this in mind we turn to the truth table for v:

X	Y	XvY
T	T	T
T	F	T
F	T	T
F	F	F

Reading from the table, we see that if X is true then XvY is true, whatever the truth-value of Y, and if Y is true then XvY is true, whatever the truth-value of X. This gives us the left-hand (signed) diagram for v:

$$\mathbf{T} \;\; XvY$$
$$/ \quad \backslash$$
$$\mathbf{T}X \qquad \mathbf{T}Y$$

There is just one row where X∨Y takes the value F, and that is the row at which both X and Y take the value F. This gives us the right-hand signed diagram for ∨:

F   X∨Y
|
F   X
F   Y

Using the same unsigning procedure as for ∧, we obtain the pair of unsigned conjugate diagrams for ∨:

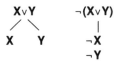

X∨Y   ¬(X∨Y)
 / \ |
X   Y   ¬X
              ¬Y

Notice the mirror symmetry between the pair of diagrams for ∧ and that for ∨: if we change ∨ to ∧ in the diagrams for ∨, and negate each sentence, eliminating all double ¬'s, we obtain the diagrams for ∧; and vice versa. This is a special case of a principle called the *Duality Principle*, which we shall return to in Chapter 3.

The same procedure as that used to obtain the diagrams for ∧ and ∨ yields the conjugate unsigned diagrams for → and ↔:

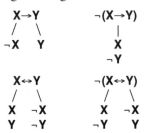

X→Y   ¬(X→Y)
/ \ |
¬X   Y   X
                 ¬Y

X↔Y   ¬(X↔Y)
/ \   / \
X   ¬X   X   ¬X
Y   ¬Y   ¬Y   Y

Where the lower sentences in these diagrams occur in pairs it is customary to write one member of the pair above the other, as above. No priority is implied in this listing, and it can be reversed without changing the diagram characteristics, as we shall see.

The reader may be wondering what has happened to ¬. It too is a truth-functional connective, defined by a truth table, and consequently it too will have a pair of unsigned diagrams representing its truth table. Since its properties have already been implicitly used in converting signed diagrams into unsigned ones, it might seem that the unsigned diagrams for negation itself are unlikely to be very informative. To some extent this is true, but by no means entirely. The signed diagrams are these:

T¬X   F¬X
| |
FX   TX

yielding the unsigned diagrams:

```
   ¬ X              ¬ ¬ X
    |                 |
   ¬ X                X
```

Clearly, the left-hand diagram of this pair is totally uninformative. This leaves us with only one non-trivial diagram, the right-hand one. Though a single diagram, it will turn out to be very useful, so useful that it is given a special name, the *Rule of Double Negation.*

Exercises

1 Construct the truth tables for the sentence Z represented in (a) and (b) below by the left-hand unsigned member of each of a pair of unsigned conjugate diagrams, and express Z as a truth-functional compound of X and Y, employing any of the connectives ∧, ∨, ¬ and → (remember that the left-hand diagram always represents the T rows of the table for Z).

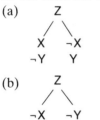

(a)
```
        Z
      /   \
     X     ¬X
    ¬Y     Y
```

(b)
```
        Z
      /   \
    ¬X     ¬Y
```

2 Construct the truth table for the compound which these conjugate diagrams determine, and rewrite the right-hand diagram so that it satisfies the condition that no diagram has more than two branches:

```
   |        /    |    \
  ¬X       X     X     ¬X
  ¬Y       Y    ¬Y     Y
```

3 TRUTH TREES

The conjugate diagrams of the previous section (together with the Rule of Double Negation) can be used to yield simple graphic demonstrations of truth-functional validity. We shall start with some very simple examples, the inferences (i)–(iii) of section 1. First (i), *modus ponens*:

```
     A→B
     A
  ∴  B
```

Asking whether it is possible for the premises A→B, A to take the truth-value T and the conclusion, B, the value F is, of course, equivalent to

asking whether A→B, A, and ¬B can all take the value T. Write down
A→B, A, ¬B, signifying that we are supposing, for the sake of argument,
that they're all true:

A→B
A
¬B

These will be called the *initial sentences*. The order in which they are listed
is immaterial: they're simply a set of three sentences assumed, for the
moment, to be all true. Now write underneath the initial sentences the
lower part of the tree diagram for A→B:

/ \
¬A B

We now have a small upside-down tree:

A→B
A
¬B
/ \
¬A B

If we define a *branch* in the tree to be a continuous path up from the
terminal lower sentences to the topmost sentence of the tree, then
the tree above has two branches, one carrying the sentences A→B, A,
¬B, ¬A, and the other A→B, A, ¬B, B.

This tree is called a *truth tree*. The information it contains is probably
more immediately conveyed by the equivalent signed version:

On the left-hand branch we see **AT** and **AF**, and on the right-hand branch
BT and **BF**; neither is a consistent assignment of truth-values. As those
two branches represent all the possibilities admitted by the initial assignment, this signed tree shows that the assumption that A→B and A are
true and B false is *impossible*: it leads to a contradictory assignment of
T and F either to B or to A. The original tree also showed this, if less
explicitly, by having both A and ¬A on one branch, and B and ¬B on
the other. At any rate, we infer *that there can be no truth-functional
counterexample to the inference*; i.e. no distribution of truth-values to A
and B which makes the premises A→B and A both true and the conclusion
B false. In other words, the inference A, A→B ∴B is truth-functionally
valid.

Of course, we already knew that, by means of an argument in section 1 that in some ways resembles an informal version of the one above. But the tree format has the advantage over the informal argument that it extends to a simple and mechanical method for deciding the validity or otherwise of any truth-functional inference whatever, no matter how complex.

Now for (ii):

$$A \wedge B$$
$$\therefore A$$

Here the sole premise is A∧B, and the conclusion is A, and we shall again use a tree – they will all be unsigned from now on – to show that the assignment of T to A∧B and F to A, i.e. of T to both A∧B and ¬A, is impossible. This time we get a tree with only one branch

$$A \wedge B$$
$$\neg A$$
$$|$$
A   (these lines are from the tree diagram
B   for X∧Y, where X is A and Y B)

on which the pair A, ¬A appear. These cannot both be true, so again we conclude that our assumption, that a truth-value distribution over A, B exists which satisfies both A∧B and ¬A, leads to a contradiction. Hence the inference from A∧B to A is truth-functionally valid.

Finally, (iii). Again, we write down the premises and negation of the conclusion, implicitly assuming them all true:

$$A \vee B$$
$$\neg A$$
$$\neg B$$
$$/ \ \backslash$$
A   B   (from A∨B, using the diagram for
X∨Y)

We see immediately that we have A and ¬A on one branch, and B and ¬B on the other. Since these branches exhaust the possible ways in which the initial sentences can be true together, we infer that those initial sentences cannot all be true together, and so (iii) is truth-functionally valid.

This all seems very promising. Let us see how it fares with a slightly more complex inference:

If the mark rises or the yen rises the dollar will fall.
The dollar will not fall.
∴ It is not the case that the mark rises and the yen rises.

This has the truth-functional form

$$(A \lor B) \to C$$
$$\neg C$$
$$\therefore \ \neg(A \land B)$$

As in the previous examples, we list the premises and the negated conclusion, so:

$$(A \lor B) \to C$$
$$\neg C$$
$$\neg \neg(A \land B)$$

and, starting from this set of initial sentences, we shall use the conjugate diagrams for the connectives to decompose the compound sentences into simpler ones until the tree generated in the process finally tells us, by depositing a sentence and its negation on every branch, that there is no way all the initial sentences can be true.

The final sentence on the list of initial sentences is the double negation $\neg \neg(A \land B)$, which seems a good enough place to start. Applying the rule of double negation to $\neg \neg(A \land B)$, we extend a branch downwards as follows, numbering the lines as we go:

```
1   (A∨B)→C
2   ¬C
3   ¬¬(A∧B)        √
         |
4        A∧B
```

In the terminology we shall use from now on, $\neg \neg(A \land B)$ has been *used*. For book-keeping purposes we can indicate this by placing a tick beside it – we don't want inadvertently to use it twice.

Proceeding downwards, we can now write the diagram for $A \land B$ directly beneath $A \land B$:

```
1   (A∨B)→C
2   ¬C
3   ¬¬(A∧B)        √
         |
4        A∧B        √
         |
5        A
6        B
```

Now what? We now look around for another compound sentence to use by writing the tree diagram for it under the lowest point of the tree. There is only one such sentence, the topmost, the conditional $(A \lor B) \to C$. This has antecedent $A \lor B$ and consequent C. Directly beneath B on line 6 write the diagram for the conditional with that antecedent and consequent:

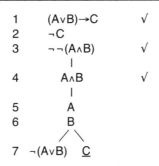

We have now used (A∨B)→C, and in so doing extended the tree to one with two branches. The right-hand branch, terminating in C, contains the negation ¬C of C as well as C, and therefore (visualise the tree signed with truth-values) represents an impossible truth-value assignment. Accordingly, we shall *close* that branch by writing a line beneath it to signify that it must not be continued.

> As soon as any two sentences occur on a branch, one of which is the negation of the other, that branch is closed.

No further attention is paid to closed branches; they merely represent failed attempts to make the initial sentences all true.

The remaining unclosed branches on any tree are said to be *open*. There is now one open branch on the tree above, the left-hand one. It also contains a compound sentence for which there is a tree diagram, namely ¬(A∨B). Accordingly we continue the left-hand branch by writing the tree diagram for ¬(A∨B) beneath ¬(A∨B):

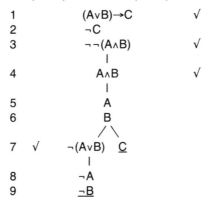

Now all the branches have closed. *When this happens the tree itself is said to close*, a phenomenon we have now learned to interpret as meaning that no distribution of truth-values at all over A, B and C will make the initial sentences jointly true. Therefore the inference we started with is truth-functionally valid: no distribution of truth-values over its sentence letters makes the premises true and the conclusion false.

It makes little difference in what order we use the sentences on a tree. *In particular, it makes no difference to whether the tree closes or not* (we shall give a rigorous proof of this in Chapter 4). We can check that this is so in the example above by constructing a tree in which the sentence (A∨B)→C is used first:

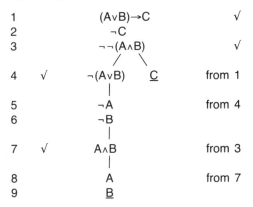

Important note *In the event of there being more than one open branch at the point at which a sentence is used, place the tree diagram for that sentence at the end of every such branch.* Bearing in mind that the tree diagrams give the truth-conditions for their respective connectives, it's not difficult to see why this should be done: each open branch of the tree represents a different way in which the sentences on it which have already been used can be jointly true. Each time a further sentence is used, that represents a further constraint, and one which has to be applied uniformly to all open continuations of that branch. Hence *when a sentence is used in a tree, its diagram must be placed on every open branch.*

We have observed that we can interpret a closed tree as indicating that there is no distribution of truth-values over its sentence letters which will make the initial sentences all true. What if we eventually use all the usable sentences on the tree and it doesn't close? The tree in these circumstances is said to be *finished* and *open*. Can we infer that there is a truth-value distribution over the sentences letters that will make all the initial sentences true? The answer is 'yes'. Informally, the argument is as follows: each open branch of the tree represents a way in which the sentences on it which have been used can be true. If there is no further sentence to be used and there are still open branches, this means that there are ways in which all the sentences on those branches, including the initial sentences, can all be true.

To sum up:

Truth trees constructed from a set of initial sentences tell us whether there is a truth-value distribution over their sentence letters which will make the initial sentences true. If there is no such distribution, the tree will close. If there is one, it won't.

So far we have admittedly given only rather intuitive arguments for these claims, especially the last, but eventually we shall be in a position to give a more rigorous one.

We shall end this section with a resumé of how to build trees.

First, write the initial sentences (when testing inferences, these are the premises and the negation of the conclusion) in any order. Then select what looks like the simplest compound sentence and write its diagram under the initial sentences. That sentence is now used. Now choose another compound and write its diagram under the last sentence on each open branch if there is more than one. Continue doing this, closing every branch on which appears a sentence and its negation, until the tree itself either closes or else terminates without closing.

Procedural remark   Neither numbering the lines of a tree nor ticking branches is an essential part of tree construction; for extended trees these are useful devices, for simple ones usually unnecessary.

Historical note   Despite the fact that tree proofs of validity are a relatively modern development, they are really just a way of representing what logicians have traditionally called *reductio ad absurdum* arguments. In these you assume as true the premises and also the *negation* of the conclusion which is alleged follows from them, and you try to deduce a contradiction ('reduce them to absurdity'). If you succeed, that shows that the negation of the conclusion is inconsistent with the premises. The tree construction is a powerful modern systematisation of this ancient method of proof.

Exercises

1 Formalise the following inferences using sentence letters and the appropriate connectives, and construct truth trees to show that each is truth-functionally valid.

   (i)   The butler did it or the gardener did it. The gardener did not do it. ∴ The butler did it.

   (ii)   The butler did it or the gardener did it. ∴ If the butler did not do it then the gardener did.

   (iii) If the butler did not do it then the gardener did. ∴ The butler did it or the gardener did it.

   (iv)   If the butler did it then the gardener did not. ∴ If the gardener did it then the butler did not.

   (v)   'If naive realism is true then naive realism is false [not true]. ∴ Naive realism is false' (Bertrand Russell).

   (vi)   If the government raises interest rates then there will be inflation.

If the government does not raise interest rates then there will be inflation. ∴. There will be inflation.

2 Suppose you have constructed a tree to test the validity of an inference, and all the branches close with one of the initial sentences still unused. What does this tell you (i) if the unused sentence is a premise, and (ii) if the unused sentence is the negated conclusion?

4 TAUTOLOGIES AND CONTRADICTIONS

Consider the compound $A \lor \neg A$. This takes the truth-value T whatever the truth-value of A might be. So does $\neg(A \land \neg A)$, while $A \to (B \to A)$ and $(A \land \neg A) \to B$ take the value T whatever the truth-values of each of A and B might be. Compounds like these which take the value T for all distributions of truth-values over their sentence letters are called *tautologies*. Compounds which take the value F for all values of their sentence letters are called *contradictions*. We can immediately infer that the negation of a tautology is a contradiction, and the negation of a contradiction is a tautology.

We can use truth trees to test for tautologousness and for contradictoriness. No truth-value distribution over sentence letters can make a contradiction true, which means that if we construct a truth tree from it then eventually the tree will close. Conversely, if the tree closes then there is no truth-value distribution over sentences letters that makes the initial sentence true, and it is therefore a contradiction.

Example

$$\neg(A \to B) \land \neg A$$
$$|$$
$$\neg(A \to B)$$
$$\neg A$$
$$|$$
$$A$$
$$\underline{\neg B}$$

i.e. $\neg(A \land B) \to \neg A$ is a contradiction.

We can now also construct a tree test for tautologousness. For if a sentence is a tautology then its negation is a contradiction, which means that if we construct a tree from its negation the tree will close. In other words, X is a tautology if and only if a tree generated from $\neg X$ closes. Beginners are always tempted to say that a compound is a tautology just in case a tree generated from it has only open branches. This is definitely incorrect, though it is left as an exercise to say why.

Example $(A \to (B \to C)) \to ((A \to B) \to (A \to C))$. This is a tautology, as the following closed tree establishes (supply the justification for each line):

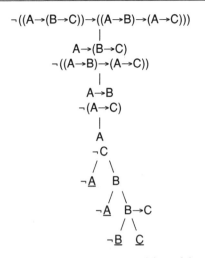

Finally, we can test for whether a compound is neither a tautology nor a contradiction. Construct a tree from ¬X, and another from X. Neither tree closes if and only if X is neither a tautology nor a contradiction.

A tautology of the form X↔Y is called a *tautological biconditional*. There is an intimate relationship between tautological biconditionality and truth-functional equivalence: where X and Y are any truth-functional compounds, *X⇔Y if and only if the compound (X↔Y) is a tautology* (this is easy to show, and is left as exercise 1 below). This means that we can use a tree test for truth-functional equivalence, for we know how to use trees to test for tautologousness. Thus we can decide whether X⇔Y by seeing whether a tree generated from ¬(X↔Y) closes; if it does, X⇔Y. We can even shorten the procedure as follows. The tree diagram for a negated biconditional is this:

```
¬(X↔Y)
 /    \
X      Y
¬Y    ¬X
```

A tree generated from ¬(X↔Y) will therefore close if and only if the two trees generated by the pairs {X, ¬Y} and {Y, ¬X} of initial sentences both close. *Hence X⇔Y if and only if trees generated from both pairs {X, ¬Y} and {Y, ¬X} of initial sentences close.* Note that this result also tells us that X⇔Y if and only if X is a truth-functional consequence of Y and Y is a truth-functional consequence of X.

Exercises

1 Let X and Y be truth-functional compounds. Explain why X⇔Y if and only if X↔Y is a tautology.

2 Show that any sentence is a truth-functional consequence of a contradiction, and that a tautology is a truth-functional consequence of any
   sentence.
3 Of the following, state which are tautologies, contradictions or neither,
   and construct trees to justify your statements.
   (i)   A→(B→A)
   (ii)   A→(¬A→B)
   (iii) A∧¬(A∨B)
   (iv)   (A∨B)→B
   (v)   (A∧B)→A
   (vi)   A→¬A
   (vii) ¬(A→¬A)
   (viii) ¬(A→A)
   (ix)   A∧¬(B→A)
4 Suppose a tree generated by a single sentence X has only open
   branches. Does this mean that X is a tautology?
5 Of the following pairs of sentences, state which are truth-functionally
   equivalent to each other, and construct trees to justify your statements.
   (a)   A→(B→C)   (A∧B)→C
   (b)   A→B   ¬A→¬B
   (c)   (C∨A)∧(B∨A)   (C∧B)∨A
   (d)   A∧C   ¬(A→¬C)
   (e)   (A→B)∧(C→B)   (A∨C)→B
   (f)   (A→B)∧(A→C)   A→(B∨C)
   (g)   (A∧¬A)∨(B∨C)   B∨C
   (h)   A∨(B→D)   ¬B∨(A∨D)
   (i)   ¬(A↔B)   (A∧¬B)∨(B∧¬A)
   (j)   A∧¬A   B∧¬B
6 In what follows let **T** be an arbitrary tautology and ⊥ an arbitrary
   contradiction, as above. Let X be any truth-functional compound. With
   reference to appropriate trees, explain why

   X→T⇔T
   T→X⇔X
   X→⊥⇔¬X
   ⊥→X⇔T

Chapter 3

Propositional languages

1 PROPOSITIONAL LANGUAGES

In Chapter 1 we introduced the notion of a *propositional language*, as a
formal model of the class of truth-functional compounds which can be
generated from some initially given set of sentences, using some specified
set of connectives. These formal languages are of interest for two reasons:
(i) they form the framework for the detailed development of truth trees
in Chapter 4; and (ii) a characteristic feature of their syntactic structure
allows a powerful method, called *inductive proof,* to be used to investigate
their properties. Nearly all the results of this chapter will be directly or
indirectly obtained by this method. However, if the reader wants to
continue the development of truth trees where the last chapter left off,
they can skip this chapter and proceed directly to Chapter 4, where enough
about propositional languages to make the discussion intelligible will be
explained at the outset.

These preliminaries over, let S be a set of sentence letters and Π some
set of connectives. Let L[S; Π] denote the set of all the truth-functional
compounds which can be constructed using sentence letters from S and
connectives from Π. *L[S, Π] is called the propositional language generated
by the sentence letters in S and the connectives in Π.* We shall often
refer to an arbitrary propositional language simply as L. Following the
notational convention introduced in Chapter 1 we shall use capitals ...,
X, Y, Z from the end of the Roman alphabet to refer to arbitrary sentences
of L. When the members of either S or Π are explicitly displayed, as they
are in L[{A, B};{¬, ∧}], for example, we shall omit the *set brackets* {, } and
simply write L[A, B; ∧, ¬].

S can be either finite or infinite, but Π will be assumed to be finite; it
does not have to be the set {∧, ∨, ¬, →, ↔}, or even include any members
of it. If we want to define a new five-place connective © where ©(A, B,
C, D, E) is true, say, when A and D are true, and false in all other 2^5
$- 2^3 = 24$ cases, then there is a perfectly respectable propositional language
whose set of connectives contains ©. For all choices of Π except the empty

set the number of distinct sentences in L[S; Π] is infinite, even when S contains just one letter. For example, suppose S is just {A} and Π is just {¬}. Then all of ¬A, ¬¬A, ¬¬¬A, ¬¬¬¬A, etc. are in L. The reader should keep in mind that though A and ¬¬A are truth-functionally equivalent, *they are nevertheless different sentences*, A has no occurences of ¬ while ¬¬A has two.

Exercises

1 How many sentences are there in (i) L[A, B; ∅] (∅ is the standard symbol for the *empty set*; in other words, there are no connectives in this language), (ii) L[A; ¬], and (iii) L[A; →]?
2 Is A↔B a sentence in L[A, B; ∧, ∨, ¬, →]? If not, does this mean that there is no biconditional sentence in L?
3 Show that there are infinitely many sentences in L[A, B; ∨, ¬] truth-functionally equivalent to A→B.

2   OBJECT-LANGUAGE AND METALANGUAGE

Throughout this book we shall be using more or less standard English to discuss the structure of the formally generated entities intended to be the symbolic representations of English (or any natural-language) sentences themselves. The language in which these structures and their relationships are discussed – in this case English – is called the *metalanguage*. The formal languages, like the propositional languages we have just introduced, whose structure is under discussion in the metalanguage, are usually called *object-languages*.

Where, as here, a special symbolism is used for the object-language, the meta-/object-level distinction is fairly explicit. However, sometimes special symbols are used also in the metalanguage. For example, ⇔ is used in this book as a metalinguistic symbol, denoting a relation between object-language sentences. The letters . . ., X, Y, Z used to refer to 'arbitrary' sentences in a propositional language L are also metalinguistic objects; their correct classification is metalinguistic *variables*, ranging over a domain consisting of all the sentences of L. The letter L itself is also a metalinguistic variable, ranging over a domain consisting of propositional languages.

In saying that English is used as a metalanguage for the discussion of a propositional object-language, we are making a meta-meta-level assertion, since we are now discussing the relationship of ordinary English itself to its object-language(s). Yet we are doing so in ordinary English! In other words, one and the same language – ordinary English in this case – is made to operate on more than one level. But this is true to a great extent even as regards the metalanguage of the object-languages we shall discuss in this book and those object-languages themselves. The reader will soon note, if they haven't already, that in our metalinguistic discussion we are using terms like 'and', 'or', 'not', 'if ... then ...' and 'if and only if', which are, in symbolic form, part of the propositional languages described. There is nothing wrong with this; after all, children are taught the structure of their own language using that language.

The results we shall establish about the properties of propositional and later first-order languages, and the system of formal deduction each will be associated with, are sometimes called *metatheorems*, because they are established using (usually rather informal) reasoning within the meta-language. This metalinguistic reasoning itself is often called *metalogical*, or *metatheoretic*. Most of what appears in textbooks of logic is in fact metalogic, since its object is to discuss properties of formal systems.

3   ANCESTRAL TREES

Consider the propositional language L[A, B, C, ...; ¬, ∧, ∨, →]. We observed in Chapter 1 that its class of sentences can be specified in a very compact way. Call any finite string of symbols drawn from the list enclosed in square brackets in L[...] an *expression of L*. Then an expression of L is a *sentence of L* if and only if it is (i) a sentence letter of L, or (ii) if it is of the form ¬Y, (Y∨Z), (Y∧Z), (Y→Z) where Y and Z are sentences of L.

These clauses define a class of objects – sentences of L – by stating that certain things (sentence letters) are in that class unconditionally, and that certain other things are in it *conditionally* on their being built in a specific way out of things already registered as members. A definition which specifies a class in terms of this sort of absolute-plus-conditional member-ship criterion is called an *inductive definition*. The ability of a class of entities to be defined inductively is a highly prized characteristic, because classes so defined obey a related *principle of induction* which can be used to elicit a range of other interesting properties shared by their members; more on this shortly.

Y is called the *immediate predecessor* of the sentence ¬Y, and Y and Z the *immediate predecessors* of each of the sentences Y∧Z, Y∨Z, Y→Z. Sentence letters are decreed to have no immediate predecessors. We can depict the immediate predecessor relation graphically as follows:

$$X = \neg Y \qquad X = Y \vee Z \text{ (or } Y \wedge Z \text{ or } Y \rightarrow Z)$$
$$\begin{array}{cc} | & / \setminus \\ Y & Y \ Z \end{array}$$

where Y in the first diagram and Y and Z in the second are the immediate predecessors of X. *Do not* confuse these diagrams with the conjugate tree diagrams for the connectives: the latter specify truth-conditions, whereas those above convey purely structural information.

If either Y or Z in the diagrams above is not a sentence letter we can continue the diagrams downwards, to include their immediate predecessors, and so on until we eventually reach sentence letters which, because they have no immediate predecessors, are terminal points of the resulting tree. By analogy with human genealogy we shall call this tree the ancestral tree of X. Here is the ancestral tree of the sentence B→(Bv(A∧¬C)):

```
  B→(Bv¬(A∧¬C))
  ╱      ╲
B      Bv¬(A∧¬C)
        ╱ ╲
       B   ¬(A∧¬C)
            |
           A∧¬C
           ╱ ╲
          A   ¬C
              |
              C
```

The nodes on this tree (i.e. the junction-points of line-segments, including the initial and terminal points) below X are all predecessors of X; another term for these is *proper subsentences* of X. Thus the ancestral tree is also the *subsentence tree* of X.

Exercises

Draw the ancestral trees of the following sentences:

(a) Av¬(A→(BvC))
(b) ¬(CvD)∧(D∧¬C)
(c) A→(B→¬(C∧¬D))

4   AN INDUCTION PRINCIPLE

The sentences in any propositional language all have ancestral trees (the ancestral tree of a sentence letter A is just the single node consisting of A), a fact which is exploited in a very useful method of proving general results about these languages called the *Principle of Induction on Immediate Predecessors*. This says the following. Suppose *P* is any property which it makes sense to speak of sentences of L having or not having. Then:

> If (1) all the sentence letters of L have *P*, and (2) from the assumption that the immediate predecessors of any non-atomic sentence X in L have *P*, it follows that so too does X, then (3) every sentence in L has *P*.

To see why the principle is true, suppose L is any propositional language including the sentence letters A, B, C and the connectives ∧, v, ¬. Let X be B→(B∨¬(A∧¬C)) for example. Look at its ancestral tree given on p. 34 above. Suppose that assumptions (1) and (2) above are satisfied. (1) tells us that A, B and C have *P*, and (2) tells us that we can think of a single line-segment or pair of line-segments in the ancestral tree as carrying possession of *P* upwards from those lower nodes to their successor node. But since, by (1), each of the terminal nodes B, B, A and C (from left to right in the tree) have *P*, it follows that possession of *P* is carried from successive level to successive level up the tree, until it is finally inherited by the topmost node X itself. Clearly, the same argument will establish that any given sentence of L has *P*.

The Induction Principle is really no more than a roundabout way of saying that every sentence in a propositional language has an ancestral tree. But it is very useful, and we shall show by means of some examples how the principle can be used as a powerful (meta)proof-technique. We shall start with a very simple example. Consider the language L[A; ∧]. We shall show, by induction, that no sentence in L is a tautology. Let the property *P* in the statement of the Induction Principle be *is not a tautology*. First, we have to show that (1) in the statement of the principle is satisfied. This means that we have to show that every sentence letter of L is not a tautology. There is only one sentence letter in L, A, and A is not a tautology because it has the truth table

$$\frac{A}{\begin{array}{c} T \\ F \end{array}}$$

which obviously contains at least one F; exactly one, in fact.

Now we must show that (2) is satisfied. This is traditionally called the *induction step*. Suppose X is any sentence of L other than a sentence letter, i.e. other than A. X must therefore contain at least one occurrence of ∧, and hence be of the form Y∧Z, for some pair of sentences Y, Z of L. X's immediate predecessors are therefore Y and Z, and we have to show that if both these have *P*, then so does X. Well, suppose that Y and Z have *P*, i.e. suppose that neither Y nor Z is a tautology. In that case, both Y and Z will have at least one F in their truth table, from which it follows that Y∧Z must have at least one F too, since we know that a conjunction is false if either conjunct is. Hence Y∧Z, i.e. X, is not a tautology. So we have shown that if X's immediate predecessors have *P*, so too does X, and we can invoke the Induction Principle to infer that all sentences in L have *P*, i.e. are not tautologies. **Q.E.D.**

(**Q.E.D.** stands for 'quod erat demonstrandum', i.e. 'which was to be demonstrated'. This is the phrase, translated into Latin from the original Greek, with which Euclid signalled the end of a demonstration in his celebrated *Elements*. The three letters, boldface, will be used to perform the same function throughout this book.)

To sum up: a proof by induction on immediate predecessors proceeds in the following three stages:

(1) establish that all the sentence letters in L have *P*, the property in question; and

(2) show that from the assumption that the immediate predecessors of some arbitrary sentence Z have *P* (this provisional assumption is called the *inductive hypothesis*), it follows that Z too must have *P*.

If stages (1) and (2) are both successfully accomplished, then we invoke the Principle of Induction to conclude that

(3) all the sentences of L have *P*.

We shall now look at another proof by induction, in which the induction step is a so-called *proof by cases*. This time L is the language L[A; →], i.e. the set of all sentences which can be constructed from A and the single connective →. Let *P* now be the property of either being a tautology or being truth-functionally equivalent to A.

(1) We first have to show that all sentence letters of L have *P*. Since there is only one, A, this amounts to showing that A has P. But obviously A has *P*, since A ⇔ A.

(2) We now have to show for every non-atomic X in L, that if X's immediate predecessors have *P*, then so does X itself. If X is non-atomic, this means that X must be of the form Y→Z for some sentences Y and Z of L. Y and Z are X's immediate predecessors, so we now have to assume that both Y and Z have *P*, and see whether from that assumption we can show that X must have *P*. So let us assume that Y is equivalent to A or Y is a tautology, and the same for Z. This is our inductive hypothesis, and it implies that there are four exclusive and exhaustive possibilities to consider:

(i) Y is a tautology and Z is a tautology; or

(ii) Y is a tautology and Z ⇔ A; or

(iii) Y ⇔ A and Z is a tautology; or finally

(iv) Y ⇔ A and Z ⇔ A.

We shall now consider these in turn.

(i) We here have the truth table

A	Y	Z	Y→Z
T	T	T	T
F	T	T	T

Clearly, X = Y→Z is a tautology, and therefore X has *P*.

(ii) Now we have the truth table

A	Y	Z	Y→Z
T	T	T	T
F	T	F	F

Here X = Y→Z is obviously equivalent to A, and so in this case too X has *P*.

(iii) This gives the truth table

A	Y	Z	Y→Z
T	T	T	T
F	F	T	T

in which case X = Y→Z is a tautology. Hence in this case X has *P*.

(iv) Here the truth table is

A	Y	Z	Y→Z
T	T	T	T
F	F	F	T

and so in this case X is a tautology, and so has *P*. We have just proved that in each of the four different possible cases, if Y and Z have *P*, so does X. The Principle of Induction on Immediate Predecessors now permits us to conclude that all sentences in L are either equivalent to A or are tautologies, and step (3) is accomplished. **Q.E.D.**

Exercises

1 What are the immediate predecessors of the following sentences?
   (a) (A∧B)∨(B∧A)
   (b) (A∧B)∨¬B
   (c) A
   (d) A→(B→C)
   (e) ¬(A→(B→C))

2 Show by induction on immediate predecessors that every sentence in L[A; ∧] and every sentence in L[A; ∨] is truth-functionally equivalent to A.

3 Show by induction on immediate predecessors that if X is any sentence in L[A; ↔] then X is either a tautology or is truth-functionally equivalent to A.

4* (*Replacement Principle*) Suppose X, U, V are sentences in L[A, B, C, . . .; ∧, ∨, ¬, →]. Define X(V/U) as follows. If U is a subsentence of X (i.e. U is a node in X's ancestral tree), X(V/U) is the result of substituting V for every occurrence of U in X; if U is not a subsentence of X, X(V/U) = X. Show by induction on immediate predecessors that if U⇔V then X⇔X(V/U).

A DIGRESSION ON MATHEMATICAL INDUCTION

(This can be skipped by those with an aversion to numbers.) Readers acquainted with the Principle of Mathematical Induction will find something very familiar about that of induction on immediate predecessors. This is as it should be, because at bottom both enunciate one and the same principle. The Principle of Mathematical Induction on the set N = {0, 1, 2, 3, . . .} of natural numbers says that if P is a property and (1) 0 has P and (2) whenever m in N has P so does m + 1, then all natural numbers have P (there is an analogous principle for the positive integers Z^+ = {1, 2, 3, . . .}, only (1) becomes the condition that 1 has P). Now m is the (sole) immediate predecessor of m + 1, and so we can restate clause (2) as . . . (2'): whenever the immediate predecessor of any non-zero number n has P so does n . . ., and we have something which differs from the Principle of Induction on Immediate Predecessors only in the fact that truth-functional sentences can have multiple immediate predecessors, whereas each positive integer has only one. To put it another way, the ancestral tree of a sentence may and usually will branch, whereas the ancestral tree of a positive integer is a line. However, there are propositional languages whose structure is formally identical (the technical term is *isomorphic*) to that of the natural numbers with their successor/predecessor structure. For example, L = L[A; ¬], where A corresponds to 0 and passing from X to ¬X in L corresponds to passing from n to n + 1 in N.

For those who have not seen a proof by mathematical induction before, here is a well-known and simple one. We want to show that 1 + 2 + 3 + . . . + n = n(n + 1)/2, for all n in Z^+ (the set of positive integers). Let S_n stand for the sum of the first n positive integers, i.e. 1 + 2 + . . . + n, and f(n) for the function n(n + 1)/2. Let n have the property P just in case S_n = f(n). It is easy to show by mathematical induction that every n in Z^+ has P. First we need to check that 1 has P. This is immediate, since clearly S_1 = 1 = f(1). Now for the induction step: we shall assume that m has P for some arbitrary m, and then show that m + 1 has P. So we suppose that S_m = f(m). Adding m + 1 to both sides, we infer that 1 + 2 + . . . + m + (m + 1) = S_{m+1} = f(m) + (m + 1) = (m(m + 1)/2) + m + 1 = (m(m + 1) + 2(m + 1))/2 = (m + 1)(m + 2)/2 = f(m + 1). Thus from m's having P we infer that m + 1 has P, and the induction step is proved. Hence we infer that for all n in Z^+, n has P. **Q.E.D.**

5 MULTIPLE CONJUNCTIONS AND DISJUNCTIONS

In this section we shall use the Principle of Induction on Immediate Predecessors to prove a very useful metaresult about truth-functional compounds which involve only the connective ∧, and compounds which only involve ∨. As a preamble we can verify by truth tables that the following two equivalences hold for any sentences X, Y and Z in any propositional language containing ∧ and ∨ (cf. exercise 1, Chapter 1, section 4):

X∧(Y∧Z) ⇔ (X∧Y)∧Z
X∨(Y∨Z) ⇔ (X∨Y)∨Z.

These two conditions amount to saying that ∨ and ∧ are associative: it does not matter where you put the brackets in a conjunction or disjunction of X, Y and Z: X∧(Y∧Z) is true just when all of X, Y and Z are true, and X∨(Y∨Z) is false just when all of X, Y and Z are false. For this reason the sentences above are usually written simply as X∧Y∧Z and X∨Y∨Z respectively.

We shall now generalise this result. Let the set S in L[S; ∧] contain n sentence letters, which we shall write $A_1, \ldots, A_n$ (these are *metalinguistic* symbols used simply to signify that S contains n sentence letters; no ordering of those letters is implied), and let X be a sentence in L[S, ∧], i.e. in L[$A_1, \ldots, A_n$; ∧]. Thus X is obtained by conjoining some or all of the sentence letters in S in any order, possibly with repetitions. Using the Principle of Induction on Immediate Predecessors we shall now show that for all X in L, X takes the value T in its truth table just when all the A_i in X take the value T. Let *P* be the property a sentence X in L has when the following condition is satisfied: X takes the value T when and only when all the A_i in X take the value T. We shall show (1) that all the A_i have *P*, and (2) that for non-atomic X, if X's immediate predecessors have *P* then so does X itself.

(1) is immediate. For to say that A_j has *P* is to say that A_j is T when and only when A_j is T, which is itself (trivially) true. Now for the induction step (2). Suppose that X is not an A_i. Then X must be of the form Y∧Z, with immediate predecessors Y and Z for some sentences Y and Z in L. Let us suppose (the inductive hypothesis) that Y and Z each have *P*, i.e. they are T just when their component A_i are all T. We have to establish that the inductive hypothesis implies that X is T if and only if all its constituent sentence letters are T. (i) Suppose X is T. Then Y and Z must both be T. Hence, by the inductive hypothesis, all the sentence letters in Y and Z are all T. But these are just the sentence letters in X itself. (ii) Suppose all the sentence letters in X are T. Hence all the sentence letters in Y and in Z are all T. Hence, by the inductive hypothesis, Y and Z are both T. Hence X is T. So the induction step (2) is established and the result follows. **Q.E.D.**

This result tells us that any two sentences in L containing the same sentence letters are truth-functionally equivalent. A corollary is that we do not need to introduce a new n-place connective to represent the truth function of $A_1, \ldots, A_n$ which is true just when all the A_i are true; *any* compound of the A_i built up using just the binary connective ∧ has the same truth table, namely T when all the A_i are T, and F in every other case. A corollary is that if X contains $A_1, \ldots, A_n$ then X can be written without ambiguity as $A_1 \wedge \ldots \wedge A_n$: the bracketing inside X makes no difference to its truth-value. This is unlike the situation with $\rightarrow$, for example, where $A \rightarrow (B \rightarrow C)$ is not equivalent to $(A \rightarrow B) \rightarrow C$.

By a similar use of the Induction Principle, we can show that a truth-functional compound X obtained by *disjoining* the sentences $A_1, \ldots, A_n$ in any order is *false* just when all of $A_1, \ldots, A_n$ are *false*, and we can therefore write X without ambiguity as $A_1 \vee A_2 \vee \ldots \vee A_n$.

Exercises

1 Write out in full the inductive proof that if X is in $L[A_1, \ldots, A_n; \vee]$ then X is false just when all the A_i in X are false.
2 Show that if $X_1, \ldots, X_n$ and Y are truth-functional compounds, then Y is a truth-functional consequence of the set $\{X_1, \ldots, X_n\}$ if and only if Y is a truth-functional consequence of the sentence $X_1 \wedge \ldots \wedge X_n$.

6   THE DISJUNCTIVE NORMAL FORM THEOREM

Consider the following list of truth-functional equivalences (if they are not already familiar, commit them to memory now):

$$
\begin{aligned}
X \rightarrow Y &\Leftrightarrow \neg X \vee Y \\
&\Leftrightarrow \neg(X \wedge \neg Y) \\
X \vee Y &\Leftrightarrow \neg X \rightarrow Y \\
&\Leftrightarrow \neg(\neg X \wedge \neg Y) \\
X \wedge Y &\Leftrightarrow \neg(X \rightarrow \neg Y) \\
&\Leftrightarrow \neg(\neg X \vee \neg Y) \\
X \leftrightarrow Y &\Leftrightarrow (X \rightarrow) \wedge (Y \rightarrow X)
\end{aligned}
$$

Historical note The equivalences $X \wedge Y \Leftrightarrow \neg(\neg X \vee \neg Y)$ and $X \vee Y \Leftrightarrow \neg(\neg X \wedge \neg Y)$ are traditionally called *de Morgan's Laws*, after the nineteenth-century mathematician Augustus de Morgan.

This list of equivalences shows that in principle we could make do with only negation and one other of the connectives in the set $\{\wedge, \vee, \neg, \rightarrow, \leftrightarrow\}$, for each of the remainder is definable in terms of those two (a connective C is *definable in terms of others in a set* Π just in case for every sentence in $L[A, B, C \ldots; C]$ there is an equivalent one in $L[A, B, C \ldots; \Pi]$). In practice, it is convenient to have more than the bare minimum: for example, it is not immediately obvious that $\neg(X \rightarrow \neg Y)$ is equivalent to $X \wedge Y$, and so while we could make do with $\neg$ and $\rightarrow$ to formulate conjunctions, it is simpler and clearer to add $\wedge$ to the stock of basic vocabulary.

Having too much basic vocabulary can also be inefficient. One would not in practice want to introduce a separate four-place truth-functional operator ç, where ç(A, B, C, D) is defined to be true when A and C are both true, true when A and B are false and D true, and false in all other cases: we simply do not have enough occasion to make this particular type of assertion to warrant giving it a special name. It is nevertheless nice to know that should such occasion actually arise, we should not be lost for words as long as we have ∧, ∨ and ¬. For ç(A, B, C, D) can easily be shown to be truth-functionally equivalent to a sentence in L[A, B, C, D; ∧, ∨, ¬]. Indeed, by a simple procedure we shall describe shortly, *any* n-place truth-functional operator $\partial(A_1, \ldots, A_n)$ can be shown to be truth-functionally equivalent to some sentence in $L[A_1, \ldots A_n; \wedge, \vee, \neg]$.

We shall first illustrate how the procedure works with ç(A, B, C, D). ç(A, B, C, D) was defined to be true when A and C are true, true when A and B are false and D true, and false in all other cases. So ç(A, B, C, D) is true for the following six rows, and only those rows, of its truth table:

A	B	C	D
T	T	T	T
T	F	T	T
T	T	T	F
T	F	T	F
F	F	T	T
F	F	F	T

The assertion that ç(A, B, C, D) is true is therefore equivalent to the sixfold disjunction:

(A is T and B is T and C is T and D is T) or
(A is T and B is F and C is T and D is T) or
(A is T and B is T and C is T and D is F) or
(A is T and B is F and C is T and D is F) or
(A is F and B is F and C is T and D is T) or
(A is F and B is F and C is F and D is T).

We know that for any sentence X, X is false if and only if ¬X is true, i.e. X is F if and only if ¬X is T. So, for example, we can rewrite the second disjunct as 'A is T and ¬B is T and C is T and D is T', which is itself equivalent to '(A∧¬B∧C∧D) is T.' We also know that for any sentences X and Y, X is T or Y is T if and only if X∨Y is T. From these facts we infer that ç(A, B, C, D) has the same truth table as the disjunction

(A∧B∧C∧D)∨(A∧¬B∧C∧D)∨(A∧B∧C∧¬D)∨(A∧¬B∧C∧¬D)∨
(¬A∧¬B∧C∧D)∨(¬A∧¬B∧¬C∧D)

and hence is truth-functionally equivalent to it.

We can easily generalise this procedure. Suppose X is a sentence in a propositional language whose sentence letters are A, B, C, ... For each row of X's truth table, write out a corresponding conjunction $\pm A \wedge \pm B \wedge \pm C \wedge$ ..., where $\pm A$ is defined to be A if A takes the value T at that row, and is $\neg A$ if A takes the value F at that row; similarly for $\pm B$, $\pm C$, etc. (the alphabetical ordering of A, B, C, etc. in the conjunctions is quite arbitrary; any other could be chosen instead). Now form the disjunction of all these conjunctions which correspond to T rows of X's truth table. This disjunction is a sentence in L[A, B, C, . . .; $\wedge$, $\vee$, $\neg$], which by the reasoning above is truth-functionally equivalent to X. This construction obviously presupposes that X takes the value T on at least one row of its truth table; if X doesn't, i.e. if X is a contradiction, then X is equivalent to $A \wedge \neg A$, which is, of course, also a sentence in L[A, B, C, . . .; $\wedge$, $\vee$, $\neg$].

We have in effect proved the following theorem:

Theorem 1 (Disjunctive Normal Form Theorem)

Suppose X is a sentence in a propositional language L with n sentence letters, which we shall denote by $A_1, \ldots, A_n$. If X is not a contradiction, then it is truth-functionally equivalent to a disjunction of conjunctions of the form $\pm A_1 \wedge \ldots \wedge \pm A_n$, where $+ A_i = A_i$, $-A_i = \neg A_i$.

Corollary

Any truth-functional assertion is equivalent to one which uses just the connectives $\wedge$, $\vee$ and $\neg$.

Another way of stating the corollary is that every sentence in the language L in the theorem is truth-functionally equivalent to a sentence in L[$A_1, \ldots, A_n$; $\wedge$, $\vee$, $\neg$]. This is one of the fundamental results of (meta)logic. It tells us that $\wedge$, $\vee$, $\neg$ are the most one needs in terms of truth-functional operations to formulate *any* truth-functional assertion, whereby a truth-functional assertion is meant one which can be evaluated as true or false by means of a truth table. Nor is this set of connectives the smallest with this 'universal' property: we know that either disjunction or conjunction can be defined in terms of each other together with $\neg$; indeed, as we shall see in the next section, we can actually find a single binary connective with the same 'universal' property.

A non-contradictory sentence X which is already a disjunction of conjunctions $\pm A_1 \wedge \ldots \wedge \pm A_n$, all with the same number n of conjuncts, is said to be in *Disjunctive Normal Form* (DNF). When X is a sentence not in DNF, then by the theorem above it is equivalent to one that is. There will be as many of these DNF equivalents of X as there are sentences representable in this form in L. Recall that there will be infinitely many of these in general, allowing for differences in bracketing, the order in which the sentence letters occur, and possible repetitions of sentence letters (see pp. 39–40). We could nevertheless select one of these to be the canonical representative, call it DNF(X), as the disjunctive normal form of any sentence X in L, if we wished. One way might be as follows. Order the sentence letters in X, say alphabetically, and take as DNF(X) that disjunction in L whose disjuncts D_1, D_2, D_3 ... are of the form $((\pm A \wedge \pm B) \wedge \pm C) \wedge$ ... and then write the disjuncts similarly as $(((D_1 \vee D_2) \vee D_3) \vee$ .... Any other choice of canonical representative would in principle be just as good, however, and we shall simply write DNF(X) as a multiple disjunction $D_1 \vee D_2 \vee D_3$ ..., without internal pairwise bracketing, of multiple conjunctions $\pm A \pm B \pm C$ ..., also without internal pairwise bracketing.

Example

Let X be the sentence $C \rightarrow \neg (B \vee A)$. To find DNF(X), first construct the truth table for X:

	A B C	$C \rightarrow \neg (B \vee A)$
1	T T T	F F T
2	T T F	T F T
3	T F T	F F T
4	F T T	F F T
5	F F T	T T F
6	F T F	T F T
7	T F F	T F T
8	F F F	T T F

X is true at rows 2, 5, 6, 7 and 8. These rows will determine DNF(X). Since the letters in the conjuncts of DNF(X) will appear in the order A, B, C, we have DNF(X) = $(A \wedge B \wedge \neg C) \vee (\neg A \wedge \neg B \wedge C) \vee (\neg A \wedge B \wedge \neg C) \vee (A \wedge \neg B \wedge \neg C) \vee (\neg A \wedge \neg B \wedge \neg C)$.

Exercises

1 If X contains k sentence letters, what is the maximum number of disjuncts DNF(X) can possess?
2 Find the Disjunctive Normal form of each sentence below.
   (i) $A \rightarrow B$
   (ii) $A \vee B$
   (iii) $A \wedge B$
   (iv) $A \leftrightarrow B$
   (v) $A \neg A \vee B$
   (vi) $A \wedge \neg (B \vee \neg (C \rightarrow \neg A))$
   (vii) $\neg (B \vee A)$

7 ADEQUATE SETS OF CONNECTIVES

A set of connectives in terms of which all truth-functions can be defined is said to be *adequate for truth-functional logic*, or just *adequate*, for short. The Disjunctive Normal Form Theorem tells us that the set {∧, ∨, ¬} is adequate. So, of course, is any set which includes these connectives. Also, in view of the fact that ∨ (respectively ∧) is definable, by de Morgan's Laws, in terms of ¬ and ∧ (respectively ∨), we infer that both sets {¬, ∧} and {¬, ∨} are adequate. Because X∧Y ⇔ ¬(X→¬Y), and X∨Y ⇔ ¬X→Y, we know that {→, ¬} is also adequate. Surprisingly, we can find a binary connective which by itself turns out to be adequate. In fact, we can find two, symbolised | and ↓, whose truth tables are these:

A B	A|B		A B	A↓B
T T	F		T T	F
T F	T		T F	F
F T	T		F T	F
F F	T		F F	T

| is sometimes called *alternative denial*, because A|B is true just when one at least of A and B is false, and ↓ is sometimes called *joint denial*, because A↓B is true just when both A and B are false. Other names for | and ↓ are '*nand*' and '*nor*' respectively (we shall see why shortly).

It might not seem obvious, looking at these truth tables, that we can define negation in terms both of | and ↓. But, as can easily be checked with a truth table, if X is any sentence

$$\neg X \Leftrightarrow X|X \Leftrightarrow X{\downarrow}X \quad (5)$$

We can also see from the truth table for | that

$$A|B \Leftrightarrow \neg(A{\wedge}B)$$

which is why | is called 'nand', nand abbreviating 'not-and'. Hence

$$\neg(A|B) \Leftrightarrow A{\wedge}B$$

and substituting A|B for X in (5) we get

$$(A|B)|(A|B) \Leftrightarrow A{\wedge}B$$

In other words, we have shown that both ¬ and ∧ are definable in terms of |. Hence, since {¬, ∧} is an adequate set, | must also be adequate.

Now for ↓. From its truth table we can see that

$$A{\downarrow}B \Leftrightarrow \neg(A{\vee}B)$$

which is why ↓ is often called 'nor', i.e. 'not-or', or for that matter the ordinary English 'nor'. Hence

$$\neg(A{\wedge}B) \Leftrightarrow A{\vee}B$$

and so, by (5) again,

$(A\downarrow B)\downarrow(A\downarrow B) \Leftrightarrow A\vee B$

So both $\neg$ and $\vee$ are definable in terms of $\downarrow$; hence, since $\{\neg, \vee\}$ is an adequate set, $\downarrow$ is adequate.

Exercises

1 Write down the (unsigned) conjugate tree diagrams for $|$ and $\downarrow$.
2 Find a sentence X in L[A, B; $|$] such that $A\vee B \Leftrightarrow X$, and a sentence Y in L[A, B; $\downarrow$] such that $A\wedge B \Leftrightarrow Y$.
3 Find sentences X in L[A, B; $|$] and Y in L[A, B; $\downarrow$] such that $A\rightarrow B \Leftrightarrow X$ and $A\rightarrow B \Leftrightarrow Y$.
4 Which of the following are tautologies, contradictions and neither?
   (i) $(A|B)|(B|A)$
   (ii) $(A\downarrow(A\downarrow A))\downarrow(A\downarrow(A\downarrow A))$
   (iii) $(A|(A|A))|(A|(A|A))$
   (iv) $(A|B)\downarrow(A|B)$
5 Find the DNFs of
   (i) $(A|B)|(B|A)$
   (ii) $A\downarrow(B\downarrow C)$
6 Explain why it makes no sense to write $A|B|C$ or $A\downarrow B\downarrow C$.
7* Show by induction on immediate predecessors that if X is any sentence in L[A, B; $\leftrightarrow$, $\neg$], then X has 0 or 2 or 4 Ts in its truth table (i.e. in the truth table with *four* rows determined by the four truth-value distributions over A and B). Explain why this shows that $\{\leftrightarrow, \neg\}$ is not adequate. Hint: think of conjunction and disjunction.

8*   THE DUALITY PRINCIPLE

An interesting and elegant result that can be easily proved using the Principle of Induction on Immediate Predecessors is the *Duality Principle*:

Theorem 2 (Duality Principle)

Let X be any sentence in L[A_1, ... A_n; $\wedge$, $\vee$, $\neg$]. Let X* be obtained from X by replacing every occurrence of $\wedge$ in X by $\vee$, every occurrence of $\vee$ by $\wedge$, and every occurrence of A_i by $\neg A_i$. Then $X\Leftrightarrow\neg X^*$. (X* is called the dual of X.)

Proof

A sentence X of L, where L is as in the theorem, will be said to have the property P if $X\Leftrightarrow\neg X^*$. We shall prove by induction on immediate predecessors that all sentences of L have P. So we have to establish that the following two conditions are satisfied: (1) each A_i has P; and (2) for any non-atomic X, from the inductive hypothesis that the immediate predecessors of X have P, it follows that X does also.

(1) Each A_i clearly has no occurrence of $\vee$ or $\wedge$, and so $A_i{}^*$ is just $\neg A_i$. So showing that A_i has P merely requires showing that $A_i \Leftrightarrow \neg \neg A_i$, which we know to be the case.

(2) The induction step is an argument by cases. If X is not an A_i then X must have one of the following three forms: (i) $X = Y \vee Z$, (ii) $X = Y \wedge Z$, or (iii) $X = \neg Y$, where Y and Z are sentences of L. If X is of the form (i) or (ii) it has as immediate predecessors Y and Z, while if it is of the form (iii) it has the one immediate predecessor Y. We shall check that the induction step holds in each of the cases.

(i) Suppose that Y and Z each have P, i.e. that $Y \Leftrightarrow \neg Y^*$ and $Z \Leftrightarrow \neg Z^*$. This supposition, recall, is the inductive hypothesis. From this we infer that $Y \vee Z \Leftrightarrow \neg Y^* \vee \neg Z^*$ (exercise 1 below). By de Morgan's Laws $\neg Y^* \vee \neg Z^* \neg \Leftrightarrow (Y^* \wedge Z^*)$. But $Y^* \wedge Z^* = (Y \vee Z)^*$ (exercise 2 below), and $Y \vee Z = X$. So we have shown that the inductive hypothesis implies that $X \Leftrightarrow \neg X^*$, i.e. X has P as required.

(ii) We have the same inductive hypothesis as in (i). So again $Y \Leftrightarrow \neg Y^*$ and $Z \Leftrightarrow \neg Z^*$. Hence $Y \wedge Z \Leftrightarrow \neg Y^* \wedge \neg Z^*$. By de Morgan again, $\neg Y^* \wedge \neg Z^* \Leftrightarrow \neg (Y^* \vee Z^*)$. But $Y^* \vee Z^* = (Y \wedge Z)^* = X^*$. So $X \Leftrightarrow \neg X^*$ in this case too.

(iii) Here the inductive hypothesis is simply that $Y \Leftrightarrow \neg Y^*$. Hence $\neg Y \Leftrightarrow \neg \neg Y^*$. But $\neg Y^* = (\neg Y)^* = X^*$. Hence $X \Leftrightarrow \neg X^*$. **Q.E.D.**

Exercises

1 Show that if $X \Leftrightarrow Y$ and $V \Leftrightarrow W$ then
   (a) $X \wedge V \Leftrightarrow Y \wedge W$
   (b) $X \vee V \Leftrightarrow Y \vee W$
2 For any sentences Y, Z in the language $L[A_1, \ldots, A_n; \wedge, \vee, \neg]$, explain why
   (a) $\neg Y^* = (\neg Y)^*$
   (b) $Y^* \wedge Z^* = (Y \vee Z)^*$
   (c) $Y^* \vee Z^* = (Y \wedge Z)^*$
   (Imagine you are a computer programmed with the instructions for converting a sentence X in L into its dual. The program performs its function by working from left to right through X, examining every symbol, changing it appropriately or leaving it unaltered.)
3 Show that if $X \Leftrightarrow Y$ then $X^* \Leftrightarrow Y^*$

9*   CONJUNCTIVE NORMAL FORMS

An important application of the Duality Principle is in finding what are called the Conjunctive Normal Forms of truth-functional compounds. Define a *literal* to be a sentence letter or the negation of one. DNF(X), where X is any non-contradictory sentence, is a disjunction of conjunctions of literals. Now it is easy to show from the Disjunctive Normal Form Theorem and the Duality Principle that X is also equivalent to a conjunction of disjunctions of literals. Since for any sentence X in any language L, X ⇔ DNF(X), we must have ¬X ⇔ DNF(¬X). DNF(¬X) is of course a sentence whose connectives are only ∧, ∨ and ¬, and so by Duality, DNF(¬X) ⇔ ¬(DNF(¬X))*, where as before (DNF(¬X))* is the dual of DNF(¬X). Hence we have ¬X ⇔ ¬(DNF(¬X))*, and so X ⇔ (DNF(¬X))*. If we now eliminate any double negation ¬¬ that might appear in (DNF(¬X))* we obtain a conjunction of disjunctions of sentence letters and their negations, and this conjunction is called the *Conjunctive Normal Form CNF(X) of X*. For example, suppose X is the compound ¬(A∧(B→C)). As a first step, write out DNF(¬X). This is (A∧B∧C) ∨ (A∧¬B∧¬C) ∨ (A∧¬B∧C) (as in 6, we are assuming that the ordering of sentence letters relative to which the DNF's are defined is alphabetical). Dualising, and eliminating double negations, we get CNF(X) = (¬A∨¬B∨¬C) ∧ (¬A∨B∨C) ∧ (¬A∨B∨¬C).

To sum up: to find the CNF of a compound X you (i) find DNF(¬X), (ii) obtain its dual (DNF(¬X))*, and (iii) eliminate all double negations from (DNF(¬X))*; the result is CNF(X). If X is a tautology then its negation is a contradiction, and the DNF of ¬X is, according to the convention agreed earlier, A∧¬A. By steps (ii) and (iii) above, CNF(X) = ¬A∨A.

Another example

Let X be (C→¬(B∨A))∧¬(C∧A). DNF(¬X) = (A∧B∧C) ∨ (¬A∧B∧C) ∨ (A∧¬B∧C). Hence CNF(X) = (¬A∨¬B∨¬C) ∧ (A¬B∨¬C) ∧ (¬A∨B∨¬C).

Conjunctive Normal Forms are very important in logic programming, where the inferential technique of *resolution* works on sentences cast into this form.

Exercises

Write out CNF(X) for each sentence X below:

1   A→B
2   A∧B
3   A→(B∨C)
4   A→(B→A)

Chapter 4

Soundness and completeness

1 THE STANDARD PROPOSITIONAL LANGUAGE

We have already had some experience, in Chapter 2, of constructing truth trees. In this chapter we shall establish the procedure on a systematic basis and give rigorous proofs of their fundamental properties, namely that if all the members of a finite set of truth-functional sentences are *satisfiable*, i.e. true for some distribution of truth-values over their sentence letters, then they generate a finite open tree, while if they are not satisfiable they generate a closed one.

These results establish a relationship between a *syntactic* property of a finite set Σ of sentences, its generating a closed or open tree (this is a syntactic property because, as we shall see, rules can be given for tree construction of a purely formal character), and a *semantic* one, satisfiability. To prove them we have to state more precisely what form the rules of tree construction take. To begin with, we need to confine the discussion to a specific propositional language. Because our aim is a model of deductive reasoning of as great a generality as can be achieved, this propositional language should be *universal*, in the sense that *any* truth-functional inference can be represented in it. We know from the Disjunctive Normal Form Theorem that the truth-functional structure of all the sentences appearing as premises and conclusion in any inference can be translated into sentences of a propositional language L[S; Π] in which Π is the set {∧, ∨, ¬}. So any propositional language with those connectives and in which there is an unlimited supply of sentence letters will be universal in the sense we require. To give ourselves something a bit more like the luxury of ordinary language (which is what, after all, we are modelling), we shall add → to the set {∧, ∨, ¬}. What we shall now do is select an arbitrary one of these universal languages, which differ only in their sentence letters, and call it the *standard propositional language*; in the rest of this chapter it will be referred to as L[A, B, C, . . .; ∧, ∨, ¬, →] or just L.

↔ is not one of L's connectives; for technical reasons which will become apparent it is convenient to do without it. However, it is of course there implicitly, and we shall continue to write $X \leftrightarrow Y$ in appropriate circumstances, regarding this as merely shorthand for one of its truth-functional equivalents in L, like $(X \rightarrow Y) \wedge (Y \rightarrow X)$, for example.

2   TRUTH TREES AGAIN

We can 'collapse' all the conjugate diagrams for $\wedge$, $\vee$, $\rightarrow$ into just two in the following way. First, we rearrange them into two groups as follows:

(i) $X \wedge Y$ $\neg(X \vee Y)$ $\neg(X \rightarrow Y)$
     | | |
     X $\neg X$ X
     Y $\neg Y$ $\neg Y$

(ii) $\neg(X \wedge Y)$ $X \vee Y$ $X \rightarrow Y$
    / \   / \   / \
 $\neg X$ $\neg Y$ X   Y $\neg X$ Y

We shall classify the upper sentences in (i) and (ii) as α and β sentences as follows (with a minor variation this is Smullyan's (1968) classification):

An α *sentence of L* is of the form either $X \wedge Y$, $\neg(X \vee Y)$ or $\neg(X \rightarrow Y)$, where X and Y are sentences of L. For each of these three types of α sentence we define a corresponding pair of sentences α_1, α_2:

α	α_1	α_2
$X \wedge Y$	X	Y
$\neg(X \vee Y)$	$\neg X$	$\neg Y$
$\neg(X \rightarrow Y)$	X	$\neg Y$

A β *sentence of L* is of the form $X \vee Y$, $X \rightarrow Y$, or $\neg(X \wedge Y)$, where X and Y are sentences of L. For each of these three types of β sentence we define corresponding pairs of sentences β_1, β_2:

β	β_1	β_2
$X \vee Y$	X	Y
$X \rightarrow Y$	$\neg X$	Y
$\neg(X \wedge Y)$	$\neg X$	$\neg Y$

The two groups of diagrams above can now be represented by just the two diagrams:

         α β
         | / \
         α_1 β_1 β_2
         α_2

These diagrams will henceforth be known as the *tree rules (α) and (β)* respectively; the pairs of sentences α_1, α_2 and β_1, β_2 will be called the *descendants* of α and β respectively under the rules. Together with the Rule of Double Negation

$$\begin{array}{c} \neg\neg X \\ | \\ X \end{array}$$

these will be all the rules we shall employ in constructing truth-functional truth trees. A simple result which we shall find useful and which can be left to the reader to check is the following:

Theorem 1

If α is any α sentence and β is any β sentence then $\alpha \Leftrightarrow \alpha_1 \wedge \alpha_2$ and $\beta \Leftrightarrow \beta_1 \vee \beta_2$.

Theorem 1 explains why α sentences are sometimes called *conjunctive sentences*, and β sentences *disjunctive sentences*.

Another useful result we shall need is this: every sentence in L is either a literal, or a sentence commencing with at least one pair of consecutive occurrences of a negation symbol, or an α sentence, or a β sentence. It's hardly necessary to dignify this with the title 'theorem', and we shall leave its demonstration an exercise (you just need to note that every sentence in L is either a sentence letter or else is a sentence of the form $\neg X$, $X \wedge Y$, $X \vee Y$ or $X \rightarrow Y$, with outer brackets omitted as usual).

Before proceeding to a formal statement of the rules of tree construction, we shall briefly review some general tree-concepts. The *nodes* (see Chapter 3, section 3) are the end-points and junction-points of line-segments. The topmost node is the *root* of the tree. The nodes on an ancestral tree are all single sentences; those on a truth tree, by contrast, may also be constituted by sets of sentences: the pair $\{\alpha_1, \alpha_2\}$, appearing on a tree without the set brackets {} and with α_1 conventionally written above α_2, is a single node, as is the set of initial sentences which will, unless otherwise indicated, form the root of the tree. A *branch* in a tree is the sequence of nodes in any continuous path along line-segments upwards from the lowest node to the root, including the end-points. We can regard a single node as a degenerate branch.

Of course, we have not yet formally defined a tree. So far we have relied on the following informal characterisation. A finished tree generated by a finite set Σ of initial sentences is the entity generated by applying a tree rule to an unused sentence in Σ (if there is one; if there isn't, Σ itself is the finished tree generated by Σ), and continuing to apply the appropriate rule to every unused sentence on every branch generated, closing a branch as soon as a sentence and its negation appear on it. When either every branch has closed or there are no further sentences that can be used, the tree is finished.

A defect of this definition, apart from its informality, is that it fails to highlight one of the most important features of truth trees, namely the fact that they can be constructed in a completely mechanical way. Another way of putting this is to say that their construction can be made entirely algorithmic, or programmable on a suitably idealised computer. Here is a 'proto-program' for constructing a tree from Σ:

Start. Write the members of Σ in a column. Check that no sentence and its negation are in Σ. If there is a sentence and its negation in Σ, draw a line under Σ and stop: the tree consisting of just Σ is said to be finished and closed. If there is no sentence and its negation in Σ, check that there is at least one non-literal in Σ (as in Chapter 2, section 9*, a literal is any sentence letter or negation of a sentence letter). If there is not, stop: the tree consisting just of Σ is finished and open. If neither of these eventualities is the case, select the topmost non-literal X in Σ. We know that X is either a sentence commencing with more than one negation symbol, or else is an α or β sentence. We deal with these cases in turn.

(i) If X is a sentence commencing with more than one $\neg$, we can write it $\neg\neg Y$; now apply the double negation rule to X, i.e. write

$$| \atop Y$$

directly below Σ. X has now been used.

(ii) If X is an α sentence, apply the (α) rule to X; i.e. write

$$| \atop {\alpha_1 \atop \alpha_2}$$

directly below Σ, where α_1, α_2 are the descendants of X under that rule. X has now been used.

(iii) If X is a β sentence, apply the (β) rule to X; i.e. write

$$/ \quad \backslash \atop {\beta_1 \quad \beta_2}$$

below Σ, where β_1, β_2 are the corresponding descendants of X under that rule. X has now been used.

Now repeat the following sequence of instructions, enclosed within < and > brackets, in the order they appear, until no further repetition of the sequence is possible. When that happens, stop. The result is a finished tree generated from Σ.

<Close any branch containing a sentence and its negation by writing a bar under the lowest node on the branch. If all branches are closed, stop; the tree is finished and closed. If not all branches are closed, but the tree contains only literals or used sentences, stop: it is finished and open. If the tree is not finished, select the leftmost open branch **B** on which there is an unused non-literal. Choose the topmost of these on **B**; call it Y. Y will either be a sentence commencing with more than one $\neg$, or will be an α sentence, or will be a β sentence. In each case write the corresponding tree diagram for Y at the lower end of *every* open branch passing through Y.>

We called this set of instructions a proto-program because while it is not a computer program, it can be turned into one. When started up it will alway halt after finitely many repeats, whatever the set of initial sentences so long as that set is finite. This is because each of the rules (α) and (β) applied to a sentence eliminates a binary connective, while the Rule of Double Negation ensures that at some stage in the evolution of the tree every sentence on it commencing with a consecutive sequence of ¬'s will be reduced either to a literal, or else to an α or β sentence. As there are only finitely many occurrences of a connective in any sentence, it follows that after finitely many stages of the program all the sentences in Σ will have been decomposed into literals, or else the tree will have closed at some earlier point.

As we pointed out in Chapter 2, neither the numbering of lines on the tree nor the ticking of sentences on it as they are used is integral to the tree: they merely help the tree-grower keep stock of what they are doing. Henceforward we shall number lines where it is is obviously helpful, though instead of ticking sentences as they are used we shall state at each line, where it is not obvious, which line number was used to obtain that line.

Exercises

1 For each of the following sentences, say whether it is an α sentence, a β sentence, a literal, or none of these.
   (i)   A→(B→C)
   (ii)   ¬¬A
   (iii) (A∧B)∨¬(A∧¬C)
   (iv)   ¬B
   (v)   ¬(B→(¬C∨¬¬D))
   (vi)   ((C∨¬D)∨¬(D∧B))∧¬(A∨¬A)
2 Construct finished trees for the following sets of sentences, and say whether the trees are open or closed.
   (i)   {A→B, B→C, ¬C, A}
   (ii)   {A→B, B→C, ¬C, ¬A}
   (iii) {A∨B, ¬B∨C, ¬A, ¬C}
   (iv)   {A∨B, ¬B∨C, ¬A, C}
3 Show that every sentence in L is either a literal, or a sentence whose initial symbols are a block of more than one negation symbol, or else is an α or β sentence.

3   TRUTH-FUNCTIONAL CONSISTENCY, TRUTH-FUNCTIONALLY VALID INFERENCES, AND TREES

Suppose we have generated a finished tree from some finite set Σ of initial sentences. There are two possibilities: (i) the tree is closed, and (ii) it is open. We have already been told how to interpret open and closed trees in terms of the satisfiability or not respectively of their sets of initial sentences. This interpretation is justified by a pair of metatheorems which will be proved shortly, the Soundness and Completeness Theorems for truth-functional trees, whose names we are already familiar with but whose precise statement will now be useful:

Soundness Theorem

If τ is a truth-value distribution over sentence letters which makes all the members of Σ true, then every finished tree generated by Σ is open, and all the sentences on each open branch are made true by τ.

Completeness Theorem

If Σ generates a finished open tree, then there is a distribution of truth-values to sentence letters which makes all the members of Σ true; indeed, any truth-value assignment which makes all the literals on each open branch true is one.

   Hence if (i) is the case, the Soundness Theorem tells us that there is no truth-value distribution over the sentence letters appearing in Σ which satisfies Σ, i.e. which makes all the sentences in Σ true (this is simply the contrapositive form of the Soundness Theorem). If (ii) is the case, the Completeness Theorem tell us that assigning the value T to each literal on any open branch, and any values whatever to the remaining sentence letters in Σ, gives a truth-value distribution over the sentence letters in Σ which satisfies Σ.

   We shall say that a set of sentences in any propositional language is *truth-functionally consistent* if there is a distribution of truth-values over its sentence letters which makes all its sentences true (this is the property referred to earlier as satisfiability). If there is not, then it is truth-functionally *in*consistent. *The Soundness Theorem and Completeness Theorem tell us that a finite set of sentences in the standard propositional language is truth-functionally consistent if and only if it generates a finished open tree.* We now list some further consequences of these theorems.

   (a) Whether a tree generated from a finite set Σ closes or not does not depend on the order in which you use the unused sentences which appear at any stage in the development of the tree; you will usually get different trees, but either *all* those trees close or *all* remain open, depending only on whether Σ is truth-functionally consistent or not. If Σ is truth-functionally consistent, then from Soundness it follows that any finished tree generated from Σ has an open branch. The Completeness Theorem implies that if any tree generated from Σ has an open branch, then Σ is truth-functionally consistent; hence if Σ is truth-functionally inconsistent *any* tree generated from Σ closes.

(b) If an inference is truth-functionally valid then the set Σ consisting of its premises and the negation of its conclusion is truth-functionally inconsistent (to show this is left as exercise 1 below), and the Completeness Theorem implies that any tree generated by Σ will close. We shall say that there is a *tree proof* of the conclusion of an inference from its premises if a closed tree can be generated from its premises and the negation of its conclusion. Thus the Completeness Theorem implies that if an inference is truth-functionally valid then there is a tree proof of its conclusion from its premises (this is the sense of 'completeness' to which the name of the theorem refers).

(c) If an inference is truth-functionally invalid then the set Σ consisting of its premises and the negation of its conclusion is truth-functionally consistent. Hence by the Soundness Theorem any tree generated by Σ will remain open, and by the Completeness Theorem every truth-value distribution over sentence letters obtained by assigning all the literals the value T on each open branch is a counterexample to the inference.

(d) If the set Σ consisting of the premise and negation of conclusion of an inference generates a finished open tree, then *every* counterexample to the inference can be obtained as some open branch. For suppose τ is a distribution of truth-values to the sentence letters of the inference which makes all the sentences in Σ true. Then there is an open branch in any finished tree generated by Σ on which all the sentences, and hence all the literals, are true under τ.

Now for some examples. We shall start by showing that the inference in exercise 3(ii), section 8, Chapter 1, is truth-functionally valid. The inference, formalised

$$(\neg B \to \neg A) \wedge (\neg C \to \neg B), \ D \wedge (D \to \neg C), \ E \to A \ \therefore \ \neg E,$$

has a tree proof as follows (opposite):

1	$(\neg B \rightarrow \neg A) \wedge (\neg C \rightarrow \neg B)$	premise
2	$D \wedge (D \rightarrow \neg C)$	premise
3	$E \rightarrow A$	premise
4	$\neg\neg E$	¬conclusion

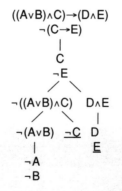

5	D	(α) on 2
6	$D \rightarrow \neg C$	
7	$\neg B \rightarrow \neg A$	(α) on 1
8	$\neg C \rightarrow \neg B$	
9	$\neg \underline{D}$ $\neg C$	(β) on 6
10	$\underline{\neg\neg C}$ $\neg B$	(β) on 8
11	$\underline{\neg\neg B}$ $\neg A$	(β) on 7
12	$\underline{\neg E}$ $\underline{A}$	(β) on 3

Now look at the inference of exercise 3(i), section 8, Chapter 1. Formalised in the standard propositional language, it becomes

$((A \vee B) \wedge C) \rightarrow (D \wedge E) \therefore C \rightarrow E$

The finished open tree below shows that it is truth-functionally invalid. The justification for each line has been omitted; as an exercise the reader should supply it.

$$((A \vee B) \wedge C) \rightarrow (D \wedge E)$$
$$\neg(C \rightarrow E)$$
$$\mid$$
$$C$$
$$\neg E$$

$\neg((A \vee B) \wedge C)$ $D \wedge E$

$\neg(A \vee B)$ $\underline{\neg C}$ D
$\mid$ $\underline{E}$
$\neg A$
$\neg B$

The tree is finished, with one open branch. The Completeness Theorem tells us that if the value T is asigned to each of the literals on this branch, the initial sentences are themselves assigned the value T. In this way, the branch determines a counterexample to the inference. In fact, it determines two, since it specifies the truth-values only on A, B, C and E, namely A–F, B–F, C–T, E–F, but it does not determine that of D. Hence the open branch determines the *two* distributions A–F, B–F, C–T, D–T, E–F and A–F, B–F, C–T, D–F, E–F, both of which are counterexamples to the inference.

Below are some simple truth-functionally valid inferences, known for so long that they have acquired classic status (and names, in the case of the first two). We have already made the acquaintance of some of them. Though not essential, it is useful to remember them.

Modus ponens:	A, A→B, ∴B
Modus tollens:	A→B, ¬B ∴¬A
Hypothetical syllogism:	A→B, B→C ∴A→C
Disjunctive syllogism:	A∨B, ¬B ∴A
Importation:	A→(B→C) ∴(A∧B)→C
Contraposition:	A→B ∴¬B→¬A

Exercises

1 Construct tree proofs for hypothetical syllogism and importation.
2 Give tree proofs of the truth-functional validity of the following
   (i)   A, ¬A ∴B
   (ii) B ∴A∨¬A
3 State which of the following inferences are truth-functionally valid, and justify your statements by constructing appropriate trees, using the sentence letters indicated. For any which is not valid, list the counter-example to it.
   (a) Tom will go to the show (A) only if Amanda will go (B), but Amanda won't go unless Henry will go (C). If Henry won't go, therefore, neither will Tom.
   (b) A person is entitled to benefit (A) only if *either* they are unemployed (B), *or* they are over 60 (C) and they have a disposable income of less than £10, 000 per year (D). Therefore, if they have an income of less than £10, 000 per year and are over 60 they are entitled to benefit.
   (c) If the Ukraine secedes from the treaty (A), and allies itself with Poland (B), then Georgia will ally itself with Russia (C). Georgia won't ally itself with the Baltic republics (¬D) if the latter support economic decentralisation (E), and if Georgia allies itself with Russia, then the Baltic republics will support economic decentralisation or ask for help elsewhere (F). Therefore if the Ukraine secedes from the treaty and Georgia allies itself with the Baltic republics, then either the Baltic republics will ask for help elsewhere or the Ukraine won't ally itself with Poland.
4 From the open trees generated by each of the following sentences, identify the distributions of truth-values over the sentences letters which make the sentences true.

   (a) B→¬(A∧¬C)
   (b) ¬(D∧(C→(D∨C)))

4* SOUNDNESS AND COMPLETENESS THEOREMS

We shall now prove the Soundness and Completeness Theorems for truth-functional trees. The Soundness Theorem requires the following lemma (a lemma is merely a preliminary result):

Lemma 1

Suppose that **B** is a branch on a tree. If all the sentences on **B** are true under some distribution of truth-values to their sentence letters, then **B** is open.

Proof

If **B** were closed it would contain a sentence and its negation; and both cannot be true together.

Theorem 2 (Soundness Theorem for Propositional Truth Trees)

Let Σ be a finite set of sentences in L. If Σ is satisfiable by a truth-value distribution τ over its sentence letters, then any finished tree generated by the rules of tree construction has an open branch, all the sentences on which take the value T under τ.

Proof

Suppose that a finished tree has been constructed from Σ and that there is some distribution τ of truth-values to the sentence letters in Σ which makes all the sentences in Σ true. We shall find an open branch in the tree.

Let **B** be the branch-segment consisting just of Σ (**B** is therefore just a single node). By Lemma 1 **B** is open. There are two possibilities: Σ contains at least one non-literal, or it does not. If it does not, **B** is a finished open branch all of whose sentences take the value T. If **B** does contain a non-literal, then **B** has an extension **B'** in the tree generated by the application of one of the rules (α) or (β) or Double Negation to some non-literal on **B**, such that all the sentences on **B'** are T under τ. For suppose rule (α) was applied. The sentences on **B'** are those in Σ and α_1 and α_2. But by assumption all the sentences on **B** take the value T under τ. Hence by Theorem 1 both α_1 and α_2 will be true under τ, and so all the sentences on **B'** will take the value T. If rule (β) was applied, Theorem 1 tells us that one of β_1 and β_2 must also be T under τ. Suppose, without loss of generality, that it is β_1. In this case let **B'** be that extension of **B** whose nodes are Σ and β_1. Again, all the sentences on **B'** take the value T. Finally, if the Rule of Double Negation was applied to a sentence $\neg\neg X$, let **B'** be the extension of **B** which includes X. Since by assumption ¬¬X takes the value T so does X, and so all the sentences on **B'** take the value T under τ.

In each case, since **B'** contains only sentences true under τ, **B'** is open, by Lemma 1. If **B'** is not finished then it has an extension in the tree obtained by applying one of the tree rules to a sentence on **B'**. Proceeding as before, we construct another open branch **B"** which extends **B'**. Continuing in the same way we obtain a sequence of open branches **B**, **B'**, **B"**, ... in the tree, each of which extends its predecessors. The sequence terminates at some finite stage, and when it does so we have a finished open branch in the tree, as required. **Q.E.D.**

Note This proof is analogous to a proof by mathematical induction on the positive integers (Chapter 3, section 4). It can indeed be converted into one explicitly, though to do so hardly adds to its force.

The proof of the Completeness Theorem requires another four easy lemmas.

Lemma 2

Suppose **B** is an open branch in a finished tree and let X be any sentence on **B**. Then, if X is an α sentence, both α_1 and α_2 will appear on **B** below X. If X is a β sentence then either β_1 or β_2 will appear on **B** below X. If X is of the form ¬¬Y then Y will appear on **B** below X.

Lemma 2 is an immediate consequence of the rules of tree construction.

For the next three lemmas we require a couple of definitions. For each connective in the standard propositional language we define its *weight* as follows: the weight of ¬ is 1, and that of each of $\wedge$, $\vee$ and $\rightarrow$ is 2. The *degree* of a sentence X in the standard propositional language is now defined to be the sum of the weights of each connective occurring in X, counting all repetitions as separate occurrences. So, for example, the degree of A is 0, of ¬¬¬A is 3, of B$\vee$¬B is 3, of C$\rightarrow$(¬C$\rightarrow$(A$\vee$¬¬B)) is 9, of ¬(¬A$\vee$B) is 4, etc. The degree of X is a property of the formal structure of X itself; in particular, the fact that ¬¬A is truth-functionally equivalent to A does *not* mean that the degree of ¬¬A is 0; it is of course 2.

Lemma 3

For any α sentence X in L, the degrees of α_1 and α_2 are each less than the degree of X, and if X is a β sentence, the degrees of β_1 and β_2 are each less than the degree of X.

The proof of Lemma 3 consists simply in checking that the α and β rules always eliminate a binary connective.

The next lemma introduces us to another type of inductive argument, sometimes called *strong induction*.

Lemma 4

Let Δ be any set of L sentences and k any integer. Suppose that (1) all the sentences of degree $\leq$ k in Δ have some property P, and (2) where X is any sentence of degree $>$ k in Δ, if all sentences in Δ of lower degree have P so does X. Then all the sentences in Δ have P.

Proof of Lemma 4

Suppose that (1) and (2) in the statement of the lemma are satisfied. By (1) all sentences of degree $\leq$ k have P. Now let k' be the smallest number greater than k such that there are degree k' sentences in Δ. By (2) all these sentences have P. Proceeding in this way, through the Δ-sentences of next highest degree, and then the next highest after that, and so on, we shall eventually infer that a sentence of any given degree will have P. Since every sentence in Δ has some degree, it follows that all the sentences in Δ must have P. **Q.E.D**.

This Induction Principle is superficially unlike the one we encountered in the previous chapter, in that instead of the induction step linking each element with a suitably defined *immediate* predecessor (or predecessors, if there is more than one), here the induction step (2) links each element with *all* those 'predecessors' determined according to the criterion of having lower degree.

Lemma 5

The only sentences of degree 0 or 1 in L are the literals of L. The proof is very simple and is left to the reader.

Theorem 3 (Completeness Theorem for Propositional Trees)

Let Σ be a finite set of sentences of L. Every finished open branch in a tree generated from Σ determines a truth-value distribution over the sentence letters in Σ which satisfies all the sentences in Σ.

Proof

Suppose that a finished open tree has been generated from Σ, and let **B** be an open branch on the tree. We shall show by strong induction on degrees that all the sentences on **B** take the value T under some distribution τ of truth-values over the sentence letters of Σ. We do this by first of all supposing τ to be any distribution of truth-values to the sentence letters in Σ such that every literal on **B** takes the value T. There does indeed exist such a distribution, because **B** is open, by assumption, and so there is no pair C, ¬C of literals on **B**. Second, we identify the set Δ in Lemma 4 with the set of all sentences on **B**, and finally we define the property P of sentences in that lemma as follows: a sentence X in Δ has P just in case X is assigned the value T by τ.

We shall now prove using Lemma 4 that all the sentences on **B** take the value T under τ. To establish the step (1) required by the lemma, note that there is at least one literal on **B** (since **B** is open and finished). Hence we infer that the lowest degree of sentences in Δ is 0 or 1. But we know that all the sentences on **B** of degree 0 or 1 are literals (by Lemma 5), and are T under τ, by assumption, and so step (1) is established.

Now for the induction step (2). Consider any sentence X on **B** of degree greater than 1. We shall suppose (inductive hypothesis) that every sentence on **B** of degree lower than that of X is true under τ, and show that from that assumption it follows that X is assigned T by τ. The reader should verify that X is either (i) an α sentence or (ii) a β sentence, or else is (iii) a multiply negated sentence (i.e. one commencing with at least two consecutive occurrences of ¬). We shall establish the induction step for each of the cases (i)–(iii). (i) If X is an α sentence, then by Lemma 1, α_1 and α_2 are also on **B**, and by Lemma 3 both are of degree less than X. So by the inductive hypothesis they are both T under τ. Hence by Theorem 1 so is X. (ii) If X is a β sentence then by Lemma 1 one of β_1, β_2 is on **B**, and by Lemma 3 both these are of degree less than X. By the inductive hypothesis, therefore, X is T under τ, and again by Theorem 1 so is X. (iii) If X is multiply negated it has the form ¬¬Y, and at some point, since **B** is finished, the Rule of Double Negation was applied to X. Hence Y is on **B**. But Y has smaller degree than X, and so by the inductive hypothesis Y is T under τ. Hence ¬¬Y is T, i.e. so is X. In each of the three possible cases, therefore, X is T under τ. The induction step (2) is now complete, and so by Lemma 4 every sentence on **B** is T under τ. In particular, all the members of Σ are T under τ, since they are all on **B**. **Q.E.D**.

Why are Soundness and Completeness so-called?

It has already been explained that the Completeness Theorem is so called because it implies that *every* truth-functional consequence of a set of premises can be shown to be a consequence by a tree proof. The Soundness Theorem is so called because it implies that *if* there is a tree proof of a sentence X from a set of premises Σ, then X is a truth-functional consequence of Σ; the tree proof, in other words, cannot prove something to be a consequence without its really being one (a theory of formal proof with this property is traditionally called sound).

Part II

First-order logic

Chapter 5

Introduction

1 SOME NON-TRUTH-FUNCTIONAL INFERENCES

Consider the following inference (it is a type known as an Aristotelian syllogism):

> (S)   All Cretans are liars.
>   All liars are wicked.
>   ∴ All Cretans are wicked.

Historical note 'All Cretans are liars' was a famous, some would say infamous, remark uttered, according to St Paul's Epistle to Titus, by Epimenides the Cretan; its self-refuting nature inspired a debate about the nature of truth which continues to this day and whose recent progress we review in Chapter 11.

Everyone from Aristotle onwards has taken (S) to be a paradigmatic example of a deductively valid inference. However, it is not *truth-functionally* valid: none of the three sentences making up the inference is a truth-functional compound of anything but itself, so within a propositional language each would have to be represented by distinct sentence letters, say A, B and C respectively. (S), in other words, has the truth-functional form

> A
> B
> ∴ C

which is truth-functionally invalid, since we have only to make the assignment T to A, T to B and F to C to get a trivial truth-functional counter-example. Of course, these can't be *real* truth-values if (S) is valid, since then it would be impossible for the two premises to be true and the conclusion false. A–T, B–T and C–F is, however, a consistent distribution of Ts and Fs over the sentence *letters* A, B and C, indicating that if (S) is valid, then it is not valid as a function of its truth-functional structure alone.

And (**S**) certainly is valid. A simple pictorial method of demonstrating its validity, and also that of the other valid Aristotelian syllogisms, was discovered by the German mathematician Euler in the eighteenth century and refined by the English mathematician John Venn in the nineteenth. Euler's method is very well known (Venn's refinement rather less so; for a brief account of it see Kneale and Kneale 1962: 421). First replace the specific class terms 'Cretan', 'liar' and 'wicked (person)' by non-specific, schematic ones, say P, Q and T. P, Q and T are now represented by circles drawn inside a rectangular box D representing a *universe of discourse*. To say that some Ps in D are Qs means that there are things in D in the intersection of P and Q, signified by placing an asterisk in that intersection (see Figure 1 (a)); to say that no Ps are Qs means that the circles do not intersect (see Figure 2 (b)) and to say that all Ps are Qs means that the circle P is either wholly contained within, or coincides with, the circle Q (see Figure (c); the fact there is no asterisk in that part of the interior of Q which is not included in that of P leaves it open whether P coincides with Q or whether there are Qs which are not Ps).

In an Euler diagram which makes the premises of the syllogism (**S**) true (whatever classes of thing P, Q and T denote), the circle P lies inside the circle Q which lies within the circle T. Hence the circle P must lie inside the circle T; i.e. all Ps are Ts and hence the conclusion of (**S**) must be true if the premises are true. As an exercise, construct an Euler diagram which will similarly demonstrate the validity of the syllogism

> All Ps are Qs.
> Some Ps are Ts.
> ∴ Some Qs are Ts.

While the method of Euler diagrams is fine for evaluating the relatively restricted class of syllogisms, it is quite inadequate for dealing with inferences in which the information is not about simple class inclusions, intersections, complements, etc. Consider, for example, the following inference:

> (*) Some positive integer is less than or equal to every positive integer.
> Therefore, for every positive integer, there is one less than or equal to it.

(*) is deductively valid, but it cannot be shown to be by an Euler diagram (try it!). We need a more powerful method and in this and the following chapters we shall develop one, called *first-order logic*.

As a first step we need to introduce some new notation, which will take us beyond the propositional languages of Chapter 3 to a class of formal languages, called *first-order languages*, capable of exhibiting much more of the logical structure of sentences than is possible within propositional languages. These more elaborate languages will still include the connectives →, ∧, ∨ and ¬, but to these will be added two other *logical* operators called the universal and existential quantifiers and a stock of *extralogical* symbols

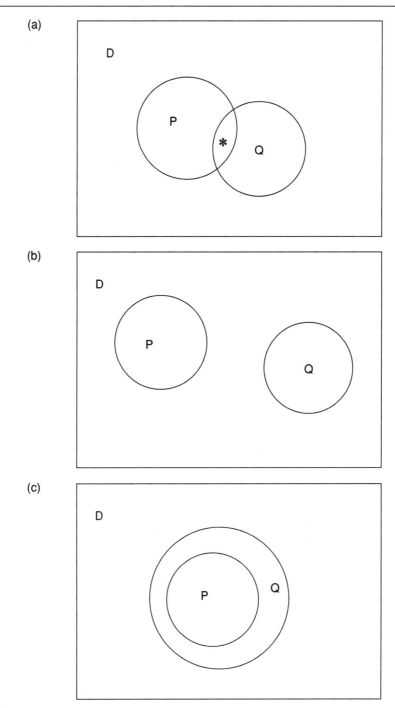

Figure 1

called predicate and relation symbols, variables and constants. We shall proceed as we did with the propositional languages, by first informally describing the syntax and semantics of these extended languages, then giving a more precise formal characterisation and finally proving Completeness and Soundness Theorems for an augmented set of tree rules.

2 QUANTIFIERS AND VARIABLES

The universal quantifier

The premises and conclusion of the syllogism (**S**) are called *universal generalisations*. This extensive and important class of statements are assertions to the effect that everything in a domain D of discourse satisfies some condition or other. 'Every' and its variant 'all' are collectively known as the *universal quantifier*, and so important is it in modern logic that it has its own special symbol, $\forall$. But $\forall$ never occurs alone like that when it is used to make an assertion; it is *always* immediately followed by what is called an *individual variable*, or simply *variable*, represented by a lower-case letter drawn from the end of the Roman alphabet, usually x, y or z. So the universal quantifer will always appear in the formalised version of an ordinary-language sentence in the composite form $\forall$x (or $\forall$y or $\forall$z).

A definite assertion is made by combining $\forall$x with a condition on x, which we can represent formally by P(x), thus: $\forall$xP(x). This is to be read 'Every individual x in the domain D satisfies the condition P(x)', or, more simply, 'For every x in D, P(x) is true' (note that there is no explicit reference to D in $\forall$xP(x), just as there is often no explicit reference to the domain of discourse in ordinary speech). $\forall$xP(x) is called a *formula* of that language (more precisely, closed formula, but 'formula' will do for now) and the occurrence of the variable x following the quantifier $\forall$x in $\forall$xP(x) is said to be bound by that quantifier.

It is easy to see that $\forall$xP(x) is true or false just when 'Everything in D satisfies P' is true or false and *we shall regard the formula $\forall$xP(x) as representing the logical form of 'Everything in D satisfies P.'* However, no variable appears explicitly in the English sentence 'Everything in D satisfies P'; in that case, why use a variable in its formalisation? Why not simply write $\forall$P, for example? The answer is that there are more complex statements than 'Everything in D satisfies P', for which it is at the very least useful, and may be indispensable, to employ variables and possibly more than one, to display clearly their logical structure. For example, try to paraphrase without using variables the statement that for any numbers x, y and z, x.(y + z) = x.y + x.z. You can do so, but not nearly so intelligibly and simply as if you use variables like x, y and z explicitly – which is, of course, why they were introduced into mathematics in the first place (this occurred in the seventeenth century and was one of the preconditions for the explosion of activity in the new mathematical sciences in that century). The great insight of the logical pioneers of the late nineteenth century was that what works so well in mathematics can work equally well in the representation of logical structure itself.

$\forall xP(x)$, $\forall yP(y)$, $\forall zP(z)$ etc. all assert that every individual in D satisfies P. Since this does not depend on D or P we can say that in all interpretations they are all true or all false. We shall express this by saying that they are all *logically equivalent* sentences and we shall use the same symbol, $\Leftrightarrow$, that we used for truth-functional equivalence to express this fact. The justification for using the same symbol is that two truth-functionally equivalent sentences are clearly logically equivalent, so that truth-functional equivalence is just a subspecies of this more extensive notion.

The existential quantifier

There is not just one but two types of quantifier in first-order logic, the second being the *existential* quantifier, symbolised $\exists$. Like the universal quantifier, it cannot exist alone in sentences but must always be accompanied by a variable to form a composite symbol $\exists x$ (or $\exists y$, $\exists z$, etc.). $\exists xP(x)$ is read as saying 'there is at least one individual x in the domain D for which $P(x)$ is true'. Similar considerations apply here as to the universal quantifier. $\exists xP(x)$ is just another way of saying that *something* in D satisfies the condition P and so $\exists xP(x)$ and $\exists yP(y)$ are logically equivalent formalisations of that same assertion.

Quantifier interdependence

There is a very important relationship between the universal and existential quantifiers: *either can be expressed in terms of the other and negation.* For $\forall xP(x)$ is true if and only if every individual in D has the property P, i.e. if and only if there is no individual in D which does not have P; but this is exactly what $\neg \exists x \neg P(x)$ says. Since these biconditionals also hold for any D and any property P, we can infer that $\forall xP(x)$ is logically equivalent to $\neg \exists x \neg P(x)$; i.e. $\forall xP(x) \Leftrightarrow \neg \exists x \neg P(x)$. A similar argument to that above, which will be left to the reader as exercise 2 below, shows that $\exists xP(x) \Leftrightarrow \neg \forall x \neg P(x)$.

Exercises

1 Suppose the domain is that of human beings, that $P(x)$ says that x is tall and that $Q(x)$ says that x is broad. State in words and without mentioning the variables x and y, what each of the following says:

(i) $\forall xP(x)$

(ii) $\exists y Q(y)$

(iii) $\exists x(P(x) \wedge Q(x))$

(iv) $\exists x P(x) \wedge \forall x Q(x)$

Do $\forall y P(y)$ and $\exists x Q(x)$ say anything different from (i) and (ii) respectively?

2 Explain carefully why $\exists x P(x) \Leftrightarrow \neg \forall x \neg P(x)$.

3 RELATIONS

A *relation* is a state of affairs that may or may not hold between individuals. 'x is less than y' is a *binary*, or *two-place*, relation between numbers; 'x is the godmother of y' and 'x is a sister of y' are binary relations between people. 'x is between y and z' is a three-place relation between individuals which may be numbers, or people on a seat, or times, or places, while 'x = (y + z)/w' is a four-place relation between numbers. Relations of more than four places might seem very arcane objects, not the sorts of things that would crop up much in practical discourse. In fact, they're commoner than might be thought, especially in the mathematical sciences, where so-called functional relations are described which can hold between enormous numbers of individuals (for example molecules of a gas).

In first-order logic, expressions of the form $R(x_1, x_2, \ldots x_n)$ symbolise n-place relations (since n is mentioned explicitly it is convenient to employ numerically subscripted variables here instead of x, y, z, . . .). In that expression R is called an *n-place relation symbol*. One-place relations are not what is normally understood by relations at all, but *properties* or *predicates* of individuals. These will be symbolised by expressions of the form $P(x)$, $Q(x)$, etc. P, Q, etc. are called *predicate symbols*. 'Is green', 'is a prime number', 'is a nuclear reactor', etc. are ordinary-language predicate terms.

It is important to grasp that $R(x, y, z, \ldots)$ signifies that x, y, z *in that order* stand in the relation R. It may well be that if x and y in that order stand in a binary relation R then so do y and x. But it may be the case that for some pair of individuals x and y, if x and y in that order stand in R, then y and x definitely do not. For example, if $R(x, y)$ represents the binary relation 'x is less than y' in the set N of natural numbers and $R(x, y)$ is true for any pair of values of x and y in N, then $R(y, x)$ is false for those values. It would be impossible to convey this information if the symbolism $R(x, y)$ did not implicitly impose an order on x and y in the way they satisfy R. This notational convention does not, however, prevent us from saying that x and y may stand in some binary relation R (for example the identity relation =) *independently* of the order in which they are written, for we can express this fact by means of the formula $R(x, y) \rightarrow R(y, x)$.

Let us pause here and look again at the inference (*) (above, p. 64). The premise and conclusion are both true statements about numbers, but at first sight they seem to be logically unrelated true statements. In fact, they are not logically unrelated at all, for (*) is a deductively valid inference: it is impossible for the premise of (*) to be true and the conclusion false. We shall prove this later, but to prepare the way it will be useful to discuss just what it *means* for it to be impossible for its premise to be true and the conclusion false. The clue lies in the observation that any demonstration of (*)'s validity should not depend on further unspecified information about the nature of the binary relation 'less than or equal to'. Were it to do so then the truth of the premise, independently of that additional information, would not be sufficient to ensure the truth of the conclusion, which it does. Hence, (*) must remain valid, in the sense of the provisional definition in Chapter 1, if we replace 'x is less than or equal to y' (x≤y) by the symbolic representation R(x, y) of a generic binary relation.

Nor should (*)'s deductive validity depend on any further unspecified information about the nature of natural numbers themselves, which implies that it is valid independently of the domain of the quantifiers. Putting these observations together, we can conclude that showing that (*) is deductively valid means showing that whatever set D is selected as the domain of the quantifiers in the formalisation below and whatever binary relation defined in D is selected as the interpretation of R in D, the premise of

$$\exists x \forall y R (x, y)$$
$$\therefore \forall y \exists x R (x, y)$$

is never true and the conclusion false.

These observations go far to redeem the promise, made in Chapter 1, that eventually we would define in a non-circular way the all-important 'cannot' in the provisional definition given there of deductively valid inference ('a valid deductive inference is one whose premises cannot all be true and conclusion false'). That provisional definition can now be updated as follows: *an inference is deductively valid if there is no structure consisting of a domain and relations defined in that domain which interpret the relation symbols in the inference, such that in that structure the premises are true and the conclusion is false.* Any structure consisting of a domain and relations defined in that domain which interprets a formalised inference we shall, naturally enough, call an *interpretation* of the inference (we shall elaborate this definition later, but it is good enough for now). An interpretation which makes the premises true and the conclusion false we shall, by analogy with the truth-functional case, call a *counterexample* to it.

When we have added tree rules for the quantifiers to the truth-functional ones of Chapter 4 we shall be in a position to prove by means of a closed tree that there is no counterexample to (*) and the various other inferences cited in this chapter. In the meantime, we need to complete the formal apparatus introduced in this chapter by adding one more item to the formal vocabulary of first-order languages. Suppose we try to formalise the following inference:

> (**)   If Mary is happy then everyone is happy.
>   ∴ If Mary is happy then so is Manfred.

In (**) two specific individuals are referred to, Mary and Manfred. We have already borrowed variables from mathematics and we shall now borrow again from it, this time *constants*, lower-case letters a, b, c, ... from the beginning of the Roman alphabet, whose function is to refer to specific individuals in the domain. Using such constants a and b to stand for Mary and Manfred respectively and the predicate symbol M to replace the predicate 'is happy', the inference above can be formalised:

> M(a)→∀xM(x)
> ∴ M(a)→M(b)

The introduction of constants completes the formal vocabulary into which we shall translate, or formalise, ordinary-language sentences. In the remainder of this chapter we shall develop some general rules and strategies for doing this.

Exercises

1 Suppose that the domain is the set of positive integers and that R(x, y) is now the relation 'x is less than or equal to y'. Explain without mentioning the variables x and y what the following sentences say and whether they are true or not.
   (i)   ∃x∃yR(x, y)
   (ii) ∃y∃xR(x, y)
   (iii) ∀xR(x, x)
   (iv) ∀x∃yR(x, y)
   (v)   ∀x∃yR(y, x)
   (vi) ∃x∀yR(x, y)
2 Which of (i)–(vi) remain true when R(x, y) is interpreted as 'x is less than y' on the same domain?
3 Explain why
   (i)   If P(a) is true in a domain D, then ∃xP(x) is true in D.
   (ii) If P(a) is true in a domain D, then ∀x¬P(x) is false in D.

4   FORMALISING ENGLISH SENTENCES

How do we know when we have the right, or a right, first-order formalisation of a natural-language sentence? Practice helps, but the following rule is a good one to try: compare the conditions in which the formalised and unformalised sentences are each true, by using informal arguments to see what seems to follow from each and what seems to imply each. This may sound a bit vague and also question-begging given that formalising ordinary discourse is just what is supposed to aid us in seeing what does and does not follow from what. But we should not despair. We already have some logical knowledge and we can use that and the machinery we subsequently develop for cross-checking our guesses.

Another good rule is to start with simple examples. The syllogism (S) at the beginning of this chapter is one such. To formalise (S), we have to formalise sentences of the form 'All Ps are Qs', where the domain D is not explicit. This at any rate seems straightforward, for another way of stating what is conveyed by 'All Ps are Qs' is by means of the universally quantified conditional 'For any x in D, if x is a P then x is a Q'. Granted this, we can formalise 'All Ps are Qs' as $\forall x(P(x) \rightarrow Q(x))$ and similarly the other sentences in the inference. Hence, letting P represent 'Cretan', Q represent 'liar' and another predicate symbol T represent 'wicked', we obtain the formalised version of (S):

$$\forall x(P(x) \rightarrow Q(x))$$
$$\forall x(Q(x) \rightarrow T(x))$$
$$\therefore \quad \forall x(P(x) \rightarrow T(x))$$

So far so good. But what about the syllogism in section 1?

> All Ps are Qs.
> Some Ps are Ts.
> $\therefore$ Some Qs are Ts.

We know how to deal with the 'All Ps are Qs' of the first premise, but what about the 'Some Ps are Ts' of the second? Most people's first thought is to formalise this analogously with 'All Ps are Qs', i.e. as $\exists x(P(x) \rightarrow T(x))$, being (mis)led by the apparent grammatical similarity of the two types of sentence, where the only difference seems to be in the initial quantifiers 'Some' and 'All'.

But $\exists x(P(x) \rightarrow T(x))$ is definitely wrong and it is easy to show why. Consider the false sentence 'There is an even positive integer not divisible by two.' In the domain of the positive integers, let P be the property of being even and T that of not being divisible by two. Thus we have a statement of the form 'Some Ps are Ts.' But $\exists x(P(x) \rightarrow T(x))$ is *true* in the domain of the positive integers and so cannot represent the logical form of 'There is an even positive integer not divisible by two.' (It is easy to show that $\exists x(P(x) \rightarrow T(x))$ is true. First, we know that 3 is a positive integer which is not even. Let the constant a denote 3. So we know that $\neg P(a)$ is true. Hence $\neg P(a) \vee T(a)$ is true, because for any sentences denoted by sentence letters A and B, $\neg A \vee B$ is a truth-functional consequence of A.

But ¬A∨B is truth-functionally equivalent to A→B. Hence we know that P(a)→T(a) is true. Define the predicate G(x) to be P(x)→T(x). Thus G(a) is true and hence so is ∃xG(x) (compare exercise 3(i) above); i.e. ∃x(P(x)→T(x)) is true.)

An interesting lesson of this demonstration is that grammatical form is not always a good guide to logical form, for we see that there is more than a quantifier difference between the logical structure of 'All Ps are Ts' and 'Some Ps are Ts.' So what formula does exhibit the logical structure of 'Some Ps are Ts'? This is not difficult to answer. 'Some Ps are Ts' says that there is at least one P which is also a T, i.e. there is at least one individual x in the domain such that x is a P and x is a T. We can straightforwardly transcribe this statement into our logical notation, whence we obtain the formula ∃x(P(x)∧T(x)). The syllogism is therefore rendered:

(***)   ∀x(P(x)→Q(x))
        ∃x(P(x)∧T(x))
    ∴ ∃x(Q(x)∧T(x))

But now suppose we are asked to formalise the two sentences 'All Ps are Qs' and 'Some Ps are Qs' as isolated sentences, (i) subject to the constraint that the domain of the variables is in each case to be the set of Ps (we assume that it is not empty), and (ii) with the domain unspecified.

(i) In the domain of Ps, 'All Ps are Qs' says that everything is a Q, while 'Some Ps are Qs' says that something is a Q. Thus 'All Ps are Qs' becomes simply ∀xQ(x) and 'Some Ps are Qs' becomes ∃xQ(x).

(ii) The answer is underdetermined. 'All Ps are Qs' could be ∀x(P(x)→Q(x)), or it could be ∀xQ(x) if you want to make the domain the set of Ps – and there is no reason either implicit or explicit in the question why you should not. Similarly, 'Some Ps are Qs' is legitimately either ∃x(P(x)∧Q(x)) or ∃xQ(x).

If, however, 'All Ps are Qs' occurs not as an isolated sentence but in the context of an inference, then the following rule must be observed: *the quantified variables must all refer to the same domain throughout*, just as we should take the unformalised sentences as referring to the same domain throughout. Thus in the syllogism (S) it would be definitely wrong to render 'All Cretans are liars' as ∀xQ(x), taking the domain to be Cretans and Q(x) the predicate 'is a liar', since the next premise states something about the members of a different class, that of the liars themselves. In formalising this syllogism, therefore the predicates 'being a Cretan', 'being a liar' and 'being wicked' must all be regarded as predicates defined in a common domain.

Now let us try something with a more complex structure. Formalise 'Some people like everyone who likes them' subject to the constraints that

(a) the domain is one of people only, and (b) the only relation or predicate symbols you are allowed to use are a single binary relation symbol L, where L(x, y) is to be read 'x likes y'. The following paraphrase is a useful first step: 'There is at least one person x such that for every person y, if y likes x then x likes y.' Since we are now considering a domain consisting of people, explicit mention of the fact that x and y are people is unnecessary and we get 'There is at least one x such that for all y, if y likes x then x likes y.' Now we can translate term by term, obtaining;

$$\exists x \forall y (L(y, x) \rightarrow L(x, y))$$

The logical structure of a sentence determines what follows deductively from it. Sometimes, however, that structure may not be made obvious by its vernacular expression, as we noted earlier. A particularly instructive example is found in what grammarians call *adverbial constructions*. For example, consider the following English sentences: 'Minerva is thinking deeply', 'Matilda is waltzing slowly' and 'It is raining heavily.' Clearly, they respectively imply that Minerva is thinking, that Matilda is waltzing and that it is raining. How are we to formalise the sentences to bring out these logical properties?

One's first answer is likely to be that 'Matilda is waltzing slowly' has the form $P(a)$, where a is a constant representing Matilda and P is a predicate symbol representing the property of waltzing slowly. The trouble with this answer is that it is powerless to reveal why 'Matilda is waltzing' is a deductive consequence of 'Matilda is waltzing slowly.' For there is no way to extract from $P(a)$ the information that waltzing is part of P. P itself has no 'parts'; it is just a letter. Since 'Matilda is waltzing' obviously is a consequence of 'Matilda is waltzing slowly', we seem justified in inferring that $P(a)$ does not faithfully represent the logical form of 'Matilda is waltzing slowly.' A more careful analysis is needed.

Let us go back to grammar. Words ending in '-ly', like 'slowly', 'deeply', 'heavily', etc., are adverbs; they qualify verbs, in this case the verbs 'is walking', 'is thinking' and 'is raining'. Verbs describe actions or processes, and hence the logical way to parse adverbial sentences is as statements asserting the existence of actions and processes possessing the relevant properties. 'Minerva is thinking deeply' gets parsed as 'There is a process which is a thinking process, which is deep and which is currently being undergone by Minerva'; formally, $\exists x(T(x) \wedge D(x) \wedge Q(x))$, where the domain includes processes (however we want to think of these) and T represents the predicate 'is a thinking process', $D(x)$, that x has depth in some relevant sense and $Q(x)$ that x is a process currently being undergone by Minerva. It is fairly obvious that $\exists x(T(x) \wedge Q(x))$ ('Minerva is thinking') is a logical consequence of $\exists x(T(x) \wedge D(x) \wedge Q(x))$ – we shall soon be able to prove this formally – and so our original problem is solved. The other adverbial sentences above can be dealt with similarly.

But some people are wary of a logical analysis that seems to commit them to what they see as a metaphysical position, in this case the claim that actions and processes enjoy real existence. But all the formalisation has done is to make explicit what is implicit in our ordinary speech. For in ordinary speech actions and processes are certainly things to which we assign properties and place in relation to other things. This sort of commitment pervades general usage ('Actions speak louder than words', 'Gluttony is a deadly sin', etc.), whether we like it or not. But if we don't, we shouldn't blame the logical analysis; it merely brings out what is already there.

There is another way of analysing the logical structure of adverbial sentences where there exists some scale of measurement of the quantities mentioned. Consider, for example, the sentence 'The train is moving quickly.' Physicists would most probably understand a sentence like this as describing the speed, or velocity, as they would term it (velocity is speed in a given direction), at which the train is moving. For them the sentence will therefore say something like 'there is a velocity r such that v(train) is in that (vague) range of values corresponding to our (vague) concept of going quickly (quickly for trains, that is, not for supersonic aircraft)', where v is the velocity function. We can represent 'v(train) = k', where k is a number, as a binary relation $V(train, k)$, where $V(a, b)$ holds between any pair (a, b) of individuals just in case a is a material thing and b is a number measuring the velocity of a. So now we can formalise 'the train is moving quickly' as $\exists y(V(a, y) \wedge Q(y))$, where the domain consists of numbers and material objects – and maybe more besides; where a denotes the train; and where $Q(y)$ is true for any individual y in the domain just in case y is a number falling in the range 'quick' when measuring velocities. Clearly, 'the train is moving' is formalised in this style as $\exists y V(a, y)$, which is, as we shall soon be able to show formally, a deductive consequence of $\exists y(V(a, y) \wedge Q(y))$.

In its intended interpretation $\exists y(V(a, y) \wedge Q(y))$ refers to a domain containing material objects and the values, whether actual numbers or not, of some scale of measurement. Such 'mixed' domains are, if only implicitly, referred to widely in ordinary discourse. Consider, for example, Abraham Lincoln's celebrated observation that you can fool all of the people some of the time and some of the people all of the time, but you can't fool all of the people all of the time. Lincoln's remark refers to both people and times and the domain of its quantifiers must consequently include both types of entity. Since we allow only a single domain for the quantifiers, these subdomains must be embraced within a 'super-domain' containing both types of entity, times and persons. These can then be regarded as subsets of the wider domain, distinguished formally by predicate symbols T and P respectively. We can now formalise Lincoln's utterance as

$$\exists y(T(y) \land \forall x(P(x) \rightarrow F(x, y))) \land \exists x(P(x) \land \forall y(T(y) \rightarrow F(x, y)))$$
$$\land \neg \forall x \forall y((P(x) \land T(y)) \rightarrow F(x, y)))$$

where $F(x, y)$ represents the binary relation 'x can be fooled at y' (we shall assume $F(x, y)$ is simply false when x is not a person or y is not a time).

The fact that we can introduce time into the formal discussion in this way means that we can capture within a first-order scheme a very important area of ordinary discourse that might seem otherwise out of our reach: *tensed* utterances. The following three statements are obviously very different in meaning. 'Rachel went to the cinema', 'Rachel is now going to the cinema', and 'Rachel will go to the cinema'; the first is in the past, the second in the present and the third in the future tense. A subtheory of modern formal logic called temporal logic has sprung up in the last half-century or so, which adds primitive temporal operators to the usual battery of logical items, the connectives and quantifiers, in order to formalise sentences such as these. But quantifying over times, as domain objects, achieves just the same end and requires no extension of the logical vocabulary.

In the process tensed statements become untensed; indeed, they become essentially timeless. Thus, the first of the three tensed statements about Rachel can be expressed as 'There is a time t before now (t_0) such that at t Rachel goes to the cinema' and is then readily formalised as

$$\exists t(R(t, t_0) \land S(a, t))$$

where a is a constant denoting Rachel, $S(a, t)$ says that the person a goes to the cinema at time t, t_0 is another constant signifying the present time relative to some method of measuring time, like the usual date and clock one, and $R(t, t_0)$ says that t is before t_0 according to this standard of measurement. Note that no additional predicates $T(t)$, i.e. 't is a time', or $P(a)$, 'a is a person', need be introduced explicitly, since the status of t and a is built into the interpretation of the relation symbols R and S. The formalisation of the remaining two statements about Rachel is left as an exercise.

Reasoning about time according to modern physics involves a larger set of relations and predicates. These predicates and relations are those of modern mathematics and the logical structure of mathematical reasoning deserves a separate treatment, which we shall consider later. But there is nothing in this sort of reasoning, apart from its complexity, that poses any difficulty of principle in representing it within the framework of a first-order language. However, there are other constructions in English that pose more of a challenge to first-order formalisation. We have already come across one type, the so-called counterfactual conditionals. Others are *modal* statements, i.e. assertions of possibility and impossibility and finally statements involving probabilities. All these topics are extensive and have had whole books written on them. Some attempt will be made in the final chapters to discuss them without going to book length to do so.

Exercises

1   Explain why, if the domain of 'All Ps are Qs' is some set D, the sentence is true if there are no Ps in D.

2   Formalise the following sentences. Take the quantified variables to range over a domain of people, and use the constant a to represent Jane and binary relation symbols B, S, O and Y in such a way that B(x, y) stands for the relation 'x is a brother of y', S(x, y) for 'x is a sister of y', O(x, y) for 'x is older than y' and L(x, y) for 'x likes y'.

(i)   Jane has a brother.
(ii)   Jane has no sisters.
(iii)   Some people like all people.
(iv)   Some people are liked by nobody.
(v)   Nobody is their own brother or sister.
(vi)   Some people have no brothers.
(vii)   Some people have no sisters older than them.
(viii) Some people have brothers older than them whom they like.
(ix)   Some people like no one's brother, but there are sisters of some people who are liked by everybody.
(x)   Some people like no one who likes themselves.
(xi)   Everyone likes everyone who likes someone.

3   Formalise the following using the relations, predicates and constants indicated:

(i)   Minerva is thinking deeply (domain: processes; M(x): x is undergone by Minerva; D(x): x is deep).
(ii)   Carla got home at 5p.m. yesterday (domain: times and people; S(x, y): x is a person and y is a time and x gets home at y; a: Carla; b: 5p.m. yesterday).
(iii)   Frank has seen the film and won't see it again (domain: times and people; R(x, y): x is a time and y is a time and x is before y; S(x, y): x is a time and y is a time and x is the same as y or after y; T(x, y): x is a person and y is a time and x sees the film at y; a: Frank; b: the present time).

Chapter 6

First-order languages: syntax and two more tree rules

1 FIRST-ORDER LANGUAGES

In the previous chapter we showed how we could represent more of the logical structure of English sentences, more, that is, than truth-functional structure, in a formal notation containing, besides truth-functional connectives, also predicate symbols and relation symbols of arbitrary numbers of places, variables, constants and quantifiers. These form the basic vocabulary items of a class of formal languages called *first-order languages*, whose syntax and semantics we shall investigate in this and the following chapters.

Syntactically, a first-order language is like a propositional language in that it is the set of all sentences which can be constructed from some class of 'atomic' components using a specified set of logical operations. However, there are two important differences: first, the set of connectives is fixed, the same for all first-order languages; and second, the atomic sentences of a first-order language are now not sentence letters, single and indivisible, but themselves constructed from a specified vocabulary of *logical* and *extralogical* items. The extralogical items are themselves subdivided into a 'descriptive', or *referential*, part and a *structural* part. These categories of vocabulary item are specified as follows (the boldface capital letter **L** refers to an arbitrary first-order language):

(i) **L**'s logical vocabulary contains the same connectives ∧, ∨, ¬ and → as the standard propositional language of Chapter 3 and in addition the two quantifiers ∀ and ∃.

(ii) The referential part of **L**'s extralogical vocabulary consists of a set of *predicate* and *n-place* (n>1) *relation symbols* (how many of each may vary from language to language, though there may be infinitely many of both and there must be at least one predicate symbol if there are no relation symbols and vice versa) and a set (possibly empty) of constants. The exact nature of **L**'s predicate and relation symbols need not concern us; all the discussion of them is carried out in the metalanguage (Chapter 3, section 2) and in this metalanguage we shall use the capitals P, Q and if necessary also P_1, P_2, ..., Q_1, Q_2, ... etc. to refer to distinct predicate symbols of **L**. Relation symbols of **L** will be referred to by capitals R and S and if necessary also R_1, R_2, ..., S_1, S_2, ... The number of places of any relation symbol will be assumed known without needing explicit signalling by means of a dedicated notation. Constants of **L** will be represented by lower-case letters a, b, c from the beginning of the Roman alphabet and if we run out, a_1, a_2, ..., b_1, b_2, ..., c_1, c_2, ...

(iii) The structural items in **L**'s extralogical vocabulary are two brackets (), the comma, and an indefinitely large supply of variables. We shall represent distinct variables, as before, by distinct lower-case letters x, y, z, ... from the end of the Roman alphabet and by x_1, x_2, ... if we run out of these.

Define an *expression* of **L** to be any finite string of symbols from **L**'s vocabulary. Some of these will be 'meaningful', like ∃xP(x), for example, if **L** contains the predicate symbol P; others will not, like x)∀xx, xR. We shall now proceed in stages to identify these 'meaningful' strings and in particular those of which it can sensibly be said that they are true or false when interpreted in an appropriate domain. *A notational convention*: in this and the following chapters, italic capitals *A*, *B*, *C* ... from the beginning of the Roman alphabet will be used to denote arbitrary expressions. In more precise terminology, *A*, *B*, *C* ... are metalinguistic variables ranging over the set of expressions of **L**; however, like Horace who saw and approved the better and followed the worse, we shall generally continue in the sloppier way to talk about arbitrary expressions, sentences, languages, etc.

The potential truth- and falsity-bearing expressions of **L** are what we are really interested in. By analogy with their informal counterparts these will be called the sentences of **L**. Rather than defining them directly, it is easier first to take a detour via a larger class of expressions called the *formulas* of **L**. Recall from the previous chapter that an English sentence of the form 'All Ps are Qs' can be formalised as a universally quantified conditional ∀x(P(x)→Q(x)). We can think of ∀x(P(x)→Q(x)) as built up from the basic vocabulary of a first-order language in the following increasingly large 'pieces' P(x), Q(x), P(x)→Q(x), ∀x(P(x)→Q(x)). These pieces will be called formulas of **L** and the pieces en route *subformulas* of the final formula.

Like the corresponding class of sentences of a propositional language, the class of formulas of **L** can be uniquely specified by an inductive definition (cf. Chapter 3, section 3). First we define the class of expressions which are unconditionally formulas of **L**. These are called the *atomic formulas* of **L** and they are all expressions of the form P(t), $R(t_1, ..., t_n)$, where R is an n-place relation symbol, for those values of n>1 such that **L** has relation symbols of those numbers of places and where t, t_1, ..., t_n

are any constants or variables of **L**. An expression A is now said to be in the class **F** of *formulas* of **L** if and only if A is either (i) an atomic formula of **L**, or (ii) of the form $\neg B$, $(B \wedge C)$, $(B \vee C)$, $(B \rightarrow C)$, $\forall x B$, $\exists x B$, where x is any variable and B and C are formulas of **L**.

Brackets are placed around $A \wedge B$, $A \vee B$ and $A \rightarrow B$ in (i) and (ii) so that the subformula structure of each formula in **L** is determinate: the subformulas of a formula A can be defined explicitly as all the nodes on A's ancestral tree (this is like the ancestral tree of a sentence in a propositional language, except that $\forall x B$ and $\exists x B$ each have a single vertical branch down to B). As before we shall omit outer brackets in ordinary discussion, writing 'the formula $A \rightarrow B$' rather than 'the formula (A→B)'. To aid the eye, we shall sometimes alternate curved and square brackets [] in complex formulas.

Where $\forall x B$, $\exists x B$ are formulas of **L**, the quantifiers $\forall x$ and $\exists x$ are said to have an *initial occurrence* in them (they may also have other occurrences in these formulas). The *scope* of those initially occurring quantifiers $\forall x$ and $\exists x$ is in each case said to be the occurrence of the subformula B immediately following each of them. A variable is said to *occur* in a formula if it appears in that formula at some point other than that immediately following a quantifier; for example, $\forall x P(x)$ has only one occurrence of x. An occurrence of a variable x in a formula A is said to be *free* if it is not in the scope of any quantifier $\forall x$, $\exists x$ in A. An occurrence of a variable is *bound* if it is not free, i.e. if it is *not* in the scope of a quantifier $\forall x$, $\exists x$. Thus there are four occurrences of a variable in the formula

$$(P(x) \wedge Q(y)) \rightarrow \exists y R(x, y)$$

three of which are free and one bound; the second occurrence of y is bound. From the way freedom and bondage for variables are defined, it is clear that every occurrence of a variable in a formula is either free or bound. A formula which has a free occurrence of some variable is said to be *open*. A formula which is not open is *closed*. The closed formulas are also called the *sentences* of **L**.

The sentences of **L**, so defined, are so called because they will be the expressions of **L** which can be true or false, depending on the interpretation of the predicate and relation symbols in them. But in that case the definition of **F** seems definitely over-permissive, for it includes as closed formulas expressions like $\forall x \exists x P(x)$, or even $\forall x P(a)$. These 'sentences' seem to make very little sense. They are included in **F** because to exclude them would make for a very complicated definition of formula and, as we shall see in the next chapter, they do in fact make perfectly good sense; $\forall x \exists x P(x)$ will turn out to say the same as $\exists x P(x)$ and $\forall x P(a)$ the same as $P(a)$. However, such formulas can easily be avoided in practice and we shall not be bothered by them.

We end this section by introducing some notational conventions which will be useful in the subsequent discussion. We shall signify by $A(x_1, \ldots, x_n)$ an arbitrary open formula of **L** with free occurrences of the variables $x_1, \ldots, x_n$. Thus $A(x)$ signifies a formula free in just the one variable x. Where A is any formula and t a constant or variable, $A(t/x)$ signifies the result of substituting t for every free occurrence of x in A; if A has no free occurrence of x we shall regard $A(t/x)$ as just A itself. Where A is known from the context of the discussion to have free occurrences of x and only of x, i.e. where A is $A(x)$, we shall usually write $A(t)$ instead of $A(t/x)$.

Exercises

In the following assume that the relevant first-order language contains all the constants and predicate and relation symbols mentioned.

1   Explain carefully how by reference to the clauses (i) and (ii) in the definition above of formulas of **L**, you can determine that the expression $\forall x \forall y (\exists z R(x, z) \rightarrow R(x, z))$ is a formula of **L**. List all its subformulas.

2   What is the scope of the quantifier $\forall x$ in each of the following?
   (a) $\forall x P(x)$
   (b) $\forall x (P(x) \land Q(x))$
   (c) $\forall x (P(x) \rightarrow \exists y R(x, y))$
   (d) $\forall x \exists y R(x, y)$
   (e) $\forall x \exists y \forall z S(x, y, z)$

3   All the sentences in question 1 are of the form $B = \forall x A(x)$.
   (i)   What is $A(a)$ in each case?
   (ii)   What is $B(a/x)$ in each case?

4   Specify the scope of each occurrence of a quantifier in the formula $\neg \forall x \forall y R(x, y) \rightarrow \exists z (Q(x) \lor S(z, y, x))$ and also indicate all the free occurrences of each variable.

5   Indicate all free occurrences of a variable in $\forall x R(x, y) \rightarrow \exists y R(x, y)$.

6   Is the formula $R(a, b)$ open or closed?

2   TWO MORE TREE RULES

We shall now introduce tree rules for the two quantifiers, in each case by a pair of conjugate diagrams. We shall work backwards to them by supposing that we have generated a finished tree from a set Σ of first-order initial sentences, in which there is an open branch **B**. Recall that an open branch in a truth-functional truth tree determined a 'world' in which all the initial sentences were true; 'world' is in quotes because it was really just an assignment of the value T to each literal on the branch. We shall suppose that **B** also furnishes a 'world' in which all the sentences in Σ are true, but in this case one which is a bit more like a world, with a domain of individuals and predicates and relations defined in that domain. It will also be a 'small world' in the sense, roughly the same as that which economists give the term, that the only individuals in it will be those named by a constant appearing on **B**.

This **B**-world is of course an interpretation of the first-order language whose predicate and relation symbols are those of the sentences in Σ. In the **B**-world a universally quantified sentence $\forall x A(x)$ in that language is true if $A(a)$ is true for every constant a on **B** (this is the 'small world' assumption), while $\forall x A(x)$ is false ($\neg \forall x A(x)$ is true) if for some constant c on **B** $A(c)$ is false ($\neg A(c)$ is true). Thus we obtain a pair of unsigned conjugate diagrams for the universal quantifier:

$$\forall x A(x) \qquad\qquad\qquad \neg \forall x A(x)$$
$$| \qquad\qquad\qquad\qquad\quad |$$
$$\{A(a)\text{: a is a constant on } \mathbf{B}\} \qquad \neg A(c)$$

The set-theoretic notation $\{A(a)$: a is a constant on **B**$\}$ is read 'the set of all $A(a)$ where a is a constant on **B**'.

Similarly, an existentially quantified sentence $\exists x A(x)$ is true in the **B**-world if $A(c)$ is true for some constant c on **B**, while it is false ($\neg \exists x A(x)$ true) if $A(a)$ is false ($\neg A(a)$ true) for every constant on **B**; and so we have the following pair of conjugate diagrams for the existential quantifer:

$$\exists x A(x) \qquad\qquad\qquad \neg \exists x A(x)$$
$$| \qquad\qquad\qquad\qquad\quad |$$
$$A(c) \qquad \{\neg A(a)\text{: a is a constant on } \mathbf{B}\}$$

Notice that, as with the diagrams for the connectives, we can also read these diagrams downwards, as saying that if the upper sentence in each is true, so are all the lower ones. This is important, because, as in the earlier truth-functional case, it will enable us to interpret a closed tree as signifying that the initial sentences cannot all be true together; in other words, the tree rules represented by these diagrams are *sound*.

Call a sentence of the form $\forall x A(x)$ or $\neg \exists x A(x)$ a γ sentence and one of the form $\exists x A(x)$ or $\neg \forall x A(x)$ a δ sentence. In the table below we define corresponding sentences $\gamma(a)$ and $\delta(a)$, where a is any constant of **L**:

γ	$\gamma(a)$	δ	$\delta(a)$
$\forall x A(x)$	$A(a)$	$\exists x A(x)$	$A(a)$
$\neg \exists x A(x)$	$\neg A(a)$	$\neg \forall x A(x)$	$\neg A(a)$

$\gamma(a)$ and $\delta(a)$ are called the *instantiations* of γ and δ with the constant a. We can now collapse the four unsigned quantifier diagrams into two:

$$(i) \qquad \gamma \qquad\qquad\qquad (ii) \quad \delta$$
$$| \qquad\qquad\qquad\qquad\qquad |$$
$$\{\gamma(a)\text{: a is a constant on } \mathbf{B}\} \qquad \delta(c)$$

Call {γ(a): a is a constant on **B**} the *descendant* of γ in (i) and δ(c) the *descendant* of δ in (ii).

We can adopt diagram (ii) as a new tree rule, which we shall call *the rule (δ)*, on the provisional hypothesis that the sentence to which (δ) is applied is a node on some eventually finished open branch which can be identified with **B** above. Of course, the hypothesis may be false, for all the branches passing through that node may close. But if it is not false we must somehow write into the statement of (δ) that the choice of c must be made in such a way that nothing else on **B** conflicts with c's role of satisfying the condition $A(x)$ or $\neg A(x)$, as the case may be. The following condition turns out to be necessary and sufficient: *the constant c in δ(c) must not be one which has already appeared on the branch above the point at which δ(c) is placed*. The condition is necessary, because otherwise we could have this:

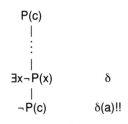

The proof that the condition is sufficient must wait until Chapter 8.

Diagram (i) cannot, however, as it stands be used as a tree rule. There is nothing wrong with the descendant of γ being a *set* of sentences rather than a single sentence: after all, the descendant of an α sentence is a set, {$α_1$, $α_2$}. The problem with (i) is that there may not be a finished open branch in the tree (it may close) and even if there is we may not know, at the stage in its development at which we want to apply (i), which constants are on it. We can't simply identify the set of constants on a branch, open or closed, with those in the initial sentences, for we now know that new constants not yet appearing may subsequently have to be added by an application of (δ)

Fortunately, we can modify (i) to get round these difficulties quite easily, while still remaining in the spirit of the enterprise. *We simply allow the instantiations γ(a) of γ to be introduced piecemeal on any branch as these new constants get added (if they do) to it*. When and only when γ has been instantiated with every constant on the branch (*including one introduced specifically for that purpose if there would otherwise have been none*) shall we say that γ is used on that branch. This is by contrast with the other tree rules, where the sentences to which they are applied are used on a branch as soon as their descendants are placed on it.

In the light of all these considerations, we can formulate the tree rules (γ) and (δ) as follows (*N.B.: **B** is now the as yet unfinished branch on which the descendant in each case is placed*):

(γ) γ
 |
 γ(a)

for any choice of constant a from those appearing on **B** above γ(a). If there is none, introduce one.

(δ) δ
 |
 δ(c)

where c is a constant not appearing on B above δ(c).

As earlier, a tree will be said to be *finished* when either it closes or every usable sentence on every open branch is used on that branch.

This is still not quite the final form of these rules, but it is final enough for our purposes now. Two features of the rules should be noted. First, though the constraints on them are inspired by semantic considerations, *the rules themselves are purely formal (syntactical)*. They can be implemented without reference to any interpretation of the language; all one has to know at the point of applying them are the sentences so far generated on the branch. Second, their validity is not restricted in any way by the 'small world' assumption made at the outset; it will turn out that if a set of first-order sentences is true in any world then it is true in a 'small' one and conversely (this is the content of a celebrated result called the Löwenheim–Skolem Theorem, which we shall prove in Chapter 8).

To get a feel for how the rules work, we shall construct a closed tree from the initial sentences $\forall$x(P(x)$\rightarrow$Q(x)), $\exists$yP(y), T(b) and $\neg\exists$zQ(z):

1	$\forall$x(P(x)$\rightarrow$Q(x))	
2	$\exists$yP(y)	
3	T(b)	
4	$\neg\exists$zQ(z)	
	|	
5	P(a)	(δ) on 2; note the new constant a
	|	
6	P(a)$\rightarrow$Q(a)	(γ) on 1
	|	
7	$\neg$Q(a)	(γ) on 4
	/ \	
8	$\neg$P(a) Q(a)	(β) on 6

Two features of this tree deserve comment. (i) There is a clear strategic advantage to applying (δ) before (γ). This is not only because once the (δ) rule has been applied to a sentence that sentence is used once and for all, but also because giving the (δ) rule priority minimises the number of individual constants which have to be introduced. (ii) We have extended the (α) and (β) rules in a natural way to *first-order sentences*: (β) was applied to the sentence P(a)$\rightarrow$Q(a), β_1 being $\neg$P(a) and β_2 Q(a). From now on the (α) and (β) rules are applied to any formulas which have the appropriate truth-functional form: for (α), of conjunctions, negations of disjunctions and negations of conditionals; and for (β), of disjunctions, conditionals and negations of conjunctions.

It might seem from this example that first-order truth trees are just about as well behaved as trees for sentences in the standard propositional languages. Well behaved they are, as we shall see in due course, but they are not quite as well behaved as the purely truth-functional trees. In the first place, to ensure that trees which can close do close we shall need to impose conditions on the order of application of the tree rules. Second, we now have to contemplate infinite trees, as the following example shows. Suppose we try generating a truth tree from the single initial sentence $\forall x \exists y R(x, y)$. This is what happens:

```
1       ∀x∃yR(x, y)
            |
2       ∃yR(a, y)        (γ) on 1
            |
3       R(a, b)          (δ) on 2
            |
4       ∃yR(b, y)        (γ) on 1
            |
5       R(b, c)          (δ) on 4
            |
6       ∃yR(c, y)        (γ) on 1
            |
7       R(c, d)          (δ) on 6
            |
          etc.
```

The 'etc.' signifies that the tree goes on for ever! Clearly, every time one of the new constants introduced by the application of the (δ) rule instantiates the initial γ sentence $\forall x \exists y R(x, y)$, it gives rise to yet another δ sentence, which then introduces another constant and so on ad infinitum.

The possibility that infinite trees may be generated from finite sets of initial sentences might seem to introduce an uncontrollable dimension into the theory of first-order truth trees, but actually this is not so. For the single-branched tree above, though infinite, is none the less well behaved enough. It is unambiguously a finished open tree: the initial γ sentence on it is definitely used, according to the criterion laid down earlier, since for every constant on the branch, the instantiation with that constant of the γ sentence appears on the branch.

Exercises

1 For each of the following, state whether it is a γ or δ sentence, or neither of these.
  (a) $\exists x(P(x) \land \forall y(Q(y) \to R(x, y)))$
  (b) $\neg \forall y(Q(y) \to R(a, y))$
  (c) $Q(b) \to R(a, b)$
  (d) $Q(b) \land \forall x(P(x) \to Q(x))$
  (e) $\neg \exists y(Q(y) \land P(a))$
  (f) $\neg \exists y Q(y) \lor \exists x P(x)$
  (g) $\neg P(a)$
2 For each of the γ and δ sentences in question 1, what are $\gamma(a)$, $\delta(a)$?
3 In two lines of the apparently closed tree below, generated from the initial sentences $\forall x \exists y R(x, y)$ and $\neg \exists y \forall x R(x, y)$, a rule has been misapplied. Identify the line and explain how the rule is misapplied.

  1   $\forall x \exists y R(x, y)$
  2   $\neg \exists y \forall x R(x, y)$
        |
  3     $\exists y R(a, y)$ (γ) on 1
        |
  4     $\neg \forall x R(x, a)$ (γ) on 2
        |
  5     $R(a, a)$ (δ) on 3
        |
  6     $\neg R(a, a)$ (δ) on 4

4 Identify a domain and a binary relation defined in it, such that in that interpretation both $\forall x \exists y R(x, y)$ and $\neg \exists y \forall x R(x, y)$ are true.

3   TREE PROOFS

Extending the terminology of Chapter 4, we shall say that there is a *tree proof* of a conclusion C from a set Γ of premises if the set of initial sentences consisting of Γ together with $\neg C$ generates a closed tree, using any of the rules of (α)–(δ) and Double Negation. The symbolism $\Gamma \vdash C$ will mean that there is such a tree proof of C from Γ. If there is such a proof, it follows from the Soundness Theorem that we shall prove later that there is no interpretation of the first-order language in which premises and conclusion are formalised in which those premises are true and the conclusion false; i.e. C is a valid inference from Γ.

We shall end this chapter with tree proofs for some of the inferences we discussed earlier, starting with one for the syllogism (**S**) as formalised in Chapter 5, section 2:

1	$\forall x(P(x){\rightarrow}Q(x))$	premise
2	$\forall x(Q(x){\rightarrow}T(x))$	premise
3	$\neg\forall x(P(x){\rightarrow}T(x))$	$\neg$conclusion
4	$\neg(P(a){\rightarrow}T(a))$	(δ) on 3
5	$P(a){\rightarrow}Q(a)$	(γ) on 1
6	$Q(a){\rightarrow}T(a)$	(γ) on 2
7	$P(a)$	(α) on 4
8	$\neg T(a)$	
9	$\neg P(a)$ $Q(a)$	(β) on 5
10	$\neg Q(a)$ $\underline{T(a)}$	(β) on 6

That was easy. So is the tree proof for the other syllogism of Chapter 5 (sections 1, 4):

> All Ps are Qs.
> Some Ps are Ts.
> ∴ Some Qs are Ts.

which will be left as an exercise.

The next tree proof we give is for (*), Chapter 5, sections 1, 3:

1	$\exists x\forall yR(x, y)$	premise
2	$\neg\forall y\exists xR(x, y)$	$\neg$conclusion
3	$\forall yR(a, y)$	(δ) on 1
4	$\neg\exists xR(x, b)$	(δ) on 2; note the new constant
5	$R(a, b)$	(γ) on 4
6	$\underline{\neg R(a, b)}$	(γ) on 4

We shall end by stating two useful facts about binary relations and proving one of them. Call a binary relation, symbolised by R, *reflexive* on a domain D if the sentence $\forall xR(x, x)$ is true in D. R is *irreflexive* on D if $\forall x\neg R(x, x)$ is true in D. R is *symmetric* on D if $\forall x\forall y(R(x, y){\rightarrow}R(y, x))$ is true in D; R is *asymmetric* on D if $\forall x(R(x, y){\rightarrow}\neg R(y, x))$ is true in D. R is *transitive* on D if $\forall x\forall y\forall z(R(x, y){\rightarrow}(R(y, z){\rightarrow}R(x, z)))$ is true in D. R is *intransitive* on D if $\forall x\forall y\forall z(R(x, y){\rightarrow}(R(x, y){\rightarrow}\neg R(x, z)))$ is true in D. The two useful facts are that (i) if R is asymmetric on D it is irreflexive on D and (ii) if R is transitive and irreflexive on D it is asymmetric on D. We shall prove (i) by giving a tree proof of irreflexivity from asymmetry:

1	$\forall x \forall y(R(x, y) \to \neg R(y, x))$	premise
2	$\neg \forall x \neg R(x, x)$	$\neg$ conclusion
3	$\neg \neg R(a, a)$	(δ) on 2
4	$R(a, a)$	Double Negation
5	$\forall y(R(a, y) \to \neg R(y, a))$	(γ) on 1
6	$R(a, a) \to \neg R(a, a)$	(γ) on 4
7	$\neg R(a, a)$ $\neg R(a, a)$	(β) on 5

(ii) is left as exercise 7 below.

Exercises

1 Show that
   (i) $\forall xP(x) \vdash \forall yP(y)$ (ii) $\exists xP(x) \vdash \exists yP(y)$
   (iii) $\forall xP(x) \vdash \exists yP(y)$ (iv) $P(a) \vdash \exists xP(x)$
   (v) $\forall x \forall yR(x, y) \vdash \forall y \forall xR(x, y)$ (vi) $\exists x \exists yR(x, y) \vdash \exists y \exists xR(x, y)$

2 Show that $\forall xA(x) \vdash \neg \exists x \neg A(x)$ and conversely (i.e. with premise and conclusion interchanged) and that $\exists xA(x) \vdash \neg \forall x \neg A(x)$ and conversely.

3 Show that $\neg \exists xA(x) \vdash \forall x(A(x) \to B(x))$ (cf. Exercise 1, Chapter 5, section 4).

4 A set A is a *subset* of a set B (standardly symbolised $A \subseteq B$) if every member of A is a member of B. Consider a domain D consisting of arbitrary things and sets. Let $R(x, y)$ be true in D just when y is a set and x is an element of y (in mathematics textbooks this relation is written $x \in y$). So we can formalise the statement 'y is a subset of z', i.e. 'for all x, if x is an element of y then x is an element of z', as $\forall x(R(x, y) \to R(x, z))$. It can be proved from the axioms of set theory that there is a unique set which has no members and this is called the empty set (we saw earlier that it is given the conventional symbol $\varnothing$); i.e. where a denotes $\varnothing$, $\forall x \neg R(x, a)$ is true. Show by a tree proof that $\forall x \neg R(x, a) \vdash \forall y \forall x(R(x, a) \to R(x, y))$; i.e. the empty set is a subset of every set.

5 Give a tree proof of the inference (**) in Chapter 5, section 3.

6 Show that
   (i) $\forall xP(x) \vdash \exists xP(x)$
   (ii) $\forall xP(x) \vee \forall xQ(x) \vdash \forall x(P(x) \vee Q(x))$
   (iii) $\exists x(P(x) \wedge Q(x)) \vdash \exists xP(x) \vee \exists xQ(x)$
   (iv) $\forall x(P(a) \to Q(x)) \vdash (P(a) \to \forall xQ(x))$
   (v) $(P(a) \to \forall xQ(x)) \vdash \forall x(P(a) \to Q(x))$
   Show that (iv) and (v) remain true when $\forall$ is replaced by $\exists$.

7 Give a tree proof which establishes that every transitive irreflexive binary relation is asymmetric.

8 Let Σ be some set, possibly empty, of sentences. Show that
   (i)   If there is a tree proof of a sentence A from a sentence B together with Σ then there is a tree proof of $B \rightarrow A$ from Σ.
   (ii) If there is a tree proof of a sentence C from a sentence A together with Σ and of C from a sentence B together with Σ, there is a tree proof of C from $A \lor B$ together with Σ.
   (iii) If there is a tree proof of a sentence B from $A(a)$ together with Σ, where a does not occur in the tree, then there is a tree proof of B from $\exists x A(x)$ together with Σ.

First-order languages: semantics

1 INTERPRETATIONS

Chapter 5 referred to first-order languages interpreted in some domain. To generate the results of the next chapter we need to be a bit more precise about just what sorts of *things* interpretations of **L** are. To prepare the following discussion, suppose that **L** contains a binary relation symbol R and consider the sentence (i.e. closed formula) $\forall x \exists y R(x, y)$ of **L**. As it stands it has no truth-value, because no domain has been specified. But it automatically acquires a truth-value once we specify a domain and a binary relation defined in the domain as the interpretation of R. Now suppose **L** also contains a constant a. For the sentence $\exists x R(x, a)$ to have a truth-value in that domain a must be made to refer to some individual in the domain. We can generalise these observations as follows: *specifying an interpretation of a first-order language will mean specifying a domain and interpretations in that domain of the extralogical vocabulary of that language.*

We shall use the capital Gothic $\mathfrak{I}$ to refer to a generic interpretation of **L**. The domain of $\mathfrak{I}$ will be written $D_{\mathfrak{I}}$ and the binary relation defined in $D_{\mathfrak{I}}$ interpreting R will be written $R_{\mathfrak{I}}$. An interpretation of **L** which we shall sometimes use for illustrative purposes is **N**, whose domain is N, the set $\{0, 1, 2, 3, \ldots\}$ of natural numbers and in which R_N is >; i.e. $R(x, y)$ is interpreted in **N** as the relation x>y. It is not difficult to see that so interpreted the **L**-sentence $\forall y \exists x R(x, y)$ is true, and $\exists x \forall y R(x, y)$ is false: the former sentence says (in **N**) that for every natural number there is a greater, which is true, while the second says that some natural number is greater than every natural number, including itself, which is false.

However, in Chapter 6 it was shown that the sentences $\exists x \forall y R(x, y)$ and $\neg \forall y \exists x R(x, y)$ generate a closed tree. From this and the Soundness Theorem proved in Chapter 8 we can conclude that all attempts to find ways of making those two initial sentences jointly true fail: there is *no* interpretation of **L** in which those two sentences are true. In particular, if $D_{\mathfrak{I}} = N$, there is no binary relation $R_{\mathfrak{I}}$ of natural numbers such that both those sentences are true in $\mathfrak{I} = (N, R_{\mathfrak{I}})$. We should pause at this point to think through the implications of this remark. What exactly does it *mean* to say 'there is no binary relation of natural numbers such that ...'? What is included in this class? There are many familiar binary relations of natural numbers, for example <, ≤, >, ≥ and identity =. With a little thought we can come up with some less familiar ones. Does 'all binary relations of natural numbers' mean merely those for which we currently have names?

Surely not. Knowledge develops and our conceptual portfolio develops hand in hand with it. It would be short-sighted, to say the least, to restrict a theory of deductive consequence to the items in that portfolio at any given time. On the other hand, the notion of an arbitrary binary or for that matter n-place relation on an arbitrary domain sounds so nebulous that to translate it into something concrete and acceptably objective would seem on the face of it a hopeless enterprise. Surprisingly, this turns out to be not at all the case. Indeed, the solution to the problem has been known for almost a century.

The germ of the solution lies in a distinction first drawn by logicians centuries ago, between *intensions* and *extensions*. The intension of a property, for example *being a person*, is, roughly speaking, the meaning of the phrase 'is a person'. The extension is the set of all things, in this case the set of people, that have the property. Similarly, the intension of, say, a binary relation is the meaning of a standard description of it. Its extension requires a little more consideration. Recall from an earlier discussion (Chapter 5, section 3) that implicit in the notation R(x, y) is that x and y *in that order* stand in the relation represented by R. It therefore seems natural to say that the *things* of which R(x, y) is true in any domain are *ordered* pairs of domain elements.

We have reached an important point in the discussion, for ordered sets will play a central role in our theory of interpretations of first-order languages and to explain clearly what they are we need to make a brief digression into elementary set theory. In set theory the word 'set' unqualified means 'unordered set' and it is customary to signify these by using curly brackets {} to enclose the terms denoting their members; we have already used these set brackets in earlier chapters. Thus the unordered pair consisting of Cain and Abel, say, is written {Cain, Abel} and because it is an unordered set, {Cain, Abel} = {Abel, Cain}. But the *ordered* pair of Cain and Abel, in that order, is written with *curved* brackets enclosing 'Cain' first and 'Abel' second, thus: (Cain, Abel). *For ordered sets (u, v) and (v, u), (u, v) = (v, u) if and only if u = v.* But Cain ≠ Abel and so (Cain, Abel) ≠ (Abel, Cain). Indeed, the first pair is in the extension of many binary relations (for example, *is or was a slayer of*) of which the other is not.

Another relevant feature which distinguishes ordered pairs from unordered ones is that the set {Cain, Cain} is not a pair at all: the set-theoretical *Axiom of Extensionality* says that an unordered set is uniquely determined by its members, from which it follows that {Cain, Cain} = {Cain}. By contrast, the ordered set (Cain, Cain) *is* a genuine pair and indeed there is a familiar binary relation defined in the domain D = {Cain, Abel} of whose extension both (Cain, Cain) and (Abel, Abel) are members, that of identity = (nor is this the only one: *being the same height as* is another). The set of all ordered pairs of members of D thus has four members: (Cain, Cain), (Cain, Abel), (Abel, Cain), (Abel, Abel).

Just as there is a set of all ordered pairs of members of D, so there is a set of all ordered triples, quadruples, . . . and in general n-tuples of members of D, for any positive n (the set of all 1-tuples we can regard simply as D itself). The set of all ordered triples of members of D has 8 members (Cain, Cain, Cain), (Cain, Cain, Abel), . . ., (Abel, Abel, Abel), of quadruples of members of D has 16 members and of n-tuples of members of D has 2^n members. The set of all ordered n-tuples of D is written in set-theoretic notation as D^n; it is also called the *nth Cartesian product of D with itself.*

That ends the set theory. We can now identify the extension of an n-place relation in a domain with the corresponding set of ordered n-tuples of domain elements which stand in that relation (formally, the notation $R(x_1, \ldots, x_n)$ suggests that R is a predicate of n-tuples). Being sets, extensions seem to be admirably objective in character and also – an important bonus – well understood mathematically. Intensions, by contrast, seem to be just the sort of knowledge-dependent entities that we decided we did not want to base our logical theory on. The appropriate strategy in these circumstances is to apply what the philosophers call *Occam's Razor* (allegedly introduced into philosophical debate by the Schoolman William of Occam, Occam's Razor is the injunction not to multiply entities unnecessarily) and eliminate intensions entirely from consideration, *identifying properties and relations straightforwardly with their extensions.*

The next step is to regard *any* set of n-tuples of members of some domain as the extension of some relation defined in it. Thereby the apparently nebulous notions of an arbitrary property and of an arbitrary n-place relation defined in a domain D are replaced by a well-understood and objective mathematical concept, an arbitrary *set* of the appropriate dimension (the dimension of a set of n-tuples is n; a subset of D itself is defined to have dimension 1). We are now in a position to define the notion of an interpretation of an arbitrary first-order language with complete generality; the definition, due originally to the Polish-American logician and mathematician Alfred Tarski, is as follows:

An interpretation $\mathfrak{I}$ of a first-order language **L** is a rule specifying

(i)   a non-empty set $D_{\mathfrak{I}}$ of individuals, called the *domain* of the variables of **L**. We should recall from our discussion in Chapter 5 that the individuals in $D_{\mathfrak{I}}$ are not necessarily physical objects. They can be anything which can be conceptually individuated, concrete or abstract, like processes, actions, numbers, algebraic structures, thoughts, emotions, or what have you.

(ii) for each individual constant c of L, a particular member $c_\Im$ of $D_\Im$. In other words, $c_\Im$ is the individual in $D_\Im$ named by the constant c of L. N.B.: there is no rule preventing the same individual in $D_\Im$ being the interpretation of more than one constant, i.e. there is nothing to stop $c_\Im$ being the same individual in $D_\Im$ as $b_\Im$ (this should not worry anybody familiar with the custom of many people giving their offspring more than one name).

(iii) for each predicate symbol P of L, a set $P_\Im$ of individuals in $D_\Im$ – this subset of $D_\Im$ specifies which individuals in $D_\Im$ are to have the property P in $\Im$. Thus the sentence P(c), where c is a constant, will be *true in* $\Im$ just in case $c_\Im$ is in $P_\Im$.

(iv) for each n-place relation symbol R of L (n>1), a set $R_\Im$ of ordered n-tuples of individuals in $D_\Im$. $R_\Im$ specifies those n-tuples of individuals which determine the R-relation in $D_\Im$. Thus, if $c_1, \ldots, c_n$ are constants and R an n-place relation symbol, $R(c_1, \ldots, c_n)$ is *true in* $\Im$ just in case the n-tuple $(c_{1\Im}, \ldots, c_{n\Im})$ is in $R_\Im$.

A consequence of the definition of an n-place relation as a set of ordered n-tuples of $D_\Im$ is that the empty set $\varnothing$ automatically qualifies as an n-place relation. For, as we know from exercise 4, section 3, Chapter 6, $\varnothing$ is a subset of any set and so qualifies both as a subset of $D_\Im$ and as a subset of $D_\Im^n$, the set of all n-tuples of $D_\Im$. To assign the empty set as the interpretation $P_\Im$ of a predicate symbol P means that *no* individuals in $D_\Im$ will be Ps in $\Im$; if $R_\Im$ is $\varnothing$, where r is any relation symbol of L, this means that no individuals in $D_\Im$ are R-related in $\Im$.

Exercises

1 Show that a tree generated from the set
    $\{\forall x(P(x)\rightarrow Q(x))\wedge\forall x(P(x)\rightarrow\neg Q(x)), \exists xP(x)\}$
    closes. What does this tell you about the identity of $P_\Im$ in any interpretation $\Im$ which makes the sentence $\forall x(P(x)\rightarrow Q(x))\wedge\forall x(P(x)\rightarrow\neg Q(x))$ true?

2 Show that a tree generated from the set
    $\{\forall x(P(x)\rightarrow Q(x)), \forall x\neg Q(x), \exists xP(x)\}$
    closes. What does this tell you about the identity of $P_\Im$ if $\forall x(P(x)\rightarrow Q(x))$ is true in $\Im$ and $Q_\Im$ is $\varnothing$?

3 Show that a tree generated from the set
    $\{\forall x(P(x)\rightarrow Q(x)), \forall xP(x), \neg\forall xQ(x)\}$
    closes. What does this tell you about the identity of $Q_\Im$ if $\forall x(P(x)\rightarrow Q(x))$ is true in $\Im$ and $P_\Im$ is the entire domain $D_\Im$ of $\Im$?

4 Let D be the set {0, 1}. List all the members of D^3, i.e. all the triples or 3-tuples of members of D.

2 FORMULAS AND TRUTH

In elementary mathematics we are familiar with open formulas being *true for given values* of their free variables and false for others. For example, 'x<7', interpreted in the domain N of the natural numbers, is true for the values 0, 1, 2, 3, 4, 5, 6 of x and false for all others. Interpreted in N, 'x<0' is true for no values of x and consequently $\forall x \neg (x<0)$ is true (note: not 'true for specified values of x', since x is *bound* in $\forall x \neg (x<0)$: $\forall x \neg (x<0)$ doesn't refer to an individual x at all; it says that no natural number is less than 0). Interpreted in the set R of real numbers, on the other hand, or in the set of positive and negative whole numbers, x<0 is true for infinitely many values of x, of course and so in each of those domains $\forall x \neg (x<0)$ is false.

The same rules apply straightforwardly to formulas of **L**. Suppose **L** contains a predicate symbol P and a binary relation symbol R and we are considering some interpretation $\Im$ of **L**. Then the open atomic formula P(x) will be *true in $\Im$ for the value x' of x in $D_\Im$* just in case x' is a member of the set $P_\Im$ (N.B.: x' is an element of $D_\Im$; it is the *value* in D assigned to the variable x of **L**). Similarly the atomic formula R(x, y) will be true in $\Im$ for an ordered pair of values (x', y') of x and y respectively just in case (x', y') is a member of $R_\Im$.

Formulas of the form $\forall x A(x)$ and $\exists x A(x)$ are of course closed: they are sentences of **L**. Their truth-conditions, with which we are already familiar, are naturally specified in terms of those for open formulas: *$\forall x A(x)$ is true in $\Im$* just in case $A(x)$ is true in $\Im$ for every value of x in $D_\Im$; and *$\exists x A(x)$ is true in $\Im$* just in case $A(x)$ is true in $\Im$ for at least one value of x in $D_\Im$. This is not formally watertight as a definition of the truth-conditions of the quantifiers, because $A(x)$ may itself have an occurrence of one or more quantifier in it. It is not particularly difficult, however, to give a formally watertight definition and for those curious to see one, it is provided in the Appendix to this section.

Examples Suppose L contains a binary relation symbol R and a constant a.

(i) Let $\Im$ be the interpretation of **L** whose domain is the set N of natural numbers and let $a_\Im$ be 0 and $R_\Im$ the relation ≤ in N, i.e. the set {(n,m): n≤m, n, m in N}. The formula R(a, x) of **L** is true in $\Im$ for all values of x in N, since interpreted in $\Im$ it says that all natural numbers are greater than or equal to 0. Hence $\forall x R(a, x)$ is true in $\Im$. Since $\forall x R(y, x)$ is true in $\Im$ for the value 0 of y, it follows that $\exists y \forall x R(y, x)$ is true in $\Im$.

(ii) Let $\mathfrak{I}$ be the same as above, except that $R_\mathfrak{I}$ is now $<$, not $\leq$ as in (i). $R(a, x)$ is now true only for the non-zero values of x in N, because interpreted in $\mathfrak{I}$ it says that x is greater than 0. $\forall xR(a, x)$ is therefore now *false* in $\mathfrak{I}$. $\exists yR(x, y)$ is true for every value of x in N, because it says that there is a number in n larger than x and this is true whatever value assigned to x. Hence $\forall x\exists yR(x, y)$ is true in $\mathfrak{I}$. Now consider a slightly less obvious example: the formula $R(x, y)\rightarrow R(y, x)$. For which pairs (x', y') of values in N of x and y is this formula true? Well, it is false only for those pairs of values which make the antecedent true and the consequent false. The values x', y' of x, y make $R(x, y)$ true just in case x'<y'. Moreover, *every* such pair (x', y') will make $R(y, x)$ false. But any pair of values of x and y will make $R(x, y)\rightarrow R(y, x)$ true just in case that pair doesn't make it false. Consequently, all pairs (x', y') of values of x and y such that x' is not less than y', i.e. all x', y', such that x'$\geq$y', will make $R(x, y)\rightarrow R(y, x)$ true.

(iii) Let $\mathfrak{I}$ be as above, except that $R_\mathfrak{I}$ is now the set $\{(n, n): n$ in N$\}$. The formula $R(a, x)$ is now true just for the value x' = 0. $R(x, x)$ is true for all values of x in N and so $\forall xR(x, x)$ is true in $\mathfrak{I}$.

(iv) Finally, consider an interpretation $\mathfrak{I}$ whose domain is *finite*. For example, let $D_\mathfrak{I}$ be the set $\{0, 1\}$, $a_\mathfrak{I}$ be 0, and $R_\mathfrak{I}$ be $\{(0, 1), (1, 1)\}$. Check that the sentence

$$\forall x\forall y\forall z((R(x, y)\wedge R(y, z))\rightarrow R(x, z))\wedge\exists xR(a, x)\wedge\exists x\neg R(a, x)$$

is true in $\mathfrak{I}$. There is no particular reason for selecting natural numbers as domain members, incidentally. Any two objects instead of 0 and 1 would have done just as well. An interpretation in which two distinct objects play the same roles as 0 and 1 in $\mathfrak{I}$ is said to be *isomorphic* to $\mathfrak{I}$. A very important fact which plays a central role in the investigation of first-order semantics, or first-order model theory, as it is more usually known, is that *isomorphic structures cannot be distinguished by any set of first-order sentences*. An equally important fact is that some non-isomorphic structures also cannot be distinguished by any set of first-order sentences. These are necessarily infinite structures. This is one of the limitations of first-order formalisations and one we shall discuss more fully in Chapter 11.

Exercises

1 A subset S of $D_\mathfrak{I}$ is said to satisfy an open formula A(x) if A(x) is true in $\mathfrak{I}$ just for values in S of the variable x. Suppose **L** contains the predicate symbol P. Which subsets of $D_\mathfrak{I}$ respectively satisfy the open formulas below?
   (a) $P(x)\wedge\neg P(x)$
   (b) $P(x)\vee\neg P(x)$
   (c) $P(x)\rightarrow\exists y(P(y)\wedge\neg P(y))$
   (d) $\exists y(P(y)\vee\neg P(y)\vee P(x))$

2 Let **L** possess a binary relation symbol R. Let the domain of $\Im$ be N and let $R_\Im$ be $<$ in N, i.e. $\{(n, m): n<m, n, m \text{ in } N\}$. In the following formulas identify the variables with free occurrences, if any, and say for which of their joint values, if any, the formulas are true.

(a) $\exists yR(x, y)$
(b) $\exists xR(y, x)$
(c) $\forall yR(x, y)$
(d) $\forall xR(x, y)$
(e) $R(x, y) \wedge R(y, x)$
(f) $\forall x \exists yR(x, y)$
(g) $\forall x \exists yR(x, y) \rightarrow R(x, y)$
(h) $R(x, y) \rightarrow \forall x \exists yR(x, y)$
(i) $\exists x \forall yR(x, y) \rightarrow R(x, y)$

APPENDIX*: TRUTH WITH RESPECT TO A VALUATION

Let A be any formula of L and $T(A)$ be the set of free variables and constants (if any) appearing in A. We shall start by replacing the informal notation, in which the value of a variable x is signified by x', by one which makes the formal development easier. A *valuation* v of $T(A)$ in an interpretation $\Im$ is an assignment to each item t in $T(A)$ a value $v(t)$, such that if t is a variable x, $v(x)$ is any individual in $D_\Im$ and if t is a constant a, $v(a) = a_\Im$ (thus the constants have a *constant* value for all valuations, while different valuations may assign variables *different* values in $D_\Im$; this is why constants are called constants and variables variables). What if A is a closed formula without constants, for example $\forall x \exists yR(x, y)$? Then $T(A)$ is empty. In this case the unique valuation on $T(A)$ is the empty valuation. Don't worry about what precisely this looks like; it can be shown that it coincides with the empty set, so invoking such an entity, and claiming its uniqueness, turn out to be perfectly consistent.

We shall now define the relation 'The formula A is true relative to a given valuation v of $T(A)$' inductively, for each *type* of formula A of **L** specified in the earlier inductive definition 'formula of **L**':

(1) A is atomic. Then A is of the form $R(t_1, \ldots, t_n)$, where R is an n-place relation symbol of **L** and $t_1, \ldots, t_n$ are variables or constants. Then $T(A) = \{t_1, \ldots, t_n\}$ and A is true relative to v if and only if $(v(t_1), \ldots, v(t_n))$ is an n-tuple in $R_\Im$.

(2) A is the negation of another formula; i.e. A is of the form $\neg B$, for some formula B of **L**. Note that $T(A) = T(B)$ so that any valuation of $T(A)$ is automatically a valuation of $T(B)$. Then A is true relative to v if and only if B is not true relative to v.

(3) A is of the form $B \vee C$, for formulas B, C of **L**. $T(A)$ is the union of $T(B)$ and $T(C)$ (the union of two sets is the set whose members are in either

set). Let v_B be v restricted to $T(B)$ and v_C be the restriction of v to $T(C)$ (v restricted to $T(B)$ is that valuation of $T(B)$ which takes the same values as v does on all the members of $T(B)$). Then A is true relative to v if and only if B is true relative to v_B or C is true relative to v_C.

4 A is of the form $B \wedge C$, for formulas B, C of **L**. Then A is true relative to v if and only if B is true relative to v_B and C is true relative to v_C.

5 A is of the form $B \rightarrow C$, for formulas B, C of **L**. Then A is true relative to v if and only if B is false relative to v_B or C is true relative to v_C.

6 A is of the form $\forall x B$, for some formula B of **L**. Then A is true relative to v if and only if B is true relative to *every* extension of v to $T(B)$ (an extension of v to $T(B)$ is a valuation of $T(B)$ which takes the same values on $T(A)$ as v).

7 A is of the form $\exists x B$ for some formula B of **L**. Then A is true relative to v if and only if B is true relative to *some* extension of v to $T(B)$.

Explanation Clause 1 generalises the conditions laid down earlier for particular atomic formulas to be true relative to given values of its free variables (if there are any). Clauses 2–5 merely state the truth table definitions of the connectives relative to a valuation of the free variables of the compounded formulas B and C; each such valuation will represent a particular truth-value distribution over B and C. Clause 6 says that once a valuation has fixed the values of the free variables (if any) other than x in B, then $\forall x B$ is true relative to that valuation if and only if B is true for every assignment of a value to x. Clause 7 says that once a valuation has fixed the values of the free variables other than x in B (if there are any), then $\exists x B$ is true relative to that valuation if and only if B is true for at least one assignment of a value to x. These last two clauses are therefore only a careful way of stating the familiar truth-conditions for the quantifiers.

If A is a closed formula, there is just one valuation v of $T(A)$; either the empty one if $T(A)$ is empty, or the one which sets the value of each constant a in $T(A)$ equal to $a_\Im$. For such a formula, we can say simply that A *is true in* $\Im$ if A is true with respect to v.

3   THE TREE RULES REVISITED

We have said that a closed formula of **L** will take a definite truth-value in any interpretation $\Im$ of **L**. It was pointed out in Chapter 6, section 1, that expressions like $\forall x \exists x P(x)$, $\exists y(R(a, b)$ and $\forall x \exists x \exists y P(x)$ all pass the test as legitimate sentences, according to the definition of 'formula' and 'closed formula' for the appropriate **L**. It may seem bizarre to regard such expressions as having determinate truth-values, but it turns out that any sensible systematic way of expressing the truth-conditions for quantified statements automatically endows such sentences with truth-values. In fact, it follows from the clauses in the Appendix above that if A is a formula of **L** which does not contain a free occurrence of x, then the truth-value in $\mathfrak{J}$ of $\forall xA$ or $\exists xA$ is the same as that of A itself, relative to any assignment of values in $D_\mathfrak{J}$ to any other variables which do have free occurrences in A. For example, suppose that $P(x)$ is true in $\mathfrak{J}$ for some value x in $D_\mathfrak{J}$. Then so is $\exists yP(x)$ by the stipulation just introduced. But $\exists yP(x)$ has the form of a formula $B(x)$ of **L** with a free occurrence of x and since it is true in $\mathfrak{J}$ for some value of x in $D_\mathfrak{J}$, it follows that $\exists xB(x)$, i.e. $\exists x\exists yP(x)$ is true in $\mathfrak{J}$. But $\exists xB(x)$ has no free occurrence of x and is true in $\mathfrak{J}$. Hence $\forall x\exists x\exists yP(x)$ is true in $\mathfrak{J}$. Similarly, $\exists xP(a)$ is true in $\mathfrak{J}$ just in case $P(a)$ is.

Since we also want our tree rules to be complete, we must amend them so that these features are represented in tree-derivability relations. To do this, we first extend the class of δ [respectively γ] sentences to contain any sentences of the form $\exists xA$ or $\neg\forall xA$ [respectively $\forall xA$ or $\neg\exists xA$] where A might or might not contain free occurrences of x. Next we define some new notation, $\gamma(a/x)$ and $\delta(a/x)$, as follows: where γ is $\forall xA$, $\gamma(a/x)$ is $A(a/x)$ (Chapter 6, section 1) and where γ is $\neg\exists xA$, $\gamma(a/x)$ is $\neg A(a/x)$. Define $\delta(a/x)$ similarly. We can now state the final form of the (γ) and (δ) rules: where the relevant quantifiers in γ and δ are on x, where x is any variable, the rules are

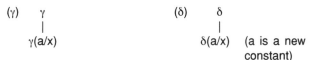

Exercises

Show that the following sentences are interderivable by trees (i.e. show that there are tree proofs of each from the other):

1 $\forall x\exists xP(x)$ and $\exists xP(x)$
2 $\exists yP(a)$ and $P(a)$
3 $\forall x\exists z\exists yP(z)$ and $\exists zP(z)$

4 CONSISTENCY AND VALIDITY

Suppose Σ is a set of sentences formalised in some first-order language **L**. A *model* of Σ is an interpretation of **L** in which all the sentences in Σ are true. Σ is *consistent* just in case it has a model. If Σ is not consistent we shall say that it is *inconsistent*. (N.B.: do not confuse this use of the word 'model' with that in the statement 'we want to build a formal model of deductive reasoning'. The sense of 'model' in that sentence is that of a relatively simple approximative *theory*, whereas 'model' in the sense we are talking about in this section refers to a *structure* in which a formalised theory is interpreted, according to the rules laid down in sections 1 and 2 of this chapter. It is an unfortunate fact of life that the same word is used to cover both, quite distinct, senses.)

In Chapter 5, we updated the provisional definition of deductive validity of Chapter 1 to this: an inference is deductively valid in first-order logic if there is no interpretation of its component sentences such that the premises are true and the conclusion false in that interpretation. Equivalently, an inference is valid in first-order logic if its premises and the negation of its conclusion cannot all be true in any interpretation (Note: to avoid cumbersome formulations we shall identify sentences with their translations into an appropriate first-order language; we shall also henceforth drop the explicit qualifier 'in first-order logic', regarding it as implicit.) But a set Σ of sentences is true in some interpretation just in case Σ consistent. So we have the alternative characterisation of deductive validity:

> An inference is deductively valid if and only if the premises and the negation of the conclusion are inconsistent.

Two important consequences of this meta-biconditional are the following:

(i) A set Σ of sentences is consistent if and only if there is no sentence C such that both C and $\neg C$ are consequences of Σ.
(ii) A set Σ of sentences is consistent if and only if there is at least one sentence which is not a consequence of Σ.

The Soundness and Completeness Theorems proved in the next chapter give us the same syntactical, proof-theoretic criteria for the semantic concept of consistency and hence for the relation of consequence, as for truth-functional logic: the Soundness Theorem for first-order trees says that if a set Σ of sentences has a model, it generates a finished open tree and the Completeness Theorem states the converse: if Σ generates a finished open tree, it is consistent.

Exercises

1 Show that (i) and (ii) above are true.
2 Show that if C is any sentence in a set Σ of sentences and Σ is inconsistent, then the inference from $\Sigma-\{C\}$ to $\neg C$ is valid ($\Sigma-\{C\}$ is what remains when C is removed from Σ).
3 Show that if A is a deductive consequence of Σ and Δ includes all the sentences in Σ, then A is a deductive consequence of Δ (this is the *monotonicity* property of deduction).
4 Show that if B is a deductive consequence of Σ and C is a consequence of Δ together with B, then C is a consequence of Σ together with Δ (this is often called the *cut* rule).
5 Show by constructing closed trees that the following sets of sentences

are inconsistent.

(a) $\{\forall xP(x), \neg P(a)\}$

(b) $\{\forall x(P(x) \rightarrow Q(x)), \exists xP(x), \forall x \neg Q(x)\}$

(c) $\{\exists y \forall xR(x, y), \neg \forall x \exists yR(x, y)\}$

(d) $\{\forall x \exists yR(x, y), \exists x \forall y \neg R(x, y)\}$

(e) $\{\exists x \forall yR(x, y), \forall x \exists y \neg R(x, y)\}$

(f) $\{\forall x(P(x) \rightarrow \exists yR(x, y)), \forall z \neg R(b, z), P(b)\}$

(g) $\{\forall x \forall y(P(x) \rightarrow Q(y)), \exists z \neg (P(z) \rightarrow \forall wQ(w))\}$

5 LOGICAL TRUTH AND LOGICAL EQUIVALENCE

The sentences of **L** which are true in every interpretation $\mathfrak{I}$ of **L** are called the *logical truths* of **L**. Clearly, a sentence is a logical truth just in case its negation has no model, i.e. just in case it by itself forms an inconsistent so-called *singleton* set (a singleton set is a set with just one member). We can therefore test for logical truth, just as we did earlier for tautologousness, by constructing a tree from the negation of the sentence in question and seeing whether it closes. Inconsistent sets of sentences are unsatisfiable, by definition and so if a tree generated from a single sentence A closes, then by the Soundness Theorem $\neg A$ is inconsistent and hence A is a logical truth. Conversely, if A is a logical truth then its negation is inconsistent and hence by Completeness $\neg A$ generates a closed tree. *Thus Soundness and Completeness tell us that A is a logical truth if and only if $\neg A$ generates a closed tree.*

We can adapt in a natural way our earlier notion of a tautology so that we can also describe sentences of **L** as tautologies if they satisfy the amended criteria. Clearly, the propositional sentence $A \rightarrow (B \rightarrow A)$ represents the truth-functional structure of $P(a) \rightarrow (\exists x[Q(x) \vee \forall yP(y)] \rightarrow P(a))$. The truth-functional representation of any first-order sentence can now be found as follows. Construct the ancestral tree of the sentence. Starting at the root, i.e. with the sentence itself at the top of the tree, follow each branch downwards until the first sentence on that branch not of the form $\neg X$, $X \rightarrow Y$, $X \vee Y$, $X \wedge Y$ is reached. Call this sentence a *propositional atom* of the first. Replace it with a sentence letter and erase the remainder of the branch below it. Assign identical propositional atoms identical sentence letters. The result will be a truncated tree whose branches now terminate in sentence letters. All the other sentences on the tree, including the root, will be truth-functional compounds of these. Going back up the branches, replace every propositional atom occurring within each mode by its corresponding sentence letter. The result will be the ancestral tree of a sentence X in the standard propositional language **L**[A, B, C, . . .; ∧, ∨, ¬, →]. X is the truth-functional representation of the original **L** sentence.

For example, P(a) and $\exists x[Q(x) \vee \forall yP(y)]$ are the propositional atoms of the first-order sentence P(a)→(∃x[Q(x)∨∀yP(y)]→P(a)). Replacing them by the sentence letters A and B respectively, we obtain X = A→(B→A), as above. If X is a tautology of the standard propositional language, as in that example, *then the corresponding first-order sentence is said to be a tautology of the first-order language* **L**. Sentences of **L** which translate by the same method into contradictions of the standard propositional language will be called contradictions of **L**. An equivalent way of defining 'tautology of **L**' is 'a sentence of **L** whose negation generates a tree which closes using only the rules (α) and (β)'. See if you can explain why the two formulations are equivalent.

There are logical truths of **L** which are not tautologies of **L**. Here are three examples:

(i)   ∀xP(x)→P(a)
(ii)   ¬∃xP(x)→¬P(a)
(iii) ∀xP(x)→∀x¬¬P(x)

So (i)–(iii) are logical truths of **L** which are not tautologies of **L**. Since the tautologies of **L** are just those logical truths which can be shown to be necessarily true by propositional means only, we can think of propositional and first-order languages as being rather like optical instruments of different resolving powers. Viewed from within a propositional language, the sentence ∀xP(x)→P(a) appears only as a sentence of the form A→B, where A and B are sentence letters and the fact that it is a logical truth is therefore not apparent.

We first used the symbol ⇔ to signify truth-functional equivalence and then extended it to sentences in a first-order language to denote logical equivalence, but without making its meaning very precise. Using model-terminology we can now do this: where *A* and *B* are sentences of some first-order language **L**, *A is logically equivalent in first-order logic to B (A ⇔ B) if and only if A and B take the same truth-value in all interpretations of* **L**.

As pointed out earlier, truth-functional equivalence is a special case of logical equivalence. We found in propositional logic that the tree method could be used to show that two truth-functional compounds X and Y were equivalent, by seeing whether both sets {X, ¬Y} and {¬X, Y} generate closed trees: if they do, and only if they do, then X and Y are truth-functionally equivalent. It should be clear that the Soundness and Completeness Theorems for first-order trees underwrite the analogous procedure when X and Y are first-order sentences. As an example, consider the following two important equivalences (a) and (b), which demonstrate the interdefinability of the universal and existential quantifiers:

(a) ∀x*A*(x) ⇔ ¬∃x¬*A*(x)
(b) ∃x*A*(x) ⇔ ¬∀x¬*A*(x)

We shall construct a pair of closed trees for (a), leaving (b) as an exercise.

(a) $\forall xA(x)$ $\neg\forall xA(x)$
       $\neg\neg\exists x\neg A(x)$ $\neg\exists x\neg A(x)$
              | |
       $\exists x\neg A(x)$ $\neg A(b)$
              | |
       $\neg A(b)$ $\underline{\neg\neg A(b)}$
              |
       $\underline{A(b)}$

Exercises

1 Show by constructing appropriate trees that the equivalence (b) above holds.
2 Explain carefully why the sentences (i)–(iii) at the beginning of this section are not tautologies. Show by the tree method that they and the following are logical truths.
   (a) $\forall x(A(x)\to B(x))\to(\forall xA(x)\to\forall xB(x))$
   (b) $\forall x(\forall yB(y)\to C(x))\to(\forall yB(y)\to\forall xC(x))$
   (c) $\forall x(\exists yB(y)\wedge C(x))\exists y(B(y)\wedge\forall xC(x))$
   (d) $\forall x(\forall yB(y)\vee C(x))\to(\forall yB(y)\vee\forall xC(x))$
   Show also that the converse of each of (b)–(d) is a logical truth (i.e. (b)–(d) are logical equivalences).
3 Show by constructing suitable closed trees that the following equivalences hold
   (a) $\neg\forall xA(x)\Leftrightarrow\exists x\neg A(x)$
   (b) $\forall x(A(x)\wedge B(x))\Leftrightarrow\forall xA(x)\wedge\forall xB(x)$
   (c) $\exists x(A(x)\vee B(x))\Leftrightarrow\exists xA(x)\vee\exists xB(x)$
   (d) $\forall x(A(x)\to B)\Leftrightarrow\exists xA(x)\to B$
   (e) $\exists x(A(x)\to B)\Leftrightarrow\forall xA(x)\to B$
   where B in (d) and (e) is any sentence which has no free occurrence of x.

Note Exercises 2 and 3 show how quantifiers can be systematically moved from being embedded in a formula to being placed at the front. A fundamental metatheorem of first-order logic, the so-called *Prenex Normal Form Theorem*, states that any formula with an embedded quantifier is equivalent to one all of whose quantifiers occur in an unbroken sequence at the 'front' of the formula. A formula commencing with a string of adjacent quantifiers, such that the final quantifier in the string includes no other quantifier in its scope, is said to be in Prenex Normal Form.

Chapter 8

Soundness and completeness

1 APPLYING THE TREE RULES

The Completeness Theorem for first-order trees, which with the corresponding Soundness Theorem will be proved in section 3, says that every open branch in a finished tree generated by a finite set Σ of sentences determines a model of Σ. It follows that if Σ is inconsistent, then every finished tree closes. If a tree closes, it closes after finitely many steps. In practice, we want to use the theorem to justify the following conditional: if a finite set is inconsistent, then it will generate a closed tree. Granted the truth of that (meta)conditional, we should then have a partial *decision procedure* for inconsistency: if a set Σ is inconsistent, then eventually we shall be able to tell it is because any tree generated from it will close (the procedure is only partial because if the tree is not going to close, i.e. if Σ is consistent, we may never know).

Unfortunately, as things stand the metaconditional above is not true, as the following examples show.

Example 1

1	$\forall x \exists y R(x, y)$	initial sentence
2	$P(a) \wedge \neg P(a)$	initial sentence
	$\mid$	
3	$\exists y R(a, y)$	(γ) on 1
	$\mid$	
4	$R(a, b)$	(δ) on 3
	$\mid$	
5	$\exists y R(b, y)$	(γ) on 1
	$\mid$	
6	$R(b, c)$	(δ) on 5
	$\mid$	
7	$\exists y R(c, y)$	(γ) on 1
	$\mid$	
	etc.	

Example 2

1	∀x∃yR(x, y)	initial sentence
2	∀y¬R(a, y)	initial sentence
3	∃yR(a, y)	(γ) on 1
4	R(a, b)	(δ) on 3
5	∃yR(b, y)	(γ) on 1
6	R(b, c)	(δ) on 5
7	∃yR(c, y)	(γ) on 1
8	R(c, d)	(δ) on 7

etc.

These two trees will not close because certain sentences fail to get used; in example 1, the sentence $P(a) \wedge \neg P(a)$ and in example 2, $\forall y \neg R(a, y)$. If, in example 2, at line 5 we had applied (γ) to the γ sentence on line 2, we would very quickly have got a closed tree:

1	∀x∃yR(x, y)	
2	∀y¬R(a, y)	
3	∃yR(a, y)	(γ) on 1
4	R(a, b)	(δ) on 3
5	¬R(a, b)	(γ) on 2

The way to remedy the defect is clearly to impose constraints on the way the tree rules are applied so that at some point those unused sentences *have* to be used. For example, we could require the tree rules to be applied in strict sequence, possibly though not necessarily in the order Double Negation, (α), (β), (δ) and (γ), allowing progression to the next rule r_{i+1} in the sequence only when each unused sentence to which r_i is applicable has had r_i applied to it and, for each open branch **B** in the tree, the descendent sentence under that application of r_i placed at the end of **B**.

Observing this or any other protocol designed to achieve the same object may, however, not provide the simplest tree proof in any given case. The solution to this problem, if it is a problem, is to be pragmatic: if you can see that a tree will close by, say, the application of a different rule before you have have finished applying the current one, apply it.

2   BRANCH MODELS

We shall now take up again the discussion of **B**-worlds from where we left it at the beginning of Chapter 6, section 2, only now we shall call them *branch models*. Let **B** be any open branch in a finished tree and L_B the first-order language whose relation symbols and constants are those appearing in the sentences occurring on **B**. The *branch model determined by B* (sometimes called the *canonical model* determined by **B**) is an interpretation $\mathfrak{I}_B$ of L_B constructed in the following way (to avoid too many subscripts we shall simply write $\mathfrak{I}$ instead of $\mathfrak{I}_B$). Suppose the set C of constants **B** is non-empty (it may be infinite, as in the case of the infinite finished tree generated by $\forall x \exists y R(x, y)$). Then

(i)   The domain $D_{\mathfrak{I}}$ of $\mathfrak{I}$ is the set C.
(ii) The denotation $c_{\mathfrak{I}}$ of each constant c of L_B is c itself.
(iii) The extension of any predicate symbol P in L_B is the set of all constants c in C such that P(c) is a sentence on **B**.
(iv) The extension $R_{\mathfrak{I}}$ in $\mathfrak{I}$ of any n-place relation symbol R in L_B is the set of all n-tuples $(c_1, \ldots, c_n)$ of constants c_i in L_B such that $R(c_1, \ldots, c_n)$ is a sentence on **B**.

We shall show in the next section that branch models are always models of the initial sentences of the tree. A distinctive feature of them is that if neither P(c) nor ¬P(c) appears as a node on **B**, then by default the individual c in the domain of $\mathfrak{I}_B$ is decreed *not* to be one of the individuals having the property P in $\mathfrak{I}_B$. The reader may initially feel uneasy about the fact that the domain of the branch model determined by a branch **B** consists of the constants of L_B named by themselves. But *any* non-empty set may be the domain of an interpretation, so there is nothing technically illegitimate about having a domain consisting of symbols of L_B, or in having those symbols denote themselves *qua* domain elements. The reader may also feel that branch models are artificial, ad hoc, cooked-up, or whatever. That is certainly true, but considered in terms of the goal of providing a model of the sentences on a finished open branch **B**, they undeniably do their job: whatever **B** may look like, $\mathfrak{I}_B$ is such a model.

Before proving this and other results about branch models, let us first look at some examples to familiarise ourselves with the construction. First, consider the set $\{\forall x(P(x) \rightarrow Q(x)), Q(a), \neg P(a)\}$ of initial sentences. From this we generate a finite finished open tree (the reader should supply the justification of each line):

$$\forall x(P(x) \rightarrow Q(x))$$
$$Q(a)$$
$$\neg P(a)$$
$$|$$
$$P(a) \rightarrow Q(a)$$
$$/ \quad \backslash$$
$$\neg P(a) \quad Q(a)$$

The γ sentence at the top of the tree cannot be instantiated any more, so the tree is finished, with both branches open. The branch model determined by each branch is actually the same, call it $\mathfrak{I}$, with domain {a}, $P_\mathfrak{I} = \varnothing$, and $Q_\mathfrak{I} = \{a\}$.

Next, consider the tree generated by the set $\{\exists x(P(x) \wedge \forall y \neg R(y, x)), P(a) \rightarrow \exists x R(a, x)\}$:

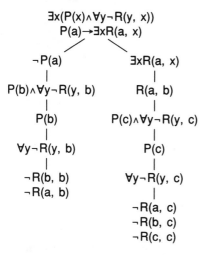

The two open branches determine two different branch models. The left-hand branch determines the model $\mathfrak{I}$ with domain {a, b}, $P_\mathfrak{I} = \{b\}$, with $R_\mathfrak{I} = \varnothing$. The right-hand branch gives the branch model $\mathfrak{I}'$ with domain {a, b, c} and with $P_{\mathfrak{I}'} = \{c\}$, $R_{\mathfrak{I}'} = \{(a, b)\}$.

Finally, consider the tree generated from the set $\{\forall x P(x) \rightarrow \exists y Q(y), \neg \forall x(P(x) \rightarrow \exists y Q(y))\}$:

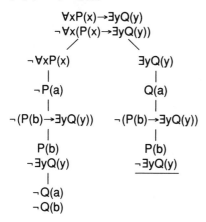

There is one open branch on this tree, which determines the branch model $\mathfrak{I}$ with domain {a, b}, $P_\mathfrak{I} = \{b\}$, $Q_\mathfrak{I} = \varnothing$. This is of course a counterexample to the inference $\forall xP(x)\rightarrow\exists yQ(y) \therefore \forall x(P(x)\rightarrow\exists yQ(y))$, and structurally the simplest one that exists.

For those who still have qualms about the way branch models are constructed, in particular about using constants of the language as elements of the domain, the following fact should be considered. Recall earlier that we pointed out that first-order sentences are incapable of distinguishing between isomorphic structures, i.e. between structures that differ only in the actual constituents of the domains, but which in every other respect are the same. Well, suppose you list all the constants in $\mathbf{L_B}$ in some particular order. For example, suppose they are subscripted $a_1, a_2, a_3, \dots.$. Now take a branch model $\mathfrak{I}$ for Σ and uniformly in the definitions of $D_\mathfrak{I}$, $a_\mathfrak{I}$, $P_\mathfrak{I}$ and $R_\mathfrak{I}$ replace a_m by m. You will now have an isomorphic structure $\mathfrak{I}_{Z+}$, but one whose individuals are positive integers. But since they're isomorphic, $\mathfrak{I}_{Z+}$ will be a model of Σ. So if you don't, for whatever reason, like branch models, you have a recipe for obtaining models in the positive integers from them.

Branch models are often the simplest models of a consistent finite set of first-order sentences if the finished tree has a finite open branch, though this is not always the case if the branch is infinite. For example, consider the infinite open branch generated by $\forall x\exists yR(x, y)$, which we examined in Chapter 6, section 2. That branch determines the branch model $\mathfrak{I}$ with domain $\{a, b, c, d, \dots\}$, where $a_\mathfrak{I} = a$, $b_\mathfrak{I} = b$, $c_\mathfrak{I} = c$, etc. and $R_\mathfrak{I} = \{(a, b), (b, c), (c, d), \dots\}$. Yet this is far from the simplest model, since there is a model with domain $\{0\}$ with R interpreted as $\{(0, 0)\}$. All branch models determined by infinite branches will always have infinite domains, though as this example shows it may well be that the initial sentences possess a small finite model. (A *finite model* is a model with an finite domain.)

Not all sets, even finite ones, of initial sentences have finite models. Here is a set of just three simple sentences which does not: $\{\forall x\exists yR(x, y), \forall x\neg R(x, x), \forall x\forall y\forall z(R(x, y)\rightarrow(R(y, z)\rightarrow R(x, z)))\}$. The second and third sentences state that R is an irreflexive and transitive relation on its domain and we know from Chapter 6, section 3, that this implies that R is also asymmetric. We also know that these are properties of the usual ordering < 'less than' on numbers and because they are infinite $\forall x\exists yR(x, y)$ is also true with R interpreted as <. In fact, these properties determine that any domain in which they are exemplified *must* be infinite; to show this is left as a not-so-easy exercise.

Exercises

1 Find one branch model for each of the following sets of sentences.
   (a) $\{\forall x(P(x)\rightarrow Q(x)), \exists x\neg P(x), \exists xQ(x)\}$
   (b) $\{\forall x(P(x)\lor Q(x)), \neg(\forall xP(x)\lor\forall xQ(x))\}$

(c) $\{\forall x \neg R(x, x), \forall x \forall y \forall z((R(x, y) \wedge R(y, z)) \rightarrow R(x, z))\}$

2   Decide by the tree method which of the inferences below are valid. For those that are invalid, produce a counterexample, i.e. a model of the premises and negation of conclusion.

(a) $\forall x(P(x) \rightarrow \exists y R(x, y)) \quad \therefore \quad \forall x \exists y(P(x) \rightarrow R(x, y))$

(b) $\forall x P(x) \rightarrow \exists y \forall z R(y, z) \quad \therefore \quad \exists x(P(x) \rightarrow \exists y \forall z R(y, z))$

(c) $\forall x P(x) \rightarrow \forall y Q(y) \quad \therefore \quad \forall x(P(x) \rightarrow \forall y Q(y))$

(d) $\exists x(P(x) \rightarrow \forall y Q(y)) \quad \therefore \quad \exists x P(x) \rightarrow \forall y Q(y)$

(e) $\forall x(P(x) \vee Q(x)) \quad \therefore \quad \forall x P(x) \vee \forall x Q(x)$

3* Show that the set
$$\{\forall x \exists y R(x, y), \forall x \neg R(x, x), \forall x \forall y \forall z(R(x, y) \rightarrow (R(y, z) \rightarrow R(x, z)))\}$$
has no finite model.

4   Why is the answer 'Because it generates an infinite tree' to question 3 incorrect?

3*   SOUNDNESS AND COMPLETENESS THEOREMS

Theorem 1 (Soundness Theorem for First-order Trees)

Suppose Σ is a finite set of first-order sentences and that Σ is consistent (i.e. has a model). Then every tree generated from Σ contains an open branch.

Proof

The proof is analogous to that of the Soundness Theorem for truth-functional trees, though a complicating factor here is that a new constant will be introduced in the sequence of extensions every time rule (δ) is applied. Let **L** be the first-order language all of whose predicate, relation and constant symbols appear in Σ and suppose that Σ is an interpretation of **L** in which all the sentences in Σ are true. Suppose a tree to have been generated from Σ. As in Chapter 4, we shall identify a sequence $\mathbf{B}_1$, $\mathbf{B}_2$, $\mathbf{B}_3$, . . . of open branch-segments in the tree, each extending its predecessors, which is either finite or infinite. In the first case the terminal member $\mathbf{B}_m$ is a finished open branch in the tree; in the second the infinite sequence determines a finished open branch.

Let $\mathbf{B}_1$ be the node consisting of Σ. All the sentences in $\mathbf{B}_1$ are true in $\Im$, by assumption. Suppose that $i \geq 1$ and that $\mathbf{B}_i$ is a branch-segment extending $\mathbf{B}_1$ such that all the sentences on $\mathbf{B}_i$ are true in an expansion $\Im_i$ of $\Im$ obtained by adding denotations in $D_\Im$ for all the new constants introduced by applications of (δ) or (γ) to earlier sentences. Clearly $\mathbf{B}_i$ must be open. If $\mathbf{B}_i$ is finished then we have the finished open branch. If not, then it is extended in the tree either by adding a member of Σ to it, or by applying one of the rules of Double Negation, (α), (β), (γ), or (δ)

to an appropriate sentence in $\mathbf{B}_i$. In each of the first three cases we let $\mathfrak{I}_i$ = $\mathfrak{I}_{i+1}$. We know from the Soundness Theorem for truth-functional trees of Chapter 4 how to extend $\mathbf{B}_i$ to a $\mathbf{B}_{i+1}$ all of whose sentences are true, and hence which is open.

It remains to consider rules (γ) and (δ). Suppose rule (γ) is applied to a γ sentence $\forall xA$ in $\mathbf{B}_i$. That sentence is by assumption true in $\mathfrak{I}_i$. If x does not have a free occurrence in A, $\gamma(a/x)$ is A which is true in $\mathfrak{I}_i$ since $\forall xA$ is, by assumption. In this case let $\mathfrak{I}_{i+1} = \mathfrak{I}_i$. If x has a free occurrence in A, we need to consider two possible cases. (i) There are already constants on $\mathbf{B}_i$. Then all of them will have been assigned denotations by $\mathfrak{I}_i$ and hence every instance $\gamma(a/x)$ must be true in $\mathfrak{I}_i$. Let $\mathbf{B}_{i+1}$ be $\mathbf{B}_i$ extended to the node $\gamma(a/x)$ and let $\mathfrak{I}_i = \mathfrak{I}_{i+1}$. Then all the sentences in $\mathbf{B}_{i+1}$ are true in $\mathfrak{I}_{i+1}$. (ii) There are no constants yet on $\mathbf{B}_i$ and one, call it a, is introduced. We now assign any value at all in $D_\mathfrak{I}$ to a, generating $\mathfrak{I}_{i+1}$, which is like $\mathfrak{I}$ except in assigning that value to a. Let $\mathbf{B}_{i+1}$ be $\mathbf{B}_i$ extended to the node $\gamma(a/x)$. Again, $\gamma(a/x)$ is true in $\mathfrak{I}_{i+1}$. The case $\gamma = \neg\exists nA$ is left to the reader.

Finally, suppose rule (δ) is applied to a sentence in $\mathbf{B}_i$, which, by assumption, is true in $\mathfrak{I}_i$. δ is either of the form $\exists xA$ or $\neg\forall xA$. We can assume that x has a free occurrence in A; if not, the discussion proceeds as in the previous case. Suppose then that $\delta = \exists xA(x)$ is true in $\mathfrak{I}_i$ for some value of x in $D_\mathfrak{I}$. Choose such a value and assign it as the denotation of the new constant a to give $\mathfrak{I}_{i+1}$. So $A(a)$ is true in $\mathfrak{I}_{i+1}$. If δ is $\neg\forall xA(x)$ then for some value of x $A(x)$ is false in $\mathfrak{I}_i$. Choose one such value and assign it as the denotation $a_\mathfrak{I}$ of a in $D_\mathfrak{I}$ to give $\mathfrak{I}_{i+1}$. So $A(a)$ is false in $\mathfrak{I}_{i+1}$ and hence $\neg\forall xA(x)$, i.e. $\delta(a)$, is true in $\mathfrak{I}_{i+1}$. Let $\mathbf{B}_{i+1}$ be $\mathbf{B}_i$ extended to the node $\delta(a)$.

Hence all the sentences in $\mathbf{B}_{i+1}$ are true in $\mathfrak{I}_{i+1}$, so $\mathbf{B}_{i+1}$ is also open. Hence all the branch-segments $\mathbf{B}_n$ are open. There are either finitely many of these, or infinitely many. If there are finitely many, then the finished branch is open, as required. If infinitely many, then the branch consisting of all those segments is infinite and it must be open because if it closed, it would do so after finitely many steps. Hence in either case the successive extensions of $\mathbf{B}_1$ trace out a finished open branch in the tree. **Q.E.D.**

(The proof of Theorem 1 is really a proof by mathematical induction on the positive integers (Chapter 3, section 4). See if you can state what the property is that is proved to hold for *all* integers.)

The proof of the Completeness Theorem is approached via a series of lemmas.

Lemma 1

Suppose $\mathfrak{I}$ is an interpretation of a first-order language **L** and that every individual in $D_\mathfrak{I}$ is named by a constant of **L**. Then (i) a γ sentence is true in $\Im$ if $\gamma(a)$ is true for every constant a in **L** and (ii) a δ sentence is true if $\delta(a)$ is true for some constant a.

The proof is very straightforward and is left to the reader.

Lemma 2

Let **B** be an open branch in a finished tree. If a sentence of the form $\neg\neg$**A** is on **B**, so is **A**. If an α sentence is on **B** then α_1 and α_2 are on **B**. If a β sentence is on **B** then one of β_1, β_2 is on **B**. If a γ sentence is on **B**, then the instances $\gamma(a/x)$, $\gamma(b/x)$, $\gamma(c/x)$, etc. are on **B**, where a, b, c, etc. are *all* the individual constants appearing in sentences on **B**. If a δ sentence is on **B**, then an instance $\delta(a/x)$ of it is on **B**.

Proof

The lemma is an immediate consequence of the definition of 'finished'.

We shall prove the main theorem by an induction similar to the one we used in the proof of the corresponding result in Chapter 4, i.e. by an induction of the 'strong' type, on the degree of a formula. Recall that the degree of a sentence in a propositional language was defined to be the sum of the weights of the connectives occurring in that sentence. The *degree of a first-order formula* is defined to be the sum of the weights of all the connectives and quantifiers occurring in it, where each of $\forall$ and $\exists$ is also assigned a weight of 2. All repetitions, as before, are counted separately. So, for example, the degree of $\exists x\neg P(x)$ is 3, of $\neg Ax\neg P(x)$ is 4, etc. Our final lemma states a principle of induction on the degree of a first-order formula.

Lemma 3

(Strong Induction on Degrees)
Let Δ be any set of first-order sentences and let P be any property. Suppose (1) that all the sentences of degree $\leq$ k in Δ have P and that (2) (the induction step) for any sentence A in Δ of degree greater than k, from the assumption that all the sentences in Δ of degree less than A have P, it follows that A has P. Then every sentence in Δ has P.

Proof

The same as for Lemma 4 in Chapter 4, section 4*.

Theorem 2 (Completeness Theorem for First-Order Trees)

If **B** is an open branch on a finished tree generated by a finite set Σ of sentences, then there is a model of Σ which is also a model of all the sentences on **B**.

Proof

To keep the discussion simple, we shall suppose that the sentences in Σ are in a first-order language **L** having just one predicate symbol P and one binary relation symbol R. Let **B** be any open branch on the finished tree generated by Σ. Define **L_B** as in section 2 to be the language containing all the extralogical vocabulary of **L** plus all the constants occurring in sentences on **B**. For the purposes of what follows, we can identify **B** with the set of those sentences on it. By Lemma 2, **B** will have the following properties:

(i)   If any sentence $\neg\neg A$ is in **B**, so is A.
(ii) If an α sentence is in **B**, so are α_1, α_2.
(iii) If a β sentence is in **B**, so is one of β_1, β_2.
(iv) If a γ sentence is in **B**, so is $\gamma(a)$ for every constant a in **L_B**.
(v)   If a δ sentence is in **B**, so is $\delta(a)$ for some constant a in **L_B**

Since **B** is open it will also be the case that no sentence and its negation are in **B**. A fortiori

(vi) No atomic sentence and its negation are in **B**.

A set of sentences with the properties (i)–(vi) is called a *Hintikka set*. Hintikka sets are of fundamental importance, for as we shall show now, a model can be found for any Hintikka set. This means that a model can be found for **B** and hence for Σ.

Let $\mathfrak{I}$ be the interpretation of **L_B** which in section 2 we called the branch model determined by **B**. Recall that $D_\mathfrak{I}$ is the set of all constants on **B**, that for any constant c occurring in a sentence in **B**, $c_\mathfrak{I} = c$, that for any constant c in **B**, c is in $P_\mathfrak{I}$ if and only if P(c) is a sentence in **B** and that for the pair of constants c, d occurring in sentences in **B**, the ordered pair (c, d) is in $R_\mathfrak{I}$ if and only if R(c, d) is a sentence in **B**.

Lemma 4

For any constant c in $D_\mathfrak{I}$, P(c) is true in $\mathfrak{I}$ if and only if P(c) is a sentence in **B**. For any constants c, d in $D_\mathfrak{I}$, R(c, d) is true in $\mathfrak{I}$ if and only if R(c, d) is a sentence in **B**. The proof is left to the reader.

We shall now show by strong induction on degrees that every sentence in **B** is true in $\mathfrak{I}$. We start by showing (1) that all sentences of degree 0 or 1 in **B** are true in $\mathfrak{I}$ and that (2), for any sentence A of degree greater than 1 in **B**, it follows from the assumption that all sentences in **B** of degree less than A are true in $\mathfrak{I}$, that A is true in $\mathfrak{I}$.

(1) The sentences of degree 0 or 1 in $\mathbf{L_B}$ are those of the form P(c), or R(c, d), or ¬P(c), or ¬R(c, d), where c, d are constants in $D_{\mathfrak{I}}$. We know by Lemma 4 that any sentences in **B** of the form P(c), R(c, d) are true in $\mathfrak{I}$. Now consider any of the form ¬P(c) or ¬R(c, d). If ¬P(c) is in **B**, then by property (v) above P(c) is not in **B**. By Lemma 4, P(c) is false in $\mathfrak{I}$ and so ¬P(c) is true in $\mathfrak{I}$. Similarly, if ¬R(c, d) is in **B**, then by (v) R(c, d) is not in **B** and by Lemma 4 R(c, d) is false in $\mathfrak{I}$. Hence ¬R(c, d) is true in $\mathfrak{I}$. This completes step (1).

(2) Induction Step: Let A be any sentence in **B** of degree greater than 1 and suppose (inductive hypothesis) that all sentences in **B** of degree less than that of A are true in $\mathfrak{I}$. We have to show that A is true in $\mathfrak{I}$. Now A must be of the form ¬¬B for some sentence B, or else an α, β, γ or δ sentence (the reader will be left to prove this as an exercise). We shall prove the induction step for each of these cases.

(i) If $A = $ ¬¬B then B has smaller degree than A (two less, in fact) and B is in **B** by Lemma 2. Hence by the inductive hypothesis B is true in $\mathfrak{I}$. Hence A is true in $\mathfrak{I}$.

(ii) If A is an α sentence then we know from Chapter 4, section 4, Lemma 3 that α_1 and α_2 each have smaller degree than A. Also, by Lemma 2 both are in **B**. Hence by the inductive hypothesis both are true in $\mathfrak{I}$. Hence by Theorem 1 of Chapter 4, A is true in $\mathfrak{I}$.

(iii) If A is a β sentence then again we know that β_1 and β_2 each have smaller degree than A. By Lemma 2, one of them is in **B**. Hence by the inductive hypothesis it is true in $\mathfrak{I}$. Hence by Theorem 1, Chapter 4, A is true in $\mathfrak{I}$.

(iv) If A is a γ sentence then for every constant a in $\mathbf{L_B}$, by Lemma 2 γ(a/x) is in **B**. Also it is easy to verify that γ(a/x) has smaller degree than γ and so by the inductive hypothesis γ(a/x) is true in $\mathfrak{I}$ for every constant a in $\mathbf{L_B}$. Since $D_{\mathfrak{I}}$ is the set of constants in $\mathbf{L_B}$ and each constant in $\mathbf{L_B}$ names itself in this domain, then by Lemma 1 A is true in $\mathfrak{I}$.

(v) If A is a δ sentence then by Lemma 2 δ(a) is in **B** for some constant a in $\mathbf{L_B}$. δ(a/x) has smaller degree than δ, so by the inductive hypothesis δ(a/x) is true in $\mathfrak{I}$. But again, every individual in $D_{\mathfrak{I}}$ is named by itself and so by Lemma 1 again A is true in $\mathfrak{I}$.

We have now completed the induction step, since we have exhausted all the possible types of sentence A can be. Hence by Lemma 3, every sentence on **B** is true in $\mathfrak{I}$. Since all the sentences in Σ are on **B**, $\mathfrak{I}$ is a model of Σ. **Q.E.D.**

Corollary 1

If a first-order sentence C is a logical consequence of a finite set Σ of first-order sentences (i.e. if every model of Σ is a model of C), then there is a tree proof of C from $\Im$.

Proof

Suppose C is a logical consequence of Σ. Let Σ' be the set consisting of all the sentences in Σ together with $\neg C$. Generate a finished tree from Σ' according to the sequential procedure of applying the tree rules prescribed in section 1. If the tree had an open branch then by the theorem above Σ' would have a model. But since C is, by assumption, a consequence of Σ, Σ' has no model. Hence all the branches close; i.e. there is a tree proof of C from Σ. **Q.E.D.**

To state the next corollary we need a definition: A set is *denumberably infinite* if its members can be indexed without remainder by the natural numbers.

Corollary 2 (Löwenheim–Skolem Theorem)

If a finite set Σ of first-order sentences has a model then it has a finite or denumerably infinite model.

Proof

Suppose that Σ has a model. Then by Theorem 1 a finished tree generated from Σ will have an open branch. By Theorem 2 this determines a branch model whose domain is either finite or denumerably infinite. **Q.E.D.** As we shall see in Chapter 11, the Löwenheim–Skolem theorem has some important implications.

Exercises

1 Show that the degree of $\delta(a/x)$ is less than that of δ and that the degree of $\gamma(a)$ is less than that of γ.
2 Show that if the degree of A is greater than 1 then A is either of the form $\neg\neg B$, or is an α, β, γ or δ sentence.

4* COMPACTNESS

We know from the Corollary to Theorem 2 that if a sentence C is a logical consequence of a *finite* set Σ of sentences, then there is a tree proof of C from Σ. Yet, as we have seen in the case of the theory of identity, it is sometimes necessary to consider deductions from theories possessing infinitely many assumptions, or axioms, as they tend to be called. This raises the question of whether there is a tree proof of C from Σ when Σ is infinite.

The answer is that while there is not necessarily a tree proof of C from Σ itself, there is always one from a finite subset of Σ. This is a consequence of a result known as the *Compactness Theorem for First-Order Logic* (so-called because of its close relation to a result in topology about compact sets), which tells us that any infinite set of first-order sentences is consistent, i.e. has a model, if every finite subset of it is consistent. For suppose that a sentence A is a logical (first-order) consequence of any set Σ. Then the set Σ' consisting of Σ together with $\neg A$ is inconsistent. Hence, by the Compactness Theorem, some finite subset Σ_f of Σ' is inconsistent, from which it follows, by the Corollary to Theorem 2, that Σ_f together with $\neg A$ generates a closed tree. In other words, if A is a consequence of any set Σ of first-order sentences, there is a tree proof of A from some finite subset of Σ.

It is actually quite simple to prove the Compactness Theorem for the case (in practice the only one that need be considered) where Σ is denumerably infinite. The proof is adapted from Smullyan 1968: 64, 65). Suppose that Σ is a denumerably infinite set of sentences which is enumerated in some particular sequence $S_1, S_2, S_3, \ldots$ and that every finite subset of Σ is consistent; clearly, every finite subset of the form $\{S_1, \ldots S_n\}$ is also consistent. Choose some sequence of application of the tree rules, for example that suggested in section 1. Now construct a tree by applying that sequence *once* to S_1 and the unused sentences generated, proceeding from one rule to the next in the sequence only when the first rule has been applied to all the unused sentences it can be applied to. When this sequence of applications terminates, add S_2 to S_1 to the root of the tree and go round the cycle again, changing any constants that might have been added by an application of (δ) to others that do not appear in S_1 or S_2. At the end, add S_3 and repeat the cycle again; and so on, adding at each repeat the first sentence remaining from the original sequence S_1, $S_2, S_3, \ldots$.

All the successive trees so obtained are open, since each subset $\{S_1, \ldots S_k\}$ is consistent. Each of these trees can be regarded as an extension of a single tree with set Σ of initial sentences. This 'limiting' tree has finitely or infinitely many nodes; it will have finitely many, in fact just one, if all the S_i are atomic. If it has finitely many, it must be open and hence determines a branch model of Σ. If it has infinitely many, then by König's Lemma it has an infinite branch (*König's Lemma* states that if an infinite tree has only finitely many branchings from each node, then it has an infinite branch). This branch must be open and again it determines a branch model for Σ.

Do not, by the way, read the Compactness Theorem as saying that some finite subset generates all the consequences of an infinite set of first-order sentences. This is neither a paraphrase of, nor implied by, the Compactness Theorem and is not true. We shall see in Chapter 11 that there are infinite sets of first-order sentences such that no finite subset generates all their consequences.

Chapter 9

Identity

1 IDENTITY

Modern formal logic was developed by mathematicians and its first applications were to problems in the foundations of mathematics. As the reader probably recalls, with or without nostalgia, elementary mathematical reasoning typically involves substituting equals for equals in equations, the simplest example of which is as follows:

$$a = b \tag{1}$$
$$b = c$$
$$\therefore\ a = c$$

We usually regard (1) as a valid deductive inference. Here we seem to have a problem, however, for = would normally be formalised by a binary relation symbol R, transforming (1) into

$$R(a, b)$$
$$R(b, c)$$
$$\therefore\ R(a, c)$$

But this inference is certainly not valid in first-order logic, for the tree

$$R(a, b)$$
$$R(b, c)$$
$$\neg R(a, c)$$

is finished and open! Therefore the inference is invalid. So why do we nevertheless regard it as deductively valid?

One explanation, and the one we shall develop here, is that (1) has suppressed premises, which when rendered explicit will make it valid (the traditional name for arguments with hidden premises is *enthymemes*) and which we tend so unquestioningly to accept as true and we know that other people do too, that we do not bother to make them explicit. These premises constitute the *Theory of Identity*. Because inferences involving identity are enthymematic (on this view, which we shall defend in the final section of this chapter), when we formalise them we shall retain expressions of the form x = y unchanged, to signify that additional information about the relation = is tacitly being invoked. The aim of this chapter is to make that information explicit and to characterise it in the form of as few independent principles as possible. In modern logicians' jargon, we shall *axiomatise* the theory of identity. This means finding those fundamental features of the identity relation in terms of which all others can be determined as consequences.

The question is, what are the fundamental properties of = in this sense? Earlier we discussed the classification of binary relations into those which on their respective domains were *reflexive*, *symmetric* or *transitive*, or any combination of these. A binary relation which is all three on any domain is called an *equivalence relation*. The identity relation is clearly an equivalence relation, on every domain. If we add the following three first-order sentences saying that = is reflexive, symmetric and transitive, viz.

(reflexivity)	$\forall x(x = x)$	(2)
(symmetry)	$\forall x \forall y(x = y \rightarrow y = x)$	(3)
(transitivity)	$\forall x \forall y \forall z((x = y \wedge y = z) \rightarrow x = z)$	(4)

to the two premises explicit in (1), then we can easily obtain a tree derivation of a = c (this will be left as an exercise; in fact, only transitivity is needed for the derivation).

But being an equivalence relation does not distinguish identity from many other binary relations which are also equivalence relations. 'Being the same height as' is one, for example, but clearly two things can have the same height without being the same thing. If x is identical to y it does not merely follow that x and y have certain salient properties in common, but that *every* property which they have, they have in common (this condition is not merely necessary but also sufficient, as we shall see in Chapter 11). A natural way to express this is in terms of the 'second-order' sentence

$$\forall x \forall y(x = y \rightarrow \forall P(P(x) \leftrightarrow P(y)))$$ (5)

But we cannot simply adopt (5) as an additional axiom for identity, because first-order languages, unlike higher-order ones, do not contain predicate or relation *variables*, or quantifiers over them. We shall postpone to Chapter 11 a discussion of the advantages and disadvantages of being able to quantify over predicates and relations; the fact is that first-order languages cannot.

Surprisingly, perhaps, this limitation turns out to be of very little practical importance. The reason is simple to state. Think of what you do when you reason with identity statements. Suppose, for example, that you have acquired the information that John is the father of Sabrina. This allows you to substitute the expression 'John' everywhere for the expression 'the father of Sabrina', or vice versa, in other statements involving 'John' or 'the father of Sabrina' (except in so-called *opaque* contexts like

'Fred believes that John is happy'; Fred might well believe that John was happy but, if Fred did not also know that John was the father of Sabrina, Fred might not believe that the father of Sabrina was happy, though the identity 'John = the father of Sabrina' is true). This sort of substitution of identicals for identicals (in non-opaque contexts) is easily shown to be justified by purely first-order principles.

They do so in the following way. An interpretation $\Im$ of **L** will be called an =-*interpretation* if =$_\Im$ is actually the identity relation on $D_\Im$. Suppose that A is any first-order formula which does not contain a free occurrence of y but may have a free occurrence of x. Suppose also that values in some =-interpretation $\Im$ have been assigned to the free variables other than x in A (if there are any) and that the same value in $\Im$ is assigned to both x and y, i.e. under that evaluation the formula x = y is true. Then if relative to that evaluation A is true, $A(y/x)$ must also be true. Similarly, if A contains no free occurrence of x we can repeat the argument to show that if x = y is true under any evaluation then so is $A(x/y)$. In other words, whatever formula A is, all instances of

$$\forall z_1 \forall z_2 \ldots \forall x \forall y (x = y \rightarrow (A \rightarrow A')) \tag{5}$$

are true, where A' can be either of $A(x/y)$ or $A(y/x)$ and z_1, z_2, ... are all the free variables, if any, in A other than x or y. The only limitation on the applicability of (5) is that in A and A' x and y occur free in exactly the same places. This means that x must have no free occurrence in the scope of a quantifier on y in A and y must have no free occurrence in the scope of a quantifier on x in A; in technical jargon, *y must be free for x in A and x must be free for y respectively in A*. If A is $\exists y \neg (x = y)$, for example, the condition is not fulfilled, for $A(y/x)$ is $\exists y \neg (y = y)$ and the corresponding instance of (5),

$$\forall x \forall y (x = y \rightarrow (\exists y \neg (x = y) \rightarrow \exists y \neg (y = y))),$$

is false in every =-interpretation containing more than one individual (showing this is left as exercise 3, section 3).

The sentences (5) are called *substitution axioms*. Do these axioms provide a *complete* theory of identity, in the sense that every sentence of **L** which is true in every =-interpretation can be derived via a closed tree from those axioms? The answer, possibly surprisingly, is 'no'. However, it is fairly straightforward to show, by an extension of the branch model construction described in Chapter 8, that the single sentence $\forall x(x = x)$ is all that has to be added to achieve completeness in the sense described. In other words, *all true first-order identity sentences are logical consequences of appropriate substitution axioms and $\forall x(x = x)$*.

We shall call the *first-order theory of identity* (henceforth just 'the theory of identity') the set whose members are all substitution axioms and the sentence $\forall x(x = x)$, and say that a sentence is a consequence of a set Σ of premises and the theory of identity if it is a consequence of the union of those two sets (the union of two sets is the set whose members are in either). We shall call a first-order language a *language with identity* if it contains a binary relation symbol which is intended to be interpreted as =. Where this is the case we shall write that relation symbol simply as =.

Since all first-order languages contain an infinite set of variables, there are infinitely many formulas of the form x = y in a language with identity; hence there are infinitely many formulas *A* and hence infinitely many substitution axioms. It follows that any inference from the theory of identity even by itself is an inference from an infinite set of premises. We know from the Compactness Theorem (Chapter 8) that any consequence of an infinite set of first-order sentences is a consequence of a finite subset, but this still leaves us with the practical problem of working out which finite set of premises we shall need to use to close a tree – if any does. There is no general solution to this problem; all that one can say is that if the tree is not too complex the relevant axioms should become apparent as it develops. In the next section we shall show how to reduce the complexity somewhat.

2 TREE RULES FOR IDENTITY

The substitution axioms are γ sentences and, depending on the formula *A* involved, they may have a complex internal structure. This means that derivations using the theory of identity can turn out to be relatively complicated affairs. For example, consider the inference we started the chapter with, from a = b and b = c to a = c. Here is a tree proof of a = c from these premises and the theory of identity:

1	a = b	
2	b = c	
3	¬(a = c)	
4	$\forall x \forall y(x = y \rightarrow (y = c \rightarrow x = c))$	Substitution axiom
5	$\forall y(a = y \rightarrow (y = c \rightarrow a = c))$	(γ) on 4
6	$(a = b \rightarrow (b = c \rightarrow a = c))$	(γ) on 5
7	¬(a = b) b = c → a = c	(β) on 6
8	¬(b = c) a = c	(β) on 7

For such a simple inference as *a = b, b = c, therefore a = c* this procedure is too elaborate to be practically useful. However, we can economise. From an investigation of the proof it is apparent that we can represent the steps authorised by the substitution axioms in the compact form of a *derived tree rule*:

R_1: Where A is any sentence and a and b are any constants, if A and the sentence a = b appear on an open branch, then we may write A(a/b) or A(b/a) at any lower point on that branch.

A will be called the *major premise*, and a = b the *minor premise*, of the rule. In any tree we shall signal an application of R_1 by writing R_1(major premise, minor premise) beside the relevant line; where the lines are numbered, we shall use the respective line numbers instead. As an exercise, justify R_1 by showing that an appropriate use of a substitution axiom will yield the same result as it does.

Using R_1, the tree proof of a = c from a = b, b = c and the theory of identity now becomes trivial:

a = b
b = c
¬(a = c)
|
<u>a = c</u>　　　R_1(b = c, a = b) [or R_1 (a = b, b = c)]

Nor need we stop there. In practice, the axiom $\forall x(x = x)$ is used to justify writing sentences of the form a = a for some constant a at appropriate points in a tree. This suggests a second derived rule:

R_2: We may write a = a on any open branch at any desired point, for any constant a.

Note *R_1 and R_2 are not additions to the set of tree rules*; they merely represent routine sequences of steps justified by those rules. This is why R_1 and R_2 are called derived rules; they can always in principle be eliminated from any tree on which are appropriate substitution axioms and $\forall x(n = x)$.

Armed with R_1 and R_2 we can make short work of proving that = is symmetric (3 above) and transitive (4 above), from the theory of identity. First, symmetry:

1	$\neg \forall x \forall y(x = y \rightarrow y = x)$	¬symmetry
2	$\neg \forall y(a = y \rightarrow y = a)$	(δ) on 1
3	$\neg (a = b \rightarrow b = a)$	(δ) on 2
4	a = b	(α) on 3
5	¬(b = a)	
6	¬(a = a)	R_1(5, 4)
7	<u>a = a</u>	R_2

($\neg$(a = a) is A(a/b) where A is $\neg$(b=a)).

Now transitivity, already proved for a special case (lines 5, 7, 8 and 9 below are identical to those in the tree before last):

1    $\neg\forall x\forall y\forall z(x = y\rightarrow(y = z\rightarrow x = z))$ $\neg$transitivity

2    $\neg\forall y\forall z(a = y\rightarrow(y = z\rightarrow(a = z))$ (δ) on 1

3    $\neg\forall z(a = b\rightarrow(b = z\rightarrow a = z))$ (δ) on 2

4    $\neg(a = b\rightarrow(b = c\rightarrow a = c))$ (δ) on 3

5                    $a = b$ (α) on 4
6            $\neg(b = c\rightarrow a = c)$

7                    $b = c$ (α) on 6
8            $\neg(a = c)$

9            $\underline{a = c}$ $\mathbf{R_1}(7, 5)$

A great deal of everyday reasoning invokes the theory of identity. For example, if we know that individual a has the property P, while b does not, then we infer that a and b are distinct individuals, i.e. we infer that $\neg(a = b)$. Using the derived tree rules, the tree proof that $\neg(a = b)$ follows from $P(a)$ and $\neg P(b)$ and the theory of identity is trivial:

1    $P(a)$
2    $\neg P(b)$
3    $\neg\neg(a = b)$

4    $a = b$

5    $\underline{P(b)}$ $\mathbf{R_1}(1, 4)$

Another rather straightforward inference we can make using the theory of identity is that if $P(a)$ and $\neg P(b)$ are both true, then there are at least two individuals in the domain, whatever that may be. That there are at least two individuals in the domain we can express as $\exists x\exists y\neg(x = y)$. The tree proof of this from $P(a)$ and $\neg P(b)$ and the theory of identity is left as an exercise. A slightly less simple exercise, also left for the reader, is to find a tree proof for this inference using the theory of identity:

Everyone in this room likes someone in it other than themselves.
Jane and John are not the same person and are the only people in this room.
Therefore Jane likes John and John likes Jane.

To help you on your way, here are the appropriately formalised premises and conclusion:

(*) $\forall x \exists y (L(x, y) \wedge \neg (y = x))$
       $\neg (a = b) \wedge \forall x (x = a \vee x = b)$
       $L(a, b) \wedge L(b, a)$

We shall say that A and B are equivalent modulo the theory of identity and write $A \Leftrightarrow B$ *(mod Id)* if trees generated from the two sets of initial sentences, $\{A, \neg B\}$ and $\{\neg A, B\}$ close when identity axioms can be called on.

Example $P(a) \Leftrightarrow \exists x (x = a \wedge P(x))$ (mod Id).

Here are the two closed trees which establish the equivalence (the reader should write the justification for each line):

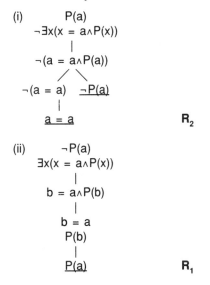

(i)   P(a)
       $\neg \exists x (x = a \wedge P(x))$
           |
       $\neg (a = a \wedge P(a))$
          /   \
   $\neg (a = a)$ $\underline{\neg P(a)}$
       |
    $\underline{a = a}$ **R$_2$**

(ii) $\neg P(a)$
       $\exists x (x = a \wedge P(x))$
            |
       $b = a \wedge P(b)$
            |
          $b = a$
          P(b)
            |
         $\underline{P(a)}$ **R$_1$**

Exercises

1 Construct a closed tree to show that $\forall x \forall y \forall z ((x = z \wedge y = z) \rightarrow x = y)$ is a consequence of the theory of identity.
2 Show that $P(a) \Leftrightarrow \forall x (x = a \rightarrow P(x))$ (mod Id).
3 Give a tree proof of 'everybody loves somebody other than themselves' from 'Nobody loves themselves' and 'Everybody loves somebody' and the theory of identity.
4 Generate a closed tree from (*) above using **R$_1$** and **R$_2$** where appropriate.

3   SOME ARITHMETIC

As we saw in the previous section, it is possible in a first-order language to say 'There are at least two things (in the domain)' without appealing to numbers as such; the sentence $\exists x \exists y \neg (x = y)$ is the simplest way of doing so. 'There are at least two things with the property P' is

$$\exists x \exists y [P(x) \wedge P(y) \wedge \neg (x = y)].$$

While one strictly does not need identity to say this ($\exists x (P(x) \wedge Q(x)) \wedge \exists x (P(x) \wedge \neg Q(x))$ does so also) it is simpler to use it, and it is indispensable for making more specific 'arithmetical' assertions.

With identity, for example, one can say that there are *exactly* two things with P, for this is true if and only if there are at least two things with P and there are at most two things with P. Consider the first conjunct: there are at most two things with P if and only if it is not true that there are at least three things with P. Hence there are exactly two things with P if and only if there are at least two things with P and there are not at least three things with P. Hence there are exactly two things with P if and only if

(7) $\exists x \exists y [P(x) \wedge P(y) \wedge \neg (x = y)] \wedge \neg \exists x \exists y \exists z [P(x) \wedge P(y) \wedge P(z) \wedge \neg (x = y) \wedge \neg (y = z) \wedge \neg (x = z)]$

is true. A simpler way of saying the same thing is

(8) $\exists x \exists y [P(x) \wedge P(y) \wedge \neg (x = y) \wedge \forall z (P(z) \rightarrow (x = z \vee y = z))];$

those who have developed a taste for constructing complicated trees might like to practise their art by showing the equivalence modulo the theory of identity of (7) and (8).

We all know that $2 + 2 = 4$. In fact, it is not difficult to show that 'there are exactly four things which are Ps or Qs' is a consequence of 'there are exactly two things which are Ps and exactly two things which are Qs and nothing which has the property P also has Q' together with the theory of identity. In other words, the theory of identity *without numbers as such* suffices for this sort of everyday arithmetical inference. But we get nothing for nothing and such baby arithmetic has little to do with the mathematics of number theory, which, precisely by regarding the integers as entities in themselves (this procedure is called 'reifying' numbers), is able to generate the deep results of modern (whole) number theory and analysis (the theory of the real and complex numbers).

Exercises

1   Formalise the sentence 'There are exactly four horsemen of the Apocalypse.'

2   Show that the conclusion 'There are exactly three things which are Ps

or Qs' is derivable from the three premises 'There are exactly two things which are Ps', 'There is just one thing which is a Q' and 'Nothing which is a P is a Q.'

3   Explain why the sentence $A = \forall x \forall y(x = y \rightarrow (\exists y \neg (x = y) \rightarrow \exists y \neg (y = y)))$ is false in every =-interpretation with a domain containing more than one individual (show that there is a tree proof of $\neg \exists x \exists y \neg (x = y)$ from A and the theory of identity).

4   FUNCTIONS AND FUNCTION SYMBOLS

A great deal of mathematical reasoning involves substituting functional terms in equations, as in the following simple example

$$\sqrt{16} = 4$$
$$\therefore \sqrt{16} + 3 = 4 + 3$$

'$\sqrt{}$' and '+' denote respectively the functions of taking the positive square root of a number and the sum of two numbers; they are functions of one and two places (traditionally, the numbers plugged into those places are called *arguments* of the functions). Had we permission to include function symbols among the descriptive vocabulary of first-order languages, then where f and g are function symbols of one and two places respectively and a, b and c are constants representing 16, 4 and 3 respectively, we could formalise the pair of equations above as

$$f(a) = b$$
$$g(f(a), c) = g(b, c)$$

It is not too difficult to see how $\mathbf{R_1}$ might be adapted to give a simple tree proof of the second sentence from the first.

In this section we shall investigate the syntax and semantics of first-order languages with identity which also contain function symbols of arbitrary numbers of places. Strictly speaking, their inclusion is unnecessary, since any inference like that above can be proved valid when formalised in language without function symbols, though at the cost of making enthymematic premises explicit. Here is a very informal and intuitive argument for this claim (a rigorous proof would be too long and involved to give). Any sentence that follows from f(a) = b together with other premises should follow from the statements (i) that a and b stand in a certain binary relation, call it R and (ii) that R is a *single-valued functional relation* of one argument, i.e. that for any x in the domain there is exactly one y such that R(x, y). (ii) is the enthymematic premise.

This procedure can be elaborated into a method of systematically eliminating n-place function symbols by (n + 1)-place relation symbols in inferences, adding the enthymematic premises explicitly as one goes. Thus we replace the premise f(a) = b in the inference above by the atomic sentence $R(a, b)$, adding as an additional premise the sentence stating that R represents a single-valued functional relation:

$\forall x \exists y (R(x, y) \wedge \forall z (R(x, z) \rightarrow z = y))$.

The conclusion $g(f(a), c) = g(b, c)$ involves another function symbol, the two-place function symbol g, which we shall eliminate with a three-place function symbol S, adding another premise saying that S represents a single-valued functional relation of two arguments. $g(f(a), c) = g(b, c)$ can be written in the equivalent form

$\forall x \forall y (((f(a) = x \wedge g(x, c)) = y) \wedge g(b, c) = y)$,

from which we can eliminate f and g to give

$\forall x \forall y ((R(a, x) \wedge S(x, c, y)) \rightarrow S(b, c, y))$.

We have now rewritten the inference as one which contains no function symbols and it is possible to construct a closed tree from the enlarged set of premises and the theory of identity. However, one does not need very much imagination to see that the tree will be unpleasantly complex. Certainly all the simplicity and intelligibility of the original inference will have been lost, combined with a large and unwanted gain in difficulty of proof. The explicit inclusion of function symbols clearly makes life a lot easier, not just in this example but in general, which is of course why they were introduced in mathematics in the first place.

Suppose, then, that first-order languages are permitted to follow mathematics in containing function symbols of any specified numbers of places and allowing functional terms of an arbitrary degree of functional composition to be constructed. This principle of functional composition is expressed for such a language – call it **L** again – in the following inductive definition of a term (of **L**): an expression t of **L** is *a term of* **L** if it is either a constant of **L** or a variable, or else t is of the form $f(t_1, \ldots t_n)$ where $t_1, \ldots t_n$ are terms of **L** and f is an n-place function symbol of **L**. The class of atomic formulas of **L** is now redefined to include any formula of the form $P(t)$ or $R(t_1, \ldots t_n)$, where $t, t_1, \ldots t_n$ are terms of **L**, P is a predicate symbol of **L** and R is an n-place relation symbol of **L** respectively. The class of formulas of **L** is defined from the class of atomic formulas in the same way as in Chapter 6, section 1.

In mathematics, a function is regarded as associating a member of one set, called the *domain* of the function, with a single member of another set called its *codomain*; the domain of a function of n arguments is therefore a set of ordered n-tuples. The codomain of any function contains the set of its values, called the *range* of the function, but is not necessarily equal to that range. In the representation of functions in first-order logic the domain of every function of one variable is always assumed to be the same domain D of individuals over which the quantifiers are interpreted, while the domain of every function of n arguments is assumed to be the set of all n-tuples of members of D. This is implicit in the above definition of *term* of **L**.

D is also assumed to be the codomain. If t is a term containing no variables (such terms are said to be *closed*), then its denotation $t_\Im$ in any interpretation $\Im$ of **L** is defined by the following two clauses:

1 If t is a constant a, then $t_\Im = a_\Im$.
2 If $t = f(t_1, \ldots t_n)$, where f is a n-place function symbol of **L** and $t_1, \ldots, t_n$ are any closed terms of **L**, then $t_\Im = f_\Im(t_{1\Im}, \ldots, t_{n\Im})$.

But what is $f_\Im$? We have said that a function of n places can be regarded as a single-valued relation of n + 1 places and in Chapter 7 we identified (n + 1)-place relations with sets of (n + 1)-tuples. Since it has been stipulated that the domain of $f_\Im$ is the set of all n-tuples of elements of $D_\Im$, and that $D_\Im$ is the codomain, this implies that $f_\Im$ in clause 2 may be any set of (n + 1)-tuples of members of $D_\Im$ such that for every $d_1, \ldots d_n$ in $D_\Im$, there is exactly one d in $D_\Im$ such that $(d_1, \ldots, d_n, d)$ is in $f_\Im$.

A language with function symbols possesses an extended class of terms for referring to specific individuals, of which the constants are a proper subclass. In view of this, we need to make some adjustments both to the derived tree rules $\mathbf{R_1}$ and $\mathbf{R_2}$ and also to (γ), because if $t_1, \ldots, t_n$ are closed terms of **L**, then in any interpretation of **L** $f(t_1, \ldots, t_n)$ will, just like a constant, denote some member of the domain. The adjustments are completely straightforward: in the statements of these rules simply replace the constants by closed terms. In (γ), therefore, the instances of the relevant g sentence that will be placed on the end of every finished open branch **B** passing through γ are all the sentences $\gamma(t/x)$ such that t is a closed term that has appeared in some sentence on **B**. The earlier forms of these rules will still hold good, of course, because all constants by definition are closed terms.

The stipulation that in every interpretation $\Im$ of **L** the domain of every n-place function is identified with the set of all n-tuples of members of $D_\Im$ can create problems when formalising some piece of discourse in which functions are only naturally defined on certain proper subsets of the domain of discourse. Examples crop up frequently, particularly in mathematics, but also in everyday talk – the functional relations 'y = the biological father of x', 'y = the legal spouse of x', for example, are not defined where x is an infant. But to allow functions to be somewhere undefined is not an option given our tree rules, for $\neg \forall y \exists x(x = f(y))$ is a demonstrable inconsistency, as the following closed tree demonstrates

1 $\neg \forall y \exists x(x = f(y))$
   |
2 $\neg \exists x(x = f(a))$ (δ) on 1
   |
3 $\neg (f(a) = f(a))$ (γ) on 2
   |
4 $\underline{f(a) = f(a)}$ $\mathbf{R_2}$

The problem here is (γ), which in effect says that $f_\gimel(a_\gimel)$ always exists. But to restrict (γ) to instantiating sentences with functional terms only where the latter are naturally defined would contravene a long-standing tradition in modern logic that syntax and semantics be sharply separated. The same objection applies to amending the formation rules so that only where $f_\gimel(a_{\gimel 1}, \ldots, a_{\gimel n})$ exists is any formula involving the term $f(a_1, \ldots, a_n)$ regarded as well formed.

Functions can always, if artificially, be made everywhere defined by being assigned a conventional value where they do not naturally take one. This strategy is often pursued in mathematics, where fear of the artificial is not such a powerful factor. Adopting it here does not, however, mean that so-called partial functions – functions not everywhere defined – cannot be discussed in first-order logic. Functions have in effect been defined as single-valued relations and these in turn have been identified with certain sets (sets of n-tuples). And there is a first-order theory of sets within which partial functions are perfectly respectable objects. Further discussion is beyond the scope of this book, though we shall say a little more about first-order set theory in Chapter 11.

Exercises

1 A n-place function f is said to be *injective* if it assigns different values in its codomain to different n-tuples of arguments. f is *surjective* if for every member c of the codomain there is some n-tuple $(d_1, \ldots, d_n)$ such that $f(d_1, \ldots, d_n) = c$. f is *bijective* if it is injective and surjective. Show how these conditions can be expressed by sentences of a first-order language with a binary relation symbol = interpreted as identity and an n-place function symbol representing f.

5   WORKING WITH EQUATIONS

As we have remarked, a good deal of mathematical activity consists in substituting in equations with a view to solving them, i.e. deriving further equations in which certain terms are equated with others whose values are known, or at any rate it is known how they can be expressed in decimal notation. We shall now do some equation solving ourselves. For ease of reading, we shall usually use standard mathematical notation in which the function symbol is infixed rather than prefixed (inserting the function symbol, as one ordinarily does with + , *between* its two arguments is to infix it; in the expression $f(g(x), y)$ both f and g are prefixed) and we shall also use numerals, like '3', '4' and '16', instead of constants a, b and c.

We shall start with the very simple example of section 4 and give a tree proof for it; i.e. we shall prove that from $\sqrt{16} = 4$ and the theory of identity it follows that $\sqrt{16} + 3 = 4 + 3$:

1	$\sqrt{16} = 4$	
2	$\neg(\sqrt{16} + 3 = 4 + 3)$	
3	$\neg(4 + 3 = 4 + 3)$	$\mathbf{R_1}\ (1, 2)$
4	$\underline{4 + 3 = 4 + 3}$	$\mathbf{R_2}$

Of course, this is hardly deep mathematics. Nor would any mathematician employ a derivation like this; they would not think the result *needed* proof. Mathematicians work at most semi-formally, using a great deal of background knowledge to cut proofs short. But mathematicians are primarily trying to discover new mathematical facts, not to analyse the process of deduction. It is the logician's task to set up formal machinery to investigate deduction itself, even in its most humble aspects. And humble inferences will often be all the more useful because they provide a source of simple models to test and illustrate the theory being evolved.

The next two examples are a little more serious. The first involves elementary group theory. A *group* is a set G and a binary operation, or function f on pairs of elements of G, such that the value of the function $f(x, y)$ for x, y in G is itself a member of G (G is said to be *closed* under f) and such that the following three conditions, or 'axioms', are satisfied, where e is a constant denoting a particular member of G called the *group identity* (it is customary to write $f(x, y)$ as xoy, i.e. to use infix notation):

(i) $\forall x \forall y \forall z((xoy)oz = xo(yoz))$
(ii) $\forall x(xoe = x \wedge eox = x)$
(iii) $\forall x \exists y(xoy = e \wedge yox = e)$

(i) says that o is *associative*; (ii) says that o-combining any element x of G with e, either to right or left, yields the same element x; and (iii) says that every element x of G has an *inverse*, i.e. an element y of G such that when x is o-combined with y the result is the identity element. The set of positive and negative integers with 0 as identity and addition as the group operation o, is a group, in which –n is the inverse of n. Examples of groups crop up all over the place and they are of fundamental importance in both mathematics and physics (*symmetry* is one of the most important notions of modern physics and it is characterised in terms of those properties of a system which are left unchanged, or *invariant*, when that system is acted on by the operations in some specified group of operations).

Group theory is the set of deductive consequences of (i)–(iii). We shall confine our attention here to one important consequence, that of the *uniqueness of the group identity*, or the statement that there is one and only one element satisfying the axioms (ii) and (iii). In fact, we can show that (ii) alone (together with the theory of identity) implies that e is unique. The uniqueness of e is expressed by the sentence

$\forall z(\forall x(xoz = x \wedge zox = x) \rightarrow e = z);$

i.e. if any element z of G satisfies condition (ii), then z is identical to e. As an exercise the reader should supply the justifications for each line in the following tree proof.

$$\forall x(xoe = x \wedge eox = x)$$
$$\neg \forall z(\forall x(xoz = x \wedge zox = x) \rightarrow e = z)$$
$$|$$
$$\neg(\forall x(xoa = x \wedge aox = x) \rightarrow e = a)$$
$$|$$
$$\forall x(xoa = x \wedge aox = x)$$
$$\neg(e = a)$$
$$|$$
$$eoa = e \wedge aoe = e$$
$$|$$
$$eoa = e$$
$$aoe = e$$
$$|$$
$$aoe = a \wedge eoa = a$$
$$|$$
$$aoe = a$$
$$eoa = a$$
$$|$$
$$\underline{e = a}$$

Our next and final example involves so-called *First-order Peano Arithmetic*. Peano's Axioms, which define the basic arithmetical properties of the natural numbers, will be described in detail in Chapter 11. In this example we shall be concerned with just two of them. These set out the properties of addition on N and they are (a) $\forall x(x + 0) = x$ and (b) $\forall x \forall y(x + s(y) = s(x + y))$, the intended domain being of course N. The one-place function symbols signify the successor of x in the usual enumeration of the natural numbers, in order of increasing magnitude. For ease of reading we write $x + y$ in the usual way rather than using a two-place function symbol g, say, and writing g(x, y). We shall regard the numerals '0', '1', '2', '3', etc. as defined in terms of '0' and s; thus, '1' is defined as 's(0)', '2' as 'ss(0)' (with two brackets omitted), '3' as 'sss(0)' and so on (enthusiasts of the use–mention distinction will observe a stylistic inconsistency here, in that the numeral for 0 is distinguished by being put in quotes, but that s is not; I trust no confusion will arise).

We end with a tree proof of $1 + 1 = 2$, i.e. $s(0) + s(0) = ss(0)$, from (a) and (b) and the theory of identity (as in the previous example, the reader should write out the justification for each line):

$$\forall x(x + 0 = x)$$
$$\forall x \forall y(x + s(y) = s(x + y))$$
$$\neg(s(0) + s(0) = ss(0))$$
$$|$$
$$\forall y(s(0) + s(y) = s(s(0) + y))$$
$$|$$
$$s(0) + s(0) = s(s(0) + 0)$$
$$|$$
$$s(0) + 0 = s(0)$$
$$|$$
$$\underline{s(0) + s(0) = ss(0)}$$

Exercises

1 Relative to which codomain would the successor function on the natural numbers be surjective?

2 Show that the conclusions of each of the following inferences follow from the premises and the theory of identity.

(a) $a = b$
   $\therefore$ $f(a) = f(b)$

(b) $f(a) = b$
     $P(b)$
   $\therefore$ $P(f(a))$

(c) $f(a) = b$
     $g(b) = h(f(a), c)$
   $\therefore$ $g(f(a)) = h(b, c)$

6   IS IDENTITY PART OF LOGIC?

Many treatments of first-order logic take '=' to be a part of the *logical* vocabulary of all first-order languages, which would entail making $\mathbf{R_1}$ and $\mathbf{R_2}$ general tree rules additional to those of Double Negation, (α), (β), (γ) and (δ). It must be admitted that the binary relation $x = y$ is a rather distinctive one. Indeed, some have questioned whether it is a relation at all, since it clearly does not relate distinct individuals. The view taken here is that = is *not* a logical item, on the ground that all other binary relations are regarded as extralogical and to make an exception of = requires a very strong justification. Yet all the justificatory arguments beg the question in one way or other.

Take the claim that = is a logical item because it does not relate distinct individuals. Without further elaboration this argument must be incorrect. 'Being the same height as' as applied to people is hardly a logical relation, yet were there no two people of the same height in a domain of people that relation too would not relate distinct individuals in that domain. It

would, in fact, have exactly the same extension as = in that domain, namely
{(*a*, *a*), (*b*, *b*), . . .}, for the individuals *a*, *b*, etc. To respond by pointing
out that 'being the same height as' *may* relate distinct individuals, whereas
= may not, simply begs the question why a relation incapable of relating
distinct individuals must be a logical relation.

Another popular reason put forward for regarding = as logical is that
its meaning is *domain independent*: it is always meaningful to say that
a = a whatever domain the denotation of a might be in. There are two
objections to this argument. One is that it is far from clear that the
meaning of identity is domain independent: for example, in set theory an
axiom (*Extensionality*) has to tell us the condition for two sets to be identical: they must have the same members. The second is that the set
membership relation ∈ is itself 'almost' domain independent, since 'x∈y',
i.e. 'x is an element of y', is true if and only if x is an element of the set
y, whatever the nature of the individuals making up the sets: we could be
discussing sets of numbers, trees, people, or whatever. Yet, for reasons
which have become celebrated in the philosophy of mathematics over the
past century and are still regarded as compelling, set theory is usually not
regarded as a part of logic, but as a mathematical theory in which 'x∈y'
is formalised as a binary relation R(x, y).

A more persuasive argument for regarding = as a logical relation is that
a = b and b = c cannot, with a strong conceptual 'cannot', both be true
and a = c false, given the meaning we assign to the symbol =. In the light
of the preliminary definition of deductive validity in Chapter 1, this fact
should make = a logical item, since otherwise that inference would be
invalid, as we saw in section 1 of this chapter. There is much to sympa-
thise with in this position, but unfortunately it cuts across another one
largely adopted by contemporary logicians. For example, the symbol < is
now *always* used to signify an irreflexive and transitive (and therefore
asymmetric) binary relation on a domain. Given this understanding of the
properties of < it is impossible for a<b to be true and b<a also to be true.
But logicians do not in general regard the inference a<b ∴ ¬(b<a) as deductively valid, although they would be happy to take it as enthymematic, i.e.
as valid once the conditions of transitivity and irreflexivity have been added
to the statement that a<b. In that case there seems no good reason not
also to regard the inference a = b, b = c ∴ a = c as enthymematic, valid
when appropriate properties of = have been added to the premises a = b,
b = c; which is what we have done.

What should and should not be classed as logical is a difficult question.
Certainly, the criterion of necessity is an important constraint, but as we
have seen, it is not a decisive one. Conventional considerations also play
a role. There are ways of presenting first-order logic in which this conventional aspect becomes more apparent – for example, within the finite-type-
theory of Church 1950, or within a theory of generalised quantifiers (as

in Bell and Slomson 1969, Chapter 13, or Lindström 1966). In both these approaches, the quantifiers $\forall$ and $\exists$, even restricted to individual variables, are merely two out of an infinity of other functions of the same type. Yet these others are not registered as logical in first-order logic; in fact they are mostly not even definable in first-order logic.

Part of the reason for denying these other operators and relations the title 'logic' is that they are too close to the more speculative parts of modern mathematics. These are subtle issues, which it is beyond the scope of this book to pursue in any detail, though they will be taken up again briefly in Chapter 11, when the question of whether second-order logic is 'really' logic will be aired. Practically speaking, it makes little difference whether any particular notion is taken to be logical or not. Mathematics may be denied the status of logic, but that doesn't diminish its importance or authority. The same can be said of the accepted parts of science generally.

In practice, it makes absolutely no difference whether = is regarded as a logical notion or not, *because neither the first order axioms of identity not any extension of them can ensure that only =-interpretations satisfy them.* For example, let **L** have one predicate symbol P apart from = and variables and the logical symbols. Now let **L** be interpreted in a domain of two elements, say 0 and 1. Let both 0 and 1 be in the extension of P in this domain, and let the extension of = be {(1,0), (0,1), (0,0), (1,1)}. It follows from a standard result (Mendelson 1987, 75, Proposition 2.24) that the identity axioms are satisfied, but obviously so interpreted = is not identity. The inability to fix the identity relation is merely a symptom of a much more general failure of first order theories to determine their intended interpretation uniquely, which we shall discuss at more length in Chapter 11. The most we can do when we want to reason about identity within any theory is append the identity axioms, or equivalently rules R_1 and R_2, to those of the theory. That theory is then called a *first order theory with equality.*

Chapter 10

Alternative deductive systems for first-order logic

1 INTRODUCTION

By a *deductive system* for a particular symbolic language, like a first-order language, we shall mean a set of rules, like the tree rules, which are purely formal, or syntactical, in character and which determine *formal proofs* of sentences from sets of sentences formalised in that language. The deductive system based on trees is not the only one for first-order logic. Indeed, there are several, all of which are known to possess analogous soundness and completeness properties. Some, like the so-called natural deduction system described in section 3, attempt to model themselves on our informal reasoning; others, like the system **H** described below, do not – or at any rate, not to the same extent.

2 H

Because of its conceptual economy ('austerity' might be a better word), **H** has played a very important role in metalogical investigations. We call the system **H** after the German mathematician David Hilbert, who first developed it. **H** is constructed within a slimmed-down first-order language which we shall call L_0. L_0's logical vocabulary contains only the one quantifier $\forall$ and the two connectives $\neg$ and $\rightarrow$. The existential quantifier $\exists x$ is taken to be defined as $\neg \forall x \neg$, while as we know $\neg(A \rightarrow \neg B)$ and $\neg A \rightarrow B$ can serve as $A \wedge B$ and $A \vee B$ respectively. We shall assume for simplicity (and without essential loss of expressive power) that L_0 contains no function symbols. We now define an infinite class of formulas of L_0 called the *logical axioms* of L_0. These are all instances of the following, where A and B are any formulas of L_0, x any variable and t any term, i.e. a variable or constant:

1. $A \rightarrow (B \rightarrow A)$
2. $(A \rightarrow (B \rightarrow C)) \rightarrow ((A \rightarrow B) \rightarrow (A \rightarrow C))$
3. $(\neg A \rightarrow B) \rightarrow ((A \rightarrow B) \rightarrow B)$
4. $\forall x A \rightarrow A(t/x)$, where, if t is a variable, it is free for x in A (see Chapter 9, section 1, for the definition of 'free for').
5. $\forall x (A \rightarrow B) \rightarrow (A \rightarrow \forall x B)$, where x does not occur free in A.

Note that where these logical axioms are closed formulas, they are logical truths. **H** contains in addition to the logical axioms two *rules of inference*. One is *modus ponens*: from formulas A and $A \rightarrow B$ infer B. The other is *generalisation*: from a formula A infer $\forall x A$. Where Σ is any set of formulas of $\mathbf{L_0}$, a *proof (in $\mathbf{H}$) from assumptions* Σ is defined to be a finite sequence $A_1, \ldots, A_n$ of formulas of $\mathbf{L_0}$, such that each A_i is either a member of Σ, or a logical axiom, or inferred from previous formulas in the sequence by modus ponens or generalisation ('assumptions' are what up to now we have been calling *premises*). A formula is a *theorem of $\mathbf{H}$* if it is provable from the empty set of assumption formulas. Since logical axioms can be lines in a proof, all of them are theorems of **H**. The Soundness Theorem for **H** implies that the theorems of **H** are all logical truths of $\mathbf{L_0}$ (the Completeness Theorem implies the converse).

The rule of generalisation deserves comment, for it sanctions a type of proof which at first sight looks strange and also appears to be unsound, namely proceeding from an assumption (premise) $P(x)$, to its closure $\forall x P(x)$. The inference seems to be unsound because $P(x)$ may be satisfied by some value of x in a given domain and yet not by all, whereas $\forall x P(x)$ is true only if every domain member satisfies $P(x)$. Yet the system **H** is known to be sound! The solution to the apparent paradox is that **H** is sound in the sense that if there is a proof in **H** of a closed formula A from a set Σ of closed formulas, then A is a logical consequence of Σ (the sentences in Σ cannot all be true in any interpretation of $\mathbf{L_0}$ and A false). The fact that there is a proof (of two lines) in **H** of $\forall x P(x)$ from $P(x)$ therefore does not contradict the soundness of **H** because $P(x)$ is not a sentence (closed formula).

A fundamental metatheorem for **H**, called the *Deduction Theorem*, states that if Σ is a set of assumptions and B is any line in a proof from the enlarged set of assumptions consisting of Σ and the formula A, then there is a proof of $A \rightarrow B$ from Σ *provided that* no line in the original proof which depends on A is obtained by applying generalisation to a variable free in B. A line in any given proof *depends on A* if and only if either that line consists of A itself, or it is obtained by a rule of inference from a formula (generalisation) or formulas (modus ponens) at least one of which depends on A. This proviso of the Deduction Theorem is clearly not satisfied in any proof in which $\forall x P(x)$ is inferred by generalisation from an assumption formula $P(x)$, as above. In fact, it follows from the soundness of **H** that $P(x) \rightarrow \forall x P(x)$ is not a theorem of **H**. (See if you explain why. Hint: use generalisation on $P(x) \rightarrow \forall x P(x)$.)

Since **H** is sound and complete it is equivalent in proving power (for closed formulas) to the set of tree rules, as long as countable (denumerably infinite or finite) sets of assumptions only are considered. However, as a glance at the definition of a proof from assumptions reveals, there is no limit on the set of assumptions; they can even be uncountable (this means not indexable by the natural numbers; there is a fuller discussion of 'sizes' of infinity in the next chapter). However, the Compactness Theorem tells us that this is only a nominal advantage. A disadvantage of **H** as an everyday proof system is that proofs of even quite simple inferences tend to be long, unwieldy and not very intuitive (the proof of even such a simple tautology as $A{\rightarrow}A$ from the empty set of assumption formulas is quite complex). On the other hand, **H** was not devised to generate easy proofs; it was devised to be a tool of what Hilbert called *Metamathematics*, or the application of mathematical methods to the investigation of logical problems. And from this point of view its conceptual minimality is a great asset.

3　ND

There are two main types of Natural Deduction system: *linear* ones, in which proofs are sequences of formulas, as in **H** and *non-linear*, in which proofs take the form of trees. **ND** is of the second type. In some ways **ND** is closer to the system of this book than it is to **H**, in others closer to **H**. It is more like **H** in its using in general a direct proof of the consequence to be established, unlike the system we have been using in which proofs are reductio proofs. On the other hand, **ND** is more like this system than it is like **H** in that in **ND** proofs are also cast in a two-dimensional tree configuration, though its trees look like the traditional method of depicting ordinary family trees rather than being like the truth trees we have developed in the previous chapters. Also, unlike **H**, **ND** makes no use of logical axioms as such, only of rules for inferring formulas. **ND** is also unlike **H** in that its rules are cast in an ordinary first-order language **L** containing both quantifiers ∀ and ∃ as well as the connective ∧, ∨, → and ¬, and to which is added also a further logical symbol, ⊥, representing logical falsehood. Again we shall assume for simplicity that **L** contains no function symbols; so wherever a term t is mentioned, t is either a variable or a constant.

ND's rules of proof are formally striking and elegant, since with the exception of two rules, they occur in conjugate pairs, one member of the pair regulating the *introduction* of a connective or quantifer into a formula and the other its *elimination*; the rule for introducing ∧, for example, will be written ∧I and the rule(s) for its elimination will be written ∧E. All these rules are rules for inferring new lines from given ones in a formal *tree derivation* (we shall talk of tree derivations to avoid confusion with the tree proofs of the earlier chapters). The upper lines may be either premises in that derivation, or be derived from earlier lines. *A*, *B*, *C*, etc. below are any formulas, open or closed.

∧I: $\dfrac{A \quad B}{A \wedge B}$ ∧E: $\dfrac{A \wedge B,}{A} \quad \dfrac{A \wedge B}{B}$

∨I: $\dfrac{A, \quad B}{A \vee B \quad A \vee B}$ ∨E: $\dfrac{A \vee B \quad \overset{A\mathbf{X}}{\underset{\text{—}}{C}} \quad \overset{B\mathbf{X}}{\underset{\text{—}}{C}}}{C}$

→I: $\dfrac{\overset{A\mathbf{X}}{\underset{\text{—}}{B}}}{A \rightarrow B}$ →E: $\dfrac{A \rightarrow B \quad A}{B}$

¬I: $\dfrac{\overset{A\mathbf{X}}{\underset{\text{—}}{\bot}}}{\neg A}$ ¬E: $\dfrac{A \quad \neg A}{\bot}$

∀I: $\dfrac{A}{\forall x A(x/y)}$ where y does not occur free in any premise on which A depends and x is free for y in A

∀E: $\dfrac{\forall x A}{A(t/x)}$ where if the term t is a variable, it is free for x in A

∃I: $\dfrac{A(t/x)}{\exists x A}$ same proviso as ∀E

∃E: $\dfrac{\exists x A \quad \overset{A(t/x)\mathbf{X}}{\underset{\text{—}}{B}}}{B}$ where t does not occur in A or in any premise other than A(t/x) on which B depends and if t is a variable it is free for x in A

The various restrictions on the quantifier rules ∀I, ∀E, ∃I and ∃E are there to prevent the derivation of a false conclusion from true premises, which can happen if the restrictions are not obeyed (Tennant 1978: 64–65, shows how).

In the rules ∨E, →I, ¬I and ∃E, the vertical sequences represent *subderivations* of the formula appearing under the dash –, among whose premises, or assumptions as they are also called in this system, may occur the upper formula (the fact that these subderivations are placed to one particular side of the main one is not significant). The boldface cross against the premise in each such subderivation means that those assumptions may be, but not necessarily must be, *discharged* in the larger derivation. To say that they are discharged is to say that they are no longer to be counted as assumptions in the derivation of the formula underneath the line. Note that in these rules there is only one formula below the line and one or more above. By analogy with family trees, we shall call the formula below the line the *child* and those above (including subderivations where they appear) the *parents* (single-parent families are allowed, and only children mandatory, in **ND**).

A somewhat complex inductive definition can be given of the notion of a derivation of a formula from a set of assumptions (see, for example Tennant 1978: 52–5), but for our purposes it is enough to say that a *derivation* is a tree constructed by combining the rules above in such a way that the child in one rule can be used as a parent in another (just as in a family tree), with all the (undischarged) initial ancestors constituting the assumptions in the derivation and the final descendent formula being that derived from those assumptions. Here, for example, is a derivation of $\forall x(P(x) \to T(x))$ from the assumptions $\forall x(P(x) \to Q(x))$ and $\forall x(Q(x) \to T(x))$:

$$
\frac{\dfrac{\dfrac{\forall x(P(x) \to Q(x))}{P(x)X \quad P(x) \to Q(x) \, [\forall E]}}{\dfrac{Q(x) \, [\to E] \qquad \dfrac{\forall x(Q(x) \to T(x))}{Q(x) \to T(x) \, [\forall E]}}{\dfrac{T(x) \, [\to E]}{\dfrac{P(x) \to T(x) \, [\to I; \text{ assumption } P(x) \text{ discharged}]}{\forall x(P(x) \to T(x)) \, [\forall I]}}}}
$$

The rule in each case is stated in brackets against the formula it is used to obtain from parent formula(s). The rule $\forall I$ allows us to reinstate the universal quantifier subject to the provisos stated in the rule, which are clearly satisfied here.

Here is another simple **ND** derivation, of $\exists x Q(x)$ from $\forall x(P(x) \to Q(x))$ and $\exists x P(x)$:

$$
\frac{\dfrac{\dfrac{\dfrac{\forall x(P(x) \to Q(x))}{P(y) \to Q(y) \, [\forall E] \qquad P(y) \, X}}{\dfrac{Q(y) \, [\to E]}{\exists x Q(x) \, [\exists I] \qquad \exists x P(x)}}}{\exists x Q(x) \, [\exists E; \text{ assumption } P(y) \text{ discharged}]}
$$

There is a certain amount of conceptual redundancy in having both $\perp$ and $\neg$ as primitive symbols and an associated redundancy in the rules. Since $\perp$ is interpreted as an arbitrary logical falsehood, it is equivalent to a contradiction. And we know that if $\perp$ is actually a contradiction (say $B \wedge \neg B$), then $\neg A$ is truth-functionally equivalent to $A \to \perp$. Using this equivalence as a *definition* of $\neg A$, we immediately infer both $\neg E$ and $\neg I$ from the rules $\to I$ and $\to E$ respectively:

$$
\frac{\dfrac{A X}{-}}{\dfrac{\perp}{A \to \perp \, [\to I]}} \qquad\qquad \frac{A \quad A \to \perp}{\perp \, [\to E]}
$$

So we don't need ¬ if we have ⊥. No matter, having both makes life easier.

However, the **ND** rules above are incomplete, in the sense that not every logical consequence of a given premise set can be proved to follow by them. To achieve completeness two more rules are required. One, known as the *Rule of Absurdity* (or *ex impossibile quodlibet*), says that you can infer any formula A from ⊥:

$$\frac{\bot}{A}$$

We know this inference to be valid whatever A may be, yet it cannot be proved to be simply from the introduction and elimination rules. Completeness can now be obtained by adding to all the foregoing any one of the following three rules:

Excluded Middle

$$\frac{\quad\quad}{A \lor \neg A}$$

i.e. you can unconditionally write $A \lor \neg A$, for any formula A and not regard it as an assumption (this is why the bar is placed above it). Again, we know that $A \lor \neg A$ is unconditionally true, but it cannot be proved on the basis of the rules so far listed.

Double Negation

$$\frac{\neg\neg A}{A}$$

Classical Reductio

$$\frac{\begin{array}{c}\neg A \ \mathbf{X}\\[2pt]\overline{}\\[2pt]\bot\end{array}}{A}$$

Excluded Middle, Double Negation and Classical Reductio are all interderivable, given the other rules. Showing this provides quite a good illustration of some characteristic proof-procedures of **ND**; in fact, we shall show that, given the other rules, (i) Excluded Middle (EM) implies Classical Reductio (CR), (ii) CR implies Double Negation (DN) and (iii) DN implies EM.

(i) EM implies CR:

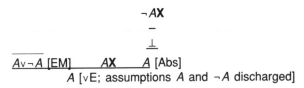

$$\frac{\qquad}{Av\neg A \text{ [EM]}} \quad \frac{A\mathbf{X} \qquad A \text{ [Abs]}}{A \text{ [}\vee\text{E; assumptions } A \text{ and } \neg A \text{ discharged]}}$$

Thus, if we have a derivation of ⊥ from ¬*A*, then, with EM, we have a derivation of *A* from no assumptions.

(ii) CR implies DN:

$$\frac{\neg A\,\mathbf{X} \qquad \neg\neg A}{\dfrac{\perp \text{ [}\neg\text{E]}}{A \text{ [CR; assumption } \neg A \text{ discharged]}}}$$

Thus, given CR, we have a derivation of *A* from ¬ ¬*A*.

(iii) DN implies EM:

$$\frac{A\,\mathbf{X}}{Av\neg A \text{ [}\vee\text{I]}} \qquad \neg(Av\neg A)\,\mathbf{X}$$
$$\frac{\perp \text{ [}\neg\text{E]}}{\dfrac{\neg A \text{ [}\neg\text{I; assumption } A \text{ discharged]}}{\dfrac{Av\neg A \text{ [}\vee\text{I]} \qquad \neg(Av\neg A)\,\mathbf{X}(2)}{\dfrac{\perp \text{ [}\neg\text{E]}}{\dfrac{\neg\neg(Av\neg A) \text{ [}\neg\text{I; assumption } \neg(Av\neg A) \text{ discharged]}}{Av\neg A \text{ [DN]}}}}}$$

The only point to note here is that the assumption ¬(*A*v¬*A*) is introduced twice and both occurrences are discharged simultaneously when the second appeal to ¬I is made.

We shall end by giving two derivations in **ND** which give another explanation of why 'If *A* then *B*' is equivalent to 'Not-*A* or *B*' (cf. our argument for the truth table for A→B in Chapter 1, section 6): (a) a derivation of ¬*A*v*B* from *A*→*B* and (b) a derivation of *A*→*B* from ¬*A*v*B*.

(a)
$$\frac{A{\to}B \qquad A\mathbf{X}}{\dfrac{B \text{ [}{\to}\text{E]}}{\dfrac{\neg Av B \text{ [}\vee\text{I]}}{}}} \qquad \frac{\neg A\mathbf{X}}{\neg Av B \text{ [}\vee\text{I]}} \qquad \frac{}{Av\neg A \text{ [EM]}}$$
$$\neg Av B \text{ [}\vee\text{E]}$$

(b)
$$\frac{A\mathbf{X} \qquad \neg A\mathbf{X}}{\dfrac{\perp \text{ [}\neg\text{E]}}{B \text{ [Abs.]}}} \qquad \frac{B\mathbf{X} \qquad \neg Av B}{B \text{ [}\vee\text{E]}}$$
$$A{\to}B \text{ [}{\to}\text{I]}$$

Exercises

1 Justify each of the lines in the proofs (a) and (b) above.
2 Construct **ND** derivations of
   (i) $\perp$ from $A \wedge \neg A$.
   (ii) $A \rightarrow B$ from $\neg A$ (hint: use Absurdity and $\rightarrow$I).

4 COMPARISONS

H is probably sound and complete; so is **ND**; clear proofs are given (for **ND**) in Tennant 1978 and (for **H**) in Mendelson 1987. These facts imply that all three deductive systems, these and the truth tree system, are equal in power. What criteria should determine which to use?

One, and the principal, reason for developing **H** has been mentioned: its efficacy in metamathematical research (though Gentzen, the German mathematician who invented Natural Deduction systems, developed another, the Sequent Calculus, specifically for the metamathematical investigation of Natural Deduction). This applies neither to truth trees nor to **ND**, which from this point of view are just about equally cumbersome. The method of truth trees is highly user-friendly from the point of view of actually developing proofs within it, because they are so algorithmic and free of redundancy. As the last four examples make clear, derivations in **ND** may well require considerable forethought and sometimes a good deal of trial-and-error before a way of formulating them is found. In particular, the selection of assumptions to discharge later often calls for considerable ingenuity. Also, tree proofs of most results are a good deal shorter than the corresponding **ND** derivations. What, then, are the merits that make **ND** and its variants of interest to logicians?

There are several. One is that informal reasoning is indeed often better matched by direct proofs of a Natural Deduction character, rather than by indirect proofs by finding closed truth trees (though this is by no means always the case; for some very basic inferences which truth trees accomplish very easily and naturally, Natural Deduction arguments are cumbersome and very unnatural: contrast, from this point of view, an **ND** derivation of $\neg(A \wedge \neg A)$ from the empty set of assumptions with a tree proof of it).

5 INTUITIONISM

Another reason why Natural Deduction systems are studied is philosophical. Truth trees are efficient largely because the rules (α) and (β) and Double Negation do no more than codify the truth tables for the respective types of truth-functional sentence. The truth tables for the connectives, and the interpretation of the quantifiers developed in Chapter

5, constitute what is called *classical semantics*. However, whether classical semantics should assume such a fundamental role has long been a matter of philosophical controversy. An influential school of thought, developed initially by the Dutch mathematician L. E. J. Brouwer and called *Intuitionism*, rejects classical semantics as the basis for reasoning in mathematics as a consequence of the repudiation of mathematical Platonism, the idea of an independently existing realm of mathematical entities like numbers. Instead, Intuitionists view these as constructions of the human mind; for them, the canonical form of mathematical reasoning is *constructive proof*, the exhibition of a procedure which will show that some constructed object or objects have a definite property. Intuitionists identify mathematical truth with constructive provability from some body of constructively acceptable mathematical principles.

This leads Intuitionists to a proof-based account of the propositional connectives, expressed in the following way (by the Dutch Intuitionistic mathematician Heyting): $A \vee B$ is true (provable) if there is a proof of A or one of B (thus the classical tautology $A \vee \neg A$ is no longer a constructively acceptable principle because there is no guarantee that there is either a proof of A or a proof of its negation); $\neg A$ is true if there is a proof-procedure which will generate an absurdity (like $0 = 1$) when applied to a proof of A; $A \rightarrow B$ is true if there is a procedure which, applied to a proof of A, will generate a proof of B. $\exists x P(x)$ is true if an object a can be constructed such that there is a procedure which applied to a generates a proof that a has P; $\forall x P(x)$ is true in a given domain D of objects if there is a procedure which generates a proof of $P(a)$ for every object a in D.

The words 'proof' and 'procedure' in the semantic rules above are not explicitly defined. Nevertheless, a system of formal deductive rules was actually proposed by Heyting, in an **H**-type format, with only these rather vague rules of interpretation as its semantic support. One of the features of the **ND** rules that recommends it to philosophical logicians is that this system is most elegantly and suggestively represented as an **ND** system. So represented it consists of the Introduction and Elimination Rules and the Rule of Absurdity. An interesting consequence of this identification is that the Intuitionistic connectives cannot be given truth-table definitions in terms of any finite number of truth-values, however these might be understood. Thus, though the *formal* difference between classical and Intuitionistic logic can be represented in terms of the acceptance and rejection respectively of any one of the rules of Excluded Middle, Double Negation and Classical Reductio (all principles, incidentally, that the Intuitionists themselves regard as illegitimate), semantically they are strongly divergent.

Though Intuitionism was the creation of philosophically minded mathematicians, a strong interest in Intuitionistic logic has recently been shown in a quite different quarter, that of computer science, where Intuitionistic logic seems to have a very natural interpretation within a general theory of programming types also built on an underlying natural deduction-style logic (see Reeves and Clarke 1990, Chapters 8 and 9). A rather different way of interpreting Intuitionistic logic, as a general theory of provability from a developing body of constructively acceptable principles, was proposed earlier by Kripke. He showed how this theory could be modelled formally within the possible-worlds semantics for modal logic which he had developed earlier, in particular within a suitably adapted form of the semantics for the modal system S4 (see Chapter 12) and that with respect to this semantics the system of Intuitionistic logic described above is provably sound and complete. For an account of what are now called Kripke models for Intuitionistic logic see Tennant 1978, Chapters 5 and 6.

Chapter 11

First-order theories

1 FIRST-ORDER THEORIES

Our scientific (including mathematical) knowledge is typically organised in the form of *theories*. Theories are characterised by sets of fundamental *laws*, or *principles*, or *postulates*, or *axioms*, from which ideally everything else held to be true is deduced as consequences, though, as we shall see, a famous theorem of Gödel shows that in most cases of interest this ideal can never be achieved. In this chapter we shall talk about the formalisation of theories in first-order languages and some of the celebrated theorems proved in this century which reveal surprising properties of these formalisations.

The first theory of identity with which we are already familiar is a particularly simple first order theory. However, much of the subsequent discussion will concern a more complex example, the first order theory of the arithmetic of the natural numbers known as first order Peano arithmetic, after the Italian mathematician Giuseppe Peano (though the axioms below were not in fact formulated by him). This *theory with equality* (above p. 131) is usually formulated in the first-order language whose extralogical vocabulary comprises a one-place function symbol s and two two-place function symbols, usually written + and ·. The variables are intended to range over N; the intended interpretation of s(x), as in Chapter 9, section 5, is the *successor* of the natural number x, that of x + y is the ordinary sum of x and y and that of x.y is the ordinary product of x and y. For each natural number n, the term s(s(... s(0) ...)), with n s's, is the *numeral* for n. In what follows, we shall abbreviate this to $s_n(0)$. The first order Peano Axiom are the following:

$$\forall x \neg (s(x) = 0)$$
$$\forall x \forall y (s(x) = s(y) \rightarrow x = y)$$
$$\forall x (x + 0 = x)$$
$$\forall x \forall y (x + s(y) = s(x + y))$$
$$\forall x (x.0 = 0)$$
$$\forall x \forall y (x.s(y) = x.y + x)$$

together with all the infinitely many instances of the 'schema of mathematical induction'

$$[A(0) \wedge \forall x(A(x) \rightarrow A(s(x)))] \rightarrow \forall x A(x)$$

for each formula $A(x)$ in the first-order language containing the constant 0 and function symbols for sum, product and successor. The informal expression of the Principle of Mathematical Induction on the natural numbers is 'For any property P, if 0 has P and if, whenever x has P so does s(x), then all natural numbers have P.' This is naturally expressed by the second-order formula

$$\forall P(P(0) \wedge \forall x(P(x) \vee P(s(x))) \rightarrow \forall x P(x));$$

but since there are no predicate variables in first-order languages, the infinitely many axioms of the first-order induction schema must be employed as a surrogate for the second-order statement (in the same way that an infinite list of substitution axioms had to do duty for a second-order sentence in the theory of identity).

In Chapter 8 it was pointed out that infinite axiom sets pose no problem in principle, because the Compactness Theorem for first-order logic tells us that if a sentence is a consequence of such a set, then it is a consequence of some finite subset of it. However, this nice property of first-order logic is offset by one that is not so nice, non-categoricity, and which is a consequence of compactness (a *categorical* axiom system is one all of whose models are isomorphic). Neither the first-order Peano Axioms nor first-order Zermelo–Fraenkel set theory (the standard axiomatisation of set theory) is categorical if they are consistent; the following simple argument indicates why Peano's Axioms are not categorical even within the class of = -interpretations.

Let PA denote the first-order Peano Axioms and assume PA has an = -model in the natural numbers (a celebrated result of Gödel, which we shall discuss shortly, is that this cannot be proved without making stronger assumptions than those represented by PA). Now add to PA the following infinite sequence of statements: $\neg(a = 0)$, $\neg(a = s_1(0))$, $\neg(a = s_2(0))$, ..., $\neg(a = s_n(0))$, ..., where a is a new constant added to $\mathbf{L}(\mathbf{N})$ and call the resulting set Ω. Let Ω' be any finite subset of Ω. Either Ω' contains some statements from the above list or it does not. If it does not then Ω' is a subset of PA and so by assumption has a model in the natural numbers. If Ω' does contain sentences from the list above, then since Ω' is finite there must be a largest n, call it n_0, such that $\neg(a = s_{n_0}(0))$ is in Ω'. But Ω' still has a model in the natural numbers, for we have only to let the interpretation of a in that model be $n_0 + 1$. Hence every finite subset of Ω has a model and by the Compactness Theorem Ω has a model $\mathfrak{I}$.

But what does $\mathfrak{I}$ look like? It cannot be anything structurally similar to the natural number sequence, since the Peano Axioms ensure that the individual a cannot be interpreted as the counterpart of any number in N. In fact, a has to be interpreted as an infinite number greater than all the counterparts in $\mathfrak{I}$ of members of N: $\mathfrak{I}$ is said to have a different *order type* from the natural number sequence. But PA is a subset of W and so Ω is a model of PA. Hence if PA has an = -model in the natural numbers, then it has another not isomorphic to that model.

2   INFINITE CARDINALS

Non-categoricity is endemic to first order theories and in the remainder of this chapter we shall discuss the implications of this, and in particular whether the use of second order formalisations offers an acceptable alternative. Since infinity and in particular different *magnitudes* of infinity will play a role in the subsequent discussion, we shall now take time out to become acquainted with some elementary results of the modern theory of infinite sets (this is nothing to be alarmed about). A profound discovery made in the late nineteenth century by the German mathematician Georg Cantor was that it is possible to give a very simple definition of two sets having the same number of members as each other, even when they're infinite! Recall from Chapter 9 that a bijective function f from one set A to another B is one which never takes the same values on distinct members of A (i.e. if x ≠ y, for any x, y in A, then f(x) ≠ f(y)) and such that every element of B is the image f(x) of some member x of A. Cantor's simple definition is that A is *equinumerous with* B, or has the same number of members as B, if there is a bijective function from A to B.

This definition merely repeats a feature of equinumerous sets we're very familiar with: if I want to show that I have the same number of apples in my sack as you do in yours, then clearly all I have to do is to pair off the apples in your sack with mine and show that there is none left over in either sack. That pairing is just Cantor's bijection. What is so remarkable about the definition, however, is that it very easily follows from it that there are infinite sets with different numbers of members, without any prior definition of what an infinite number is! It is not difficult to show this, but first we need a rather more precise account of how one infinite set can be more numerous than another. Then we shall exhibit two infinite sets such that one is demonstrably more numerous than the other.

For any set A, its *power set* **P**(A) is the set of all subsets of A; the empty set and A itself are, we know, both members of **P**(A) (for a finite set A with n members it is not difficult to see that **P**(A) has 2^n members). Now let A be any set, finite or infinite. Clearly, there is an injective function from A to **P**(A), namely the one that associates every element x of A with its singleton set {x}. This shows that A has at most as many members as **P**(A). Indeed, the existence of an injection from A to B is taken as the definition of 'has at most as many members as' and it is shown in textbooks of set theory that this ordering is transitive, reflexive and anti-symmetric, i.e. if A has at most as many members as B and B has at most as many members as A, then A and B have the same number of members according to Cantor's equinumerosity definition above (this last result, which is not trivial, is known as the Schröder–Bernstein Theorem). If we write $|A| \leq |B|$ to mean that there is an injection from A to B and $|A| = |B|$ to mean that A is equinumerous with B by Cantor's definition, then the relation $|A| < |B|$ defined by '$|A| \leq |B|$ and $|A| \neq |B|$' is easily shown to be asymmetric and so we can interpret $|A| < |B|$ as saying that A has strictly fewer members than B.

Now let f be any injection from A to $\mathbf{P}(A)$ and consider the subset $C = \{x \text{ in } A: x \text{ not a member of } f(x)\}$ of A. Suppose there is some element x of A such that $C = f(x)$. x is either in C or it's not. If it is, then by the definition of C x is in C after all. Hence x cannot be in C. But again, by the definition of C, x is in C. We have a contradiction and hence there is no x in A such that $C = f(x)$. Hence there is no bijection from A to $\mathbf{P}(A)$ and hence $|A| < |\mathbf{P}(A)|$, i.e. A has fewer members than $\mathbf{P}(A)$. This fundamental result is *Cantor's Theorem*. To keep the promise we made earlier, to display two infinite sets with different numbers of members, we have only to let A be N; it follows from Cantor's Theorem that $|N| < |\mathbf{P}(N)|$. Indeed, there is an infinite hierarchy of infinite cardinals, since $|\mathbf{P}(N)| < |\mathbf{P}(\mathbf{P}(N))| < |\mathbf{P}(\mathbf{P}(\mathbf{P}(N)))| < \ldots$ etc.

N is the smallest infinite set and is said to represent the *cardinal number* $\aleph_0$ (called aleph-zero; aleph, i.e. $\aleph$, is the first letter of the Hebrew alphabet). Thus every denumerable set has the cardinality $\aleph_0$, since there is a bijection from it to N. It follows from the fact that $\mathbf{P}(N)$ has the cardinal number of the set of all functions from N into the set $\{0, 1\}$, denoted by $2^{\aleph_0}$, that $\mathbf{P}(N)$ has the same cardinality as the set of all real numbers, or the *continuum*. For each such function can be identified with the binary expansion of a real number in the interval between 0 and 1 and any increasing function defined on that interval whose codomain is the infinite interval of all real numbers, like $\tan(x)$ or the tangent of x, establishes a bijection of the two intervals. Another fundamental result of set theory is that for any cardinal number, there is a smallest cardinal greater than it. A celebrated if not notorious problem of contemporary mathematics, called the *Continuum Hypothesis*, is whether $\aleph_1$, the least cardinal greater than $\aleph_0$, is equal to $2^{\aleph_0}$.

The Continuum Hypothesis was shown by Paul Cohen in 1963 to be logically independent of the axioms currently taken as the basis for set theory. His independence result plunged set theory into a crisis from which it has not recovered. There are two connected reasons for this. (i) No additional axiom that has been suggested and that decides the Continuum Hypothesis has found much support among mathematicians. All of them (many involve postulating the existence of extremely large cardinals) seem at least as problematic as the Continuum Hypothesis itself. (ii) Set theory had for at least the previous half-century been looked on as a plausible foundation of mathematics: with suitable bridging definitions, the whole of current mathematics, including the theories of the natural, rational, real and complex numbers, is derivable as consequence of one or other current axiomatisations of set theory (for further details consult Fraenkel, Bar-Hillel and Levy 1973).

3 LÖWENHEIM–SKOLEM THEOREMS

We now return to the categoricity problem. The Löwenheim-Skolem Theorem, proved in Chapter 8, tells us that any finite set of first-order sentences has a finite or denumerable model. It can be shown that this remains true for arbitrary sets of first-order sentences, finite or not and even when attention is restricted to =-interpretations. This result is sometimes called the 'downward' Löwenheim–Skolem Theorem because it states the existence of models of at most the cardinality $\aleph_0$. There is a corresponding 'upward' Löwenheim–Skolem Theorem, which states that if any consistent set of first-order sentences has an infinite =-model, it has one also of a higher cardinality (this result is beyond the scope of this book). These two theorems immediately tell us that even within the class of =-interpretations no sets of first-order sentences having infinite models can be categorical, because one of the conditions of isomorphism between any two interpretations of those sets of sentences is that there is a bijection between their domains (the other condition is that structure is preserved under at least one bijection) and hence that their domains are of the same cardinality.

One of the strangest consequences of the wholesale failure of categoricity for first-order formalisations goes by the name of *Skolem's Paradox*. It has been mentioned that according to set theory there is an increasing sequence of infinite cardinal numbers represented concretely by the sequence of sets N, **P**(N), **P**(**P**(N)), **P**(**P**(**P**(N))), etc. Hence if first-order set theory is consistent, then it has a denumerable model, by the downward Löwenheim–Skolem Theorem (it can be shown to have no finite model). So within set theory one proves that the universe of sets is uncountably infinite, while one can also show that all these claims are satisfied within a denumerable model if first-order set theory is consistent. This is one version of Skolem's Paradox.

Skolem's Paradox is another illustration of the inability of first-order formalisations to characterise their subject-matter with any degree of uniqueness. At this point an examination of *second*-order logic becomes highly relevant, because in some important cases second-order formalisations allow both finite axiomatisability and categoricity for several mathematical theories where first-order formalisations offer neither. The identity relation can be explicitly defined by a second-order sentence, while the structures of the natural and real numbers can be uniquely defined by second-order sentences. In view of its apparently highly desirable properties, why not use second-order logic in preference to first? In the next two sections we shall try to answer this question.

4 SECOND-ORDER LANGUAGES

Second-order languages are like first-order languages, except that they have additional classes of variables, *n-place relation variables* X^n, Y^n, ... (and possibly n-place function variables) for all $n \geq 1$. In any interpretation of a first-order language, a predicate symbol is interpreted as a subset of the domain D of individuals, i.e. of the domain of the individual variables x, y, z, ..., and an n-place relation is interpreted as a subset of the set of all n-tuples of members of D. Correspondingly, the domain of the predicate variables in a second-order language is the set $P(D)$ of all subsets of D, the power-set of D. Similarly, the domain of the n-place predicate variables will be $P(D^n)$ (D^n is the set of all n-tuples of members of D; cf. Chapter 7, section 1). In other words, second-order languages are interpreted not in a single domain D, as are first-order languages, but in the sequence of related domains $(D, P(D), \ldots, P(D^n), \ldots)$.

We have seen that axiom schemas subsuming infinitely many individual axioms in first-order logic can typically be replaced by a single second-order axiom, as in the case of the substitution axioms in the first-order theory of identity and the induction axioms in first-order Peano Arithmetic. This is not all: the theory of identity in second-order logic is not merely finitely axiomatisable; one does not actually need to axiomatise it at all, because the relation x = y turns out to be *definable* by a single second-order formula, namely

$$\forall X^1(X^1(x) \leftrightarrow X^1(y))$$

Call this formula $A_2(x, y)$ (assume that $\leftrightarrow$ is a defined symbol). It says that x is the same individual as y if and only if all the predicates X^1 which are true of x are exactly those which are also true of y. $A_2(x, y)$ *uniquely characterises the identity relation*. To see why, suppose x were not the same individual as y under some valuation x', y' of x and y in some domain D of individuals (cf Chapter 6; x' and y' are the individuals in D assigned as values to the variables x and y). Then there is a subset A of D which contains x' and does not contain y'. But this subset is itself the value of the second-order predicate variable X^1, say, under some valuation of the variables in the open formula $X^1(x) \leftrightarrow X^1(y)$, in which x and y are assigned the values x', y'. Hence, with respect to that valuation, $X^1(x)$ is true and $X^1(y)$ is false. Hence $\forall X^1(X^1(x) \leftrightarrow X^1(y))$ is false with respect to the values x', y' of x and y. The converse, that if that formula is false relative to any valuation of x and y in D then x' ≠ y', merely reverses the steps in this argument.

Other concepts are uniquely definable in second-order languages which cannot be in first-order ones, where they have to be introduced as primitive notions and their principal properties set out in the form of independent axioms. Indeed entire structures are implicitly definable 'up to isomophism'; these are the structures whose second-order axiomatisations are categorical while the first-order ones are not. The second-order Peano Axioms, call them PA_2, are categorical, for example. These are formulated in a second-order language L_{PA_2} whose only extralogical vocabulary is a one-place function symbol denoting the successor of a natural number and the numeral, i.e. constant, '0': identity, as we now know, can be defined in this language. PA_2 consists of just three axioms: $\forall x \neg (x = 0)$, $\forall x \forall y (s(x) = s(y) \rightarrow x = y)$ and the second-order induction axiom:

$$\forall X^1 [X^1(0) \rightarrow (\forall x (X^1(x) \rightarrow X^1(s(x))) \rightarrow \forall x X^1(x))]$$

where as earlier s(x) signifies the successor of x.

All models of these axioms are isomorphic: they characterise a unique structure, that of a denumerably infinite set of successors of zero. Not only that: the axioms determine also the arithmetical properties of the natural numbers, i.e. their behaviour under addition and multiplication. For there are formulas $A(x, y, z)$ and $B(x, y, z)$ of L_{PA_2} such that, if we think of $A(x, y, z)$ as 'x + y = z' and $B(x, y, z)$ as 'x.y = z', it is a consequence of PA_2 that there is a unique set of triples of domain elements satisfying each formula and which also satisfy the conditions x + 0 = x, x + s(y) = s(x + y), x.0 = 0, x.s(y) = (x.y) + x. In other words, the operations of addition and multiplication themselves are uniquely defined by PA_2.

There are also categorical second-order axiom sets for the theory of the real numbers and, with certain qualifications, for set theory; all sets in the intended model of first-order set theory have a unique ordinal 'rank' associated with them and the second-order set theory axioms define this rank structure uniquely up to a certain large infinite cardinal, called an 'inaccessible cardinal'. A consequence of this fact is that the second-order axioms decide the Continuum Hypothesis (though as true or false no one knows). Given that second-order formalisations have such advantages, why not use them in preference to first-order formalisations? Why is first-order logic regarded – as it is – as standard logic? The next section will attempt to provide an answer to this question.

5   COMPLETENESS

We know from the discussion of first-order Completeness in Chapter 8 that if an inference from a *countable* (i.e. finite or denumerably infinite) set Σ of first-order sentences to a sentence *A* is valid in first-order logic, then there is a tree proof of A from (a finite subset of) Σ. We noted in Chapter 10 that the systems **H** and **ND** have analogous completeness properties.

A proof is a way of establishing that a putative consequence of Σ really is a deductive consequence, for a proof once produced is something that should be able to be mechanically algorithmically checked for correctness (in principle; in practice, of course, the checker may fail through exhaustion, breakdown or other practical fault). There is even an algorithmic way of producing a proof when one exists. For example, the instructions for constructing truth trees laid down in the earlier chapters of this book can without too much difficulty be turned into an algorithm which will generate a closed truth tree from any finite set consisting of the premises and negation of the conclusion of a valid inference; all one has to do is specify an order in which the finite number of unused sentences on any tree at any time are to be used and this can be done (for example start with an α sentence and if there is more than one, choose the first on the leftmost open branch; keep going in this way until all are used and then repeat the procedure with the β sentences, etc.).

Nor does it matter if the set of initial sentences is infinite, so long as its members are countable and effectively enumerable, i.e. are such that there is an executable program for enumerating them as first, second, third, etc. (such sets are also called *recursively enumerable*); the discussion of the Compactness Theorem for countable effectively enumerable sets of initial sentences in Chapter 9 shows how these can be progressively added to any tree in such a way that if the countable set is inconsistent the tree will close. However, if the set of initial sentences is not inconsistent the finished open tree generated by it will not necessarily be finite. This marks the significant difference between truth-functional and first-order truth trees and explains why in the former case they furnish an effective decision procedure for consistency and in the latter they do not. Nor is this failure a feature peculiar to trees: the American mathematician and logician Alonzo Church proved in 1936 that there is no algorithm at all which will determine for every set of first-order sentences it is applied to whether it is consistent or not (this celebrated result is called *Church's Theorem on the Undecidability of First-order Logic*).

Nevertheless, in partial mitigation of Church's result, there is an effective procedure which will always yield the answer 'yes' in finite time to the question 'Is this set of sentences consistent?' if in fact it is. This state of affairs is summed up by saying that *first-order logic is positively, though not negatively, decidable*. We sketched above a way in which the process of tree construction could be made algorithmic. It follows that for every effectively enumerable set Σ of initial sentences, such an algorithm will always generate a closed tree finitely many steps if and only if Σ is inconsistent. A fact which it is beyond the scope of this book to demonstrate is that *any* formal deductive system is such that the set of sentences provable from an effectively enumerable set of premises (usually called axioms) is itself effectively enumerable, just so long as the condition is satisfied (as it is for closed trees and the formal proofs of **H** and **ND**) that the proofs themselves can all be algorithmically checked for correctness.

But second-order logic is not even positively decidable. In other words, *there is no set of rules of proof which both generate machine-checkable proofs and are complete.* This is a consequence of a famous pair of theorems, the *Incompleteness Theorems* for formalised arithmetic, first proved by the Austrian mathematician Kurt Gödel (his results were published in 1931; simplified modern treatments can be found in intermediate and advanced texts in mathematical logic, for example Mendelson 1987). I shall give a brief and informal account of these theorems, starting with the description of a method, due to Gödel himself, for encoding the formulas and proofs in the language L_{PA} of first-order Peano Arithmetic as distinct natural numbers. We shall then see that the sentences of L_{PA} can be interpreted as metalinguistic statements, in particular statements about the provability or otherwise of specified formulas from Peano's Axioms.

First, distinct numbers are assigned to the individual bits of vocabulary of L_{PA} (for this purpose we shall index the variables by the positive integers):

∀	1	,	15
∃	3	(	15
→	5	)	19
¬	7	s	21
∧	9	+	23
∨	11	.	25
=	13	0	27
		x_i	$27 + 2i$, $i = 1, 2, 3, \ldots$

s, as before, is intended to denote the successor operation and . multiplication. There is nothing sacred about this numbering; in principle, any would do. Let σ^* be the number assigned the symbol σ. The next stage exploits the prime number sequence. A (natural) number is prime if it is divisible only by itself and 1. Let p_i be the ith prime in increasing order of magnitude; thus $p_1 = 2$, $p_2 = 3$, $p_3 = 5$, etc. A formula A in **L** is a finite concatenation $\sigma_1 \sigma_2 \ldots, \sigma_n$ of symbols from the list above and A is assigned a Gödel number $A^* = 2^{g_1}.3^{g_2}.\ldots.p_n^{g_n}$, where $g_i = \sigma_i^*$.

Finally, Gödel numbers are assigned to *proofs* from PA. Proofs rendered in a linear deductive system like **H** in Chapter 10 are particularly easy to Gödel number, for they are finite sequences of formulas A_1, A_2, ..., A_n and the same prime number coding as was used to assign numbers to formulas can also assign such sequences code numbers, namely $2^{g_1}.\ldots.3^{g_2}.\ldots.p_n^{g_n}$, where $g_i = A_i^*$. Tree proofs are slightly more complicated to Gödel number.

The coding by Gödel numbers of formulas and proofs is *effective*, in the sense that, given the formulas and proofs, their numbers are mechanically computable. The inverse operation is also effective: given any natural number, it is a mechanical procedure to determine whether it is the number of a formula or proof and if so to construct the formula or proof of which it is a number. This can easily be seen for the prime number coding above. A theorem of Euclid tells us that every natural number can be represented in just one way as a product of powers of prime numbers and there is a well-known algorithm for finding what the powers are for any given natural number. Not every number encodes a sequence of symbols (for example, 25 does not – why not?), but it will be apparent which do and which do not and if any number does, which sequence of symbols it codes for and whether that sequence is a formula or proof and if so which (relative to the numbering scheme above, the exponent of 2 in the code of a formula is even; in that of a linear proof it is odd).

Recall that for any natural number k the numeral for k in $\mathbf{L}_{PA}$ is the expression s(s(s(...s(0) ..))) with k occurrences of s, or $s_k(0)$ for short. Call an n-place relation R between natural numbers *arithmetically definable* if there is a formula $A_R(x_1, ..., x_n)$ of that language such that $R(k_1, ..., k_n)$ is true for numbers $k_1, ..., k_n$ if and only if $A_R(s_{k_1}(0), ..., s_{k_n}(0))$ is true in the natural numbers; informally, R is arithmetically definable if it can be defined in terms of the identity relation and the arithmetical operations of successor, sum and product. The condition for a *property* or predicate of natural numbers to be arithmetically definable is obtained by setting n = 1 in the definition above. It is possible to show, and intermediate mathematical logic texts like Mendelson 1987 do so, that the condition for a string of primitive symbols to be a formula of $\mathbf{L}_{PA}$ translates into a corresponding arithmetically definable condition that a number must satisfy if it is to be a code of a formula of $\mathbf{L}_{PA}$. Indeed, all the metalinguistic predicate and relations used to describe the syntactic structure of a first-order language and its deductive system, like 'the variable with number m occurs free in the formula with Gödel number n', 'n is the Gödel number of a sentence of $\mathbf{L}_{PA}$', 'm is the Gödel number of one of Peano's axioms', 'm is the Gödel number of a proof from Peano's Axioms', etc, turn out to be arithmetically definable. It follows that these predicates can be expressed as formulas of $\mathbf{L}_{PA}$. Thus relative to the Gödel numbering used, each sentence of the metalanguage which states some syntactic property of first-order Peano Arithmetic will be true or false just in case the corresponding arithmetical sentence is true or false: *in other words L_{PA} can indirectly discuss its own syntactic or formal structure, including relations of provability.*

Indeed, Gödel was able to show that a sentence G of $\mathbf{L}_{PA}$ could be constructed which is true if and only if G is not provable from Peano's

Axioms. G is constructed in the following way. Where k is the Gödel number of a formula $A(x)$ of $\mathbf{L}_{PA}$ of PA, define the function d(k) to be equal to the Gödel number of the result of substituting the numeral $s_k(0)$ for k in $A(x)$. Where k is not the number of such a formula, d(k) is given some conventional value, like 0. Gödel showed that the functional relation d(m) = n is arithmetically definable by a formula $A_d(x, y)$. Let $Pr(x)$ be the formula of $\mathbf{L}_{PA}$ which defines the property 'is the Gödel number of a formula provable from Peano's Axioms'. Now consider the formula $\forall y(A_d(x, y) \rightarrow \neg Pr(y))$; it says in $\mathbf{L}_{PA}$ that whatever sentence d(x) is the number of, and there is at most one, that sentence is not provable from PA. Suppose it has Gödel number m. Let G be the sentence

$\forall y(A_d(s_m(0), y) \rightarrow \neg Pr(y))$.

The Gödel number G^* of G is therefore equal to d(m), so that G *'says' in $\mathbf{L}_{PA}$ that the sentence whose Gödel number is d(m), i.e. G, is unprovable from PA.*

Gödel demonstrated that if the Peano Axioms are consistent then G is not a logical consequence of them and that if they possess a slightly stronger type of consistency neither is $\neg G$ (*Gödel's First Incompleteness Theorem*). Rigorous proofs of these results are beyond the scope of this book, but the following informal argument due to Kleene (1952, 204–5) explains why *no* arithmetically definable set of axioms for arithmetic has as logical consequences all and only true sentences. Suppose K were such a set. Note that in the light of the Completeness Theorem for first-order logic a sentence is a consequence of K just in case it is provable from K. Suppose in G the formula $Pr(x)$ now refers to provability from K. If G is provable from K then it is not true, in view of its construction. Hence if G is true it is not provable. If it is false then it is not provable either, given the assumption that no false sentence is a consequence of K. Hence G cannot be provable from K. Hence G is true. And there will always be such a true sentence of arithmetic which is not provable from K, however much K may be extended by adding true sentences (but not *all* true sentences; a theorem we shall discuss later, due to Tarski, shows that the property of being the Gödel number of a sentence of $\mathbf{L}_{PA}$ true in the natural numbers is not arithmetically definable).

That a set of first-order axioms is consistent is another metalinguistic predicate that is arithmetically definable. For example, since $\neg(0 = s(0))$ is a consequence of the first-order Peano Axioms, 'the first-order Peano Axioms are consistent' can be expressed by the sentence $\neg Pr(s_q(0))$, where q is the Gödel number of 0 = s(0) (why?). $\neg Pr(s_q(0)) \rightarrow G$ is thus an arithmetical translation of the metatheorem 'If the Peano Axioms are consistent then G is unprovable from PA' and it is itself a consequence of the first-order Peano Axioms. Thus if $\neg Pr(s_q(0))$ were itself provable from those axioms, so too would be G. But G is not provable if the axioms are consistent; hence we infer (*Gödel's Second Incompleteness Theorem*) that *if the Peano Axioms are consistent, there is no proof of their consistency from those axioms themselves*; stronger assumptions are required.

Now back to second-order logic. It is not difficult to extend the Gödel numbering of the language of first-order Peano Arithmetic to the corresponding second-order language. Suppose that there is an extension of the first-order machinery of deduction (for example of tree rules, or **H** or **ND** rules, or any other) for second-order sentences. It does not really matter for the subsequent discussion what this might look like, though we should want it to underwrite as logical truths second-order sentences like $\forall X A \rightarrow A(P/X)$ where P is a predicate constant and

$$\exists X^n \forall x_1, \ldots, \forall x_n (X^n(x_1, \ldots, x_n) \leftrightarrow A(x_1, \ldots, x_n))$$

for every formula $A(x_1, \ldots, x_n)$ of the second-order language. We should also want it to be *sound* and in addition such that any proof within that system should in principle be machine-checkable. Let the notation $\Sigma \vdash_2 A$ signify that A is provable within such a second-order proof system from assumptions Σ.

It is possible to show that there will be a sentence G' (in fact, a *first-order sentence*) constructible in just the same way as G, which is true in the natural numbers if and only if it is not the case that $PA_2 \vdash_2 G'$, where as before PA_2 stands for the set of second-order Peano Axioms. Define a set of axioms to be *syntactically consistent* if there is no formula A such that both A and $\neg A$ are formally provable from those axioms (the Completeness property of first-order truth trees, or of **H** or **ND**, implies that first-order logic syntactical consistency and consistency in the semantic sense of having a model coincide: the reader should show this as an exercise). The argument showing that G is not provable if the first-order Peano Axioms are syntactically consistent now goes through for the second-order case in the following form: if PA_2 is syntactically consistent then it is not the case that $PA_2 \vdash_2 G'$.

Despite Gödel's second Incompleteness Theorem, it is taken for granted that the Peano Axioms, first- and second-order, *are* syntactically consistent because they are assumed to be true in their respective '*standard models*', i.e. the first- and second-order interpretations whose domain of individuals is N. If the axioms were inconsistent it would arguably imply that we have no coherent conception of the natural numbers at all and none of the reasoning above would make sense. So we can suppose that G and G' are both true in their standard models. We observed earlier that all the models of PA_2 are isomorphic and that no formalised sentence is capable of distinguishing between isomorphic structures: i.e. if such a sentence is true in one of them it is true in all. It follows that every model of PA_2 is a model of G'. *This means that G' is a logical consequence of PA_2, though by Gödel's First Incompleteness Theorem no proof of it from those axioms exists.*

However, this might seem an unwarranted conclusion – haven't we just proved that G' is a logical consequence of PA_2? In fact, we have proved in the metatheory of Peano Arithmetic that G' is true in the standard model of PA_2. But that metaproof is a proof from the assumption that the so-called standard model of those axioms is actually a model of them, which implies that they are syntactically consistent. Just as in the first-order case a closed formula of the second-order language, call it $Con(PA_2)$, can be constructed which, decoded, asserts that PA_2 is syntactically consistent and a proof exists from PA_2 of the conditional $Con(PA_2) \rightarrow G'$, giving a second-order version of the second Incompleteness Theorem. It follows that the assumption, no matter how plausible it might be, that PA_2 is syntactically consistent is actually stronger than PA_2 itself. So we have not proved G' from PA_2.

The careful reader might now point out that the argument from the First Incompleteness Theorem to the conclusion that there is no proof of G' from PA_2 likewise depends on the assumption that PA_2 is consistent. This is true, but there are alternative ways of deriving the result that do not depend on that assumption (see Grandy 1977: 119, for example). To sum up: however we extend the deductive machinery of first-order logic to encompass what we believe to be sound principles of second-order inference, it will never be complete (nor will it be compact either). This defect is extremely important in the light of what seems to be one of the most important goals, if for a long time an unconscious one, in the development of the discipline of formal logic: *the mechanisation of reasoning*. Ever since Aristotle and the Stoics substituted letters for predicates and whole sentences respectively and classified formal patterns of valid inferences, the impetus has been to removing reasoning from the domain of the intuitive to that of the mechanical. That there should be second-order inferences for which in principle there are not machine-checkable proofs means that second-order logic fails to meet an extremely important criterion that is satisfied by first-order logic.

There is another reason, of a more philosophical nature, why people feel on firmer ground with first-order logic. For second-order logic has what might be called non-trivial mathematical content. The Continuum Hypothesis, which we encountered in section 2 above, says that there is no set whose cardinality lies strictly between that of the natural numbers and that of the continuum of real numbers – hence the name 'Continuum Hypothesis'. Deciding, if that is possible, whether the Continuum Hypothesis is true has always been regarded as a specifically mathematical problem; yet in a suitable second-order language it is possible to construct a sentence C equivalent to the Continuum Hypothesis and such that if the Continuum Hypothesis is true then C is a logical truth of second-order logic and if it is false then C is a logical falsehood. The existence of C is a consequence of the fact that the structures of the natural numbers and of the real numbers can each be defined up to isomorphism in second-order logic, as can the relation 'cardinally less than' (see Etchemendy 1990: 123; Etchemendy's book is a stimulating though I believe mistaken attack on the 'standard' theory of logical consequence, that is to say the one developed in the earlier chapters of this book).

In other words, even at the second-order level the distinction between truths of mathematics and truths of logic is blurred, to say the least. Yet it is a tenet of late twentieth-century philosophical faith that mathematics is not empty of some sort of factual content – though no one is clear what this is, or how precisely to characterise it – and therefore is quite distinct from logic, which allegedly has none. To sum up: the restriction to first-order logic has its costs, but it also has demonstrable and valuable advantages. To most people, the benefits outweigh the costs of invoking higher order logic. Indeed, to most people a self-styled logic lacking a complete deductive base is not genuinely a logic at all.

6 THE LIAR PARADOX

The technique of Gödel numbering shows that part at any rate of the metalanguage of the first- or second-order language of arithmetic can be translated via that number-coding into the object-language itself. 'There is a formula in $\mathbf{L}_{PA}$ which contains two occurrences of the connective $\rightarrow$' is a metalinguistic assertion (because it talks *about* that language and the expressions in it), for example, but it is equivalent, given the particular Gödel numbering adopted, to a purely arithmetical assertion $\exists x A(x)$ in that same language. So, for someone equipped with the coding, $\exists x A(x)$ can be interpreted both as an ordinary object-language sentence about natural numbers and as a metalinguistic statement. In other words, at the symbolic or extensional level one and the same language may function in different roles.

But it is possible for these roles to get mixed up, rather like the characters in a Pirandello or Stoppard play who are simultaneously outside and inside the play. We are already familiar with this in the logical context, because it is precisely such a mixing of roles that arithmetical sentences can play and which is exploited in Gödel's Incompleteness Theorems. This confusion of levels might seem like a dangerous game to play, however, and, as if in confirmation, we have the ancient *Liar Paradox*. This proceeds from considering the self-referential sentence 'This sentence is not true.' If it is true then it seems to follow that it is not true (since that is what it asserts), while equally if it is not true then it equally seems to follow that it is true. Hence it is true if and only if it is not true, which is a truth-functional contradiction. Yet self-reference is not the cause of the problem. The Gödel sentence G, when decoded, asserts that it is not provable from Peano's Axioms, and is therefore also self-referential, even if obliquely. But instead of issuing in a contradiction, G is exploited to prove a very deep result. Why is the so-called Liar sentence productive of inconsistency and G not?

Attempts to provide a satisfactory answer to this question constitute a major contemporary logico-philosophical industry (consulting Barwise and Etchemendy 1987, Martin 1984 and McGee 1990 will give the reader some idea of the vast amount of work done in this area). What has become known as the 'orthodox' view, attributed to Tarski (his 1931 paper, reprinted in English in Tarski 1956 as 'The Concept of Truth in Formalised Languages', was seminal), is that ascriptions of truth are *essentially* metalinguistic and cannot be consistently self-applied as attempted in the Liar sentence. Backing up this claim is a metatheorem, called *Tarski's Theorem on the Definability of Truth*, proved by Tarski at about the same time as Gödel proved his Incompleteness Theorems. This theorem (of which a proof can be found in Mendelson 1987: 169) says that the extension of 'truth-for-L', for any but a very impoverished language **L**, is not definable by a formula of **L** via any coding of the formulas of **L** by members of the domain of the intended interpretation of **L** (the coding does not have to be arithmetical). The theorem is proved by reasoning closely parallel to that of the Liar Paradox itself, by supposing there to be a formula $B(x)$ which defines the set of codes of sentences of **L** true in that interpretation, constructing a corresponding Liar sentence within **L** and using the reasoning of the Liar Paradox to conclude by reductio that no such formula $B(x)$ exists in **L**.

Tarski's and Gödel's work seems, therefore, to explain why paradox arises when we attempt to construct a sentence asserting its own falsity, but not when we construct one asserting its own unprovability. Though both truth and provability are metalinguistic predicates, the latter is definable in a sufficiently rich object-language (Gödel), while the former is not (Tarski); the Liar Paradox is merely a reductio of the assumption of what is called *semantic closure*: that a language may contain its own truth-predicate. The natural inference from this conclusion is that when we talk about truth and falsity, we can do so consistently only if the sentences whose truth is discussed are assumed to be in some distinct object-language; thus any sentence asserting its own falsity is meaningless because it attempts to be simultaneously meta- and object-linguistic.

Call this the *Metalinguistic Theory of Truth*, or the Metalinguistic Theory for short. The fact that a natural language like English seems to contain its own truth-predicate and use it sensibly in many cases is explained according to this theory by the fact that it is possible to consistently model many of the *properties* of truth within a first-order language **L** containing names of its own sentences (directly or indirectly via a Gödel numbering), a predicate symbol T ('is true') and, *for suitably restricted* sentences **A**, biconditionals of the form T('A')↔A, where 'A' is a name of the sentence A in **L**. But such biconditionals amount only to a *partial* interpretation of truth in the object-language; in particular, no such biconditionals can be consistently postulated for any sentence A which asserts that this is not true, as the Liar Paradox shows.

Does the metalinguistic theory yield a good enough model of our ordinary truth-talk? One simple and now celebrated example, due to Kripke, seems to show that it does not. A little dated now, Kripke's example is an imaginary exchange between two of the protagonists of the 1974 Watergate scandal, the then US President Richard Nixon and one of his White House staff, John Dean (I have changed some details of Kripke's example). Suppose Dean said 'Everything Nixon says about Watergate is false' and that Nixon said 'Everything Dean says about Watergate is false'. Since each's statement is in the scope of the other's universal quantifier, they cannot fit into an object-/metalanguage hierarchy of the sort proposed by the Metalinguistic Theory and one or both dismissed as meaningless. But just suppose that Dean were to have said at some point 'Watergate is Watergate' and that at some point Nixon had said 'Watergate is in the US' (a willing suspension of disbelief is in order here). Both these last two statements are true, from which it ought to follow that Nixon's and Dean's initially quoted statements are not only meaningful but in fact unambiguously false.

But how are we to square such examples with Tarski's Theorem? Well, one of the assumptions of Tarski's Theorem is *bivalence*, the principle that for any sentence A, either A is true or A is false ($\neg A$ is true). This suggests an alternative explanation of the Liar Paradox, as a reductio not of the existence of an object-language truth-predicate, but instead of the assumption of uniform bivalence. In the 1970s there were two developments of a theory of truth for a non-bivalent but otherwise standard first-order language **L** containing among other extralogical vocabulary a predicate Tr whose intended interpretation is 'is true' as applied to the sentences of **L** itself. These two accounts, one due to Martin and Woodruff (1975), the other to Kripke (1975), assume that

(i) the domain D of the intended interpretation of **L** contains as a subdomain either the set of sentences of **L**, or codes of them like their Gödel numbers. (ii) **L** contains a sentence L which in its intended interpretation says of itself that it is not true. If D contains sentences explicitly then L can be taken to be the sentence $\neg\text{Tr}(a)$, where a is a constant of **L** which in D denotes $\neg\text{Tr}(a)$. If **L** is the language of first-order Peano Arithmetic, then L can be constructed analogously to the Gödel sentence G for first-order Peano Arithmetic.

(iii) the truth table for negation is:

A	$\neg A$
T	F
F	T
u	u

where u is to be read simply as 'neither T nor F'. Three-valued truth tables for the other connectives are given, which together with that above are called the Strong Kleene tables (Kleene 1952: 334–5).

Suppose that 'A' is a name in **L** of the sentence A. Where D contains sentences, 'A' can be a constant of **L**, as above. Where A has to be referred to by a Gödel number, say, then we can let 'A' be the numeral for that number. Two subsets A_T and A_F of D can be constructed (their construction is the centrepiece of both Kripke's and Martin and Woodruff's papers, though the pairs of sets are not identical in both cases) such that A_T and A_F are disjoint, i.e. they have no member in common and

(1) In the intended interpretation, call it $\mathfrak{I}_0$, of **L**, Tr is assigned as its denotation not a single subset of D but a *pair* (A_T, A_F), which Kripke called the *extension* and *anti-extension* respectively of Tr. Tr('A') is true if 'A' is in A_T and false if 'A' is in A_F.

(2) A_T contains all and only the sentences, or codes of sentences, true in $\mathfrak{I}_0$ and A_F contains the set of all sentences false in $\mathfrak{I}_0$ (and possibly also the non-sentences in D).

(3) There are sentences, or sentence-codes, in neither A_T or A_F. In particular, none of L, $\neg L$, Tr('L') and $\neg$Tr('L') is in either A_T nor A_F. They have no truth-value in the conventional sense (they take the value u).

(4) The truth-value (T, F or u) of any sentence A in $\mathfrak{I}_0$ is the same as the truth-value of Tr('A'). However, the biconditional $A \leftrightarrow$Tr('A') does not always take the truth-value T; it takes the value u when A takes the value u. Hence the biconditional $L \leftrightarrow$Tr('L') takes the value u; it is not a contradiction and the Liar Paradox is avoided.

Kripke's construction attracted the attention of philosophers because in it membership of A_T and A_F is completely determined by the truth-values of the sentences of **L** which do not themselves contain any occurrence of the predicate Tr. The truth-values of sentences, therefore, which do contain occurrences of Tr are *grounded* (Kripke's term) in the truth-values of purely object-language sentences (one has to be careful with this terminology, because **L** is itself an object-language). Because of this feature his construction was held to satisfy an important criterion, namely that sentences with multiple embeddings of 'it is true that . . .' are true or false depending only on the facts about the primary domain, of ordinary objects, numbers, space-time points, or whatever.

Though this approach shows that there is a systematic and consistent alternative to the Metalinguistic Theory, it has been subjected to some severe criticism. The most serious objection proceeds as follows. The 'Liar sentence' L has no truth-value. Hence the following sentence seems to be true: 'The Liar sentence is not true.' But the sentence of **L** asserting that the Liar sentence is not true is, of course, the Liar sentence itself, which is not true! Hence Kripke's theory appears to suffer from the same defect as that with which he charged the Metalinguistic Theory, namely that examples of intuitively valid reasoning are not valid within it.

The obvious – but as we shall see incorrect – reply is that $\neg$ as defined by the truth table above does not express the sense of negation in 'The

Liar sentence is not true'; the sense expressed by ¬ is not mere absence of truth but definite falsity. What is allegedly needed to express that other sense, of simply not being true as opposed to being false, is the following notion of negation, called *exclusion negation*, which to distinguish it from ¬ we shall write as ~:

A	~A
T	F
F	T
u	T

Thus ~Tr('A') is true if Tr('A') takes the value u. But unfortunately for this proposal, the addition of ~ to the logical vocabulary of **L** prevents the construction of a separate extension and anti-extension for Tr containing respectively all the truths and falsehoods of the extended language. Consider a sentence B of the form ~Tr('B') (sometimes called a 'Strengthened Liar' sentence; 'B' is a constant directly denoting ~Tr('B') but essentially the same argument goes through for a Gödel-type construction) and suppose there were a disjoint extension/anti-extension for Tr. B must be in one or another, since B is ~Tr('B') and the truth table for ~ shows that ~Tr('B') must take the value T or F. But B cannot be in the extension of T, for then Tr('B') would be true and ~Tr('B'), i.e. B, would be false and hence in the anti-extension. B cannot be in the anti-extension either, for if it were, B, i.e. ~Tr('B'), would be false and Tr('B') true, which would mean that B is in the extension of Tr.

That the sentence asserting its own falsity is not true and not false in an adequate three-valued semantics is therefore not a truth of that semantics. It is on the contrary a metatheorem proved within classical, i.e. bivalent, logic. That such a metatheory has to be employed to establish the properties of a non-bivalent object theory must undermine the claim of the latter to be regarded as the correct theory of truth, particularly when the metatheory disagrees in its verdict about what is true with the object theory. For better or worse classical logic, i.e. the logical theory developed in this and other texts, is based on bivalence and much of what is regarded as standard deductive reasoning would have to be given up in a theory of deduction in which bivalence is not assumed. Whether giving up bivalence advances the search for a solution of the Liar Paradox must, in the light of all these considerations, be regarded as doubtful.

There are other proposals, quite different from the Metalinguistic Theory and that appealing to three-valued logic. One, called variously Naive Semantics or Rule-of-Revision Semantics, uses as its formal model also a language containing its own truth-predicate Tr and employs a construction in some ways similar to Kripke's to evaluate sentences involving Tr. Where it differs principally is in using classical two-valued, and not a three-valued, semantics, with the result that at every ordinal level the Liar sentence changes its truth-value. Another approach, that of Barwise and Etchemendy (1987), employs an altogether distinct way of modelling truth-bearing utterances (as what they call Austinian propositions), in which *situation* parameters and a non-standard type of set theory are involved essentially. There is no opportunity here to review all these candidates and for further discussion the reader is invited to consult the references given. For what it is worth, my opinion is that the Metalinguistic Theory is, despite Kripke's examples, still the least problematic overall.

Chapter 12

Beyond the fringe

1 COUNTERFACTUAL CONDITIONALS

In the first chapter we said that we would construct a formal model of deductive reasoning. The result was first-order logic. The ambition of every model-builder is that their model should be as accurate a representation of the reality modelled as possible. There are, however, types of deductive reasoning that do not seem well modelled, if modelled at all, by first-order logic. One is *modal* reasoning, that is to say reasoning involving the modalities *necessarily* and *possibly*. The other has already had attention drawn to it, in Chapter 1: this is reasoning involving so-called *counterfactual conditionals*, i.e. conditional sentences whose grammatical structure indicates that the antecedent is false. This grammatical structure is typically manifested in the use of the subjunctive mood for the verbs involved, as, for example, in 'Had A been the case, so would B have been.' In this chapter we shall briefly review attempts to extend the apparatus of first-order logic to accommodate counterfactuals. We shall adopt Lewis's notation, symbolising the counterfactual with antecedent A and consequent B as $A\square\!\!\rightarrow B$. Since any formal language for counterfactuals is obtained simply by adding the new connective to the truth-functional ones, we can regard the language as propositional and A, B, etc. as sentence letters.

That counterfactual conditionals make up a distinct species of conditional sentence in ordinary language is now doubted by practically no-one and for good reason: 'If Oswald did not kill Kennedy then someone else did' is clearly not equivalent to the counterfactual 'If Oswald had not killed Kennedy then someone else would have.' Among the analyses which have been proposed for counterfactuals, probably the most widely accepted are the '*possible worlds*' accounts of Stalnaker (1968) and Lewis (1973), though Stalnaker considered his theory as a theory of conditionals generally, not just counterfactuals.

The fundamental thesis of both their theories is that a counterfactual conditional $A\square\!\!\rightarrow B$ is true or not depending on whether B is *actually* true or not in certain 'possible worlds' in which A is *actually* true. Stalnaker proposed his theory first, and Lewis's can be seen as a modification of Stalnaker's account to accommodate certain difficulties arising within it and which we shall discuss shortly. The informal idea underlying Stalnaker's theory goes back to the English mathematician-economist-philosopher F. P. Ramsey and is sometimes called *Ramsey's Test.* Suppose the set of all truths about this world is changed in as minimal a way as possible to be consistent with the truth of A and A is added to that stock of information. If the truth of B is a consequence of this augmented set of truths, then A□→B is true. Stalnaker's version of the Ramsey Test analyses the idea of a minimal change in a set of sentences in terms of a *selection function* picking out a single 'world' in which A is true and which otherwise differs minimally from this one, or more generally, from any given reference world. For Stalnaker, A□→B is true at world w if in the world selected as being most like w in which A is true, B is also true.

A consequence of Stalnaker's analysis is that for every consistent pair of sentences A, B, *exactly one* of A□→B, A□→¬B is true at any world w. For if A is consistent, a unique world among those that make it true is always selected as the most like this one and in that world B will be true or false. Consider, however, the pair of statements 'If Bizet and Verdi had been compatriots, they would both have been Italian', and 'If Bizet and Verdi had been compatriots, they would both have been French.' There seems no good reason for supposing that among worlds in which both men were compatriots, one in which they are both French is any more like this world than one in which both are Italian.

To accommodate this and similar problematic examples Lewis proposed the following variant analysis: A□→B is true at a world w if no world which makes A true and B false is at least as close to w as any world in which both A and B are true. Thus in Lewis's theory (A□→B)v (A□→¬B) is not a logical truth, since it is possible that for every world in which A and B are true, there is a closer one in which A is true and B false and for every world in which A is true and B false, there is a closer one in which both A and B are true. In Lewis's theory, 'If Bizet and Verdi had been compatriots they would both have been Italian' and 'If Bizet and Verdi had been compatriots they would both have been French' seem both to be false; given the symmetry of the two sentences, then however close to this world are worlds in which both composers are compatriots, there will presumably be one in which they are both French and one in which they are both Italian and so for neither sentence are Lewis's truth-conditions satisfied.

Despite their different explications of the Ramsey Test, Stalnaker's and Lewis's theories generate logics of counterfactual conditionals with a substantial common content. The three inference patterns below, for example, would all be valid were $\Box\!\!\rightarrow$ to be replaced by $\rightarrow$, but are all invalid for both Lewis and Stalnaker conditionals:

(i) $\dfrac{A\Box\!\!\rightarrow B \\ B\Box\!\!\rightarrow C}{A\Box\!\!\rightarrow C}$

(ii) $\dfrac{A\Box\!\!\rightarrow B}{\neg B\Box\!\!\rightarrow\neg A}$

(iii) $\dfrac{A\Box\!\!\rightarrow B}{(A\wedge C)\Box\!\!\rightarrow B}$

It is not difficult to see why these inference patterns fail to be valid in those theories. Let us look in particular at Lewis's, in which $A\Box\!\!\rightarrow B$ is true (in our world) if and only if, if there is some world in which A is true, then all worlds in which A is true and B false are more unlike this world than some world in which both A and B are true. The 'Lewis diagram' of Figure 2 shows how (i) can fail on this interpretation. The circles represent contours of equi-similarity with respect to the world w, larger radii corresponding to smaller degrees of similarity to w.

It is clear from Figure 2 that (i) fails through having the antecedent A of $A\Box\!\!\rightarrow B$ true only in 'remoter' worlds than those in which the antecedent B of $B\Box\!\!\rightarrow C$ is true. The following is an example of this type, in which the two premises are apparently true, while the conclusion could easily be false:

Were I Dutch I would be able to speak Dutch fluently.
Were I able to speak Dutch fluently I would be bilingual in English and Dutch.
Therefore were I Dutch I would be bilingual in English and Dutch.

Simple diagrams of the type in Figure 2 also show how to construct counterexamples to (ii) and (iii) (Lewis 1973: 31–6).

Whether one regards the situations portrayed in these diagrams as truly counterexamples to (i)–(iii) will depend on whether or not one accepts the Lewis–Stalnaker type of analysis of counterfactuals, in which it is legitimate to consider the truth-values of different premises in different worlds. Some do not accept it. The inference above is invalid in the Lewis–Stalnaker scheme precisely because one is allowed to vary the 'reference world' in which the antecedent is true from premise to premise: the 'I' in the first premise is Dutch whereas the 'I' in the second is a native English-speaker. But once it is conceded that this is a legitimate ploy, it can plausibly be argued that the intended sense of the second premise should be made explicit by conjoining a sentence equivalent to 'I am a native English-speaker' to its antecedent. This done, the consequent of the first premise is no longer the same as the antecedent of the second and the inference ceases to look like a counterexample to transitivity.

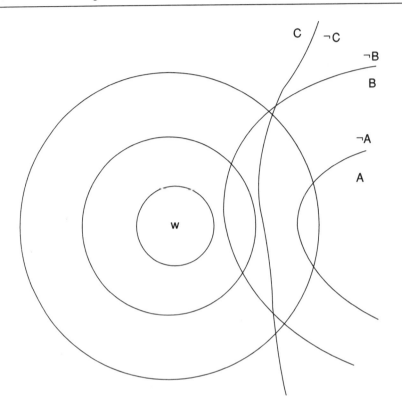

Figure 2

An objection of this type is brought against the Lewis–Stalnaker approach by Lowe (1983), who argues that counterfactuals do obey the transitivity condition. There has also been powerful criticism of the Lewis–Stalnaker machinery of possible worlds and similarity relations between them. While there may be no need to view the possible worlds as other than a formal device (this is most people's view of the way they are employed, though Lewis himself does not take this view of them), what decides the truth-values of counterfactuals is the similarity relation. But how is a possible world to be assessed as more, less or equally similar to another? Things are similar in different ways and from different points of view. Yet to concede that the choice of similarity relation is necessarily subjectively based would be an implicit confession that no objective truth-values attach to counterfactuals.

Nevertheless, some counterfactuals do seem to possess objective truth-values. For example, there seems very good reason to believe it true that had I dropped this pen in free fall it would have fallen to the floor in approximate obedience to Galileo's law s = $1/2gt^2$ (s is distance travelled, t is time elapsed and g is the gravitational constant). The reason we believe that claim to be true is that the conditional 'If this pen is dropped at t_0 [the time at which I uttered the counterfactual] it will approximately obey the Galilean law' is a consequence of a scientific theory which is accepted as true. Thus, where the counterfactuals correspond in this way to predictive consequences of accepted laws, then there seems to be a case for regarding them as true if the laws are true, since if the laws are true then so must be their consequences also. In view of the apparent arbitrariness attending the possible worlds semantics for counterfactuals, why not then simply renounce it and all other formal semantics for counterfactuals and let their truth, where they are plausibly regarded as true, be derivative from that of laws in the way suggested by the account above?

This account, which is quite close to Ramsey's own, thus makes the truth of counterfactuals depend on derivability relations of ordinary conditionals from laws. It might be objected, indeed it has been objected, that invoking laws to settle truth-claims for counterfactuals merely replaces one obscure notion – counterfactuals – by another, laws. It could even be argued that such an account begs the question – for what is a law but something that entails counterfactuals? However, there is a different way of regarding laws. This is to regard them as true universally quantified factual sentences, which are also capable of being inductively confirmed and disconfirmed by empirical data; that is to say, such data can furnish inconclusive but none the less good reason to suppose them true or false.

That laws differ from non-laws in this way does seem to be how most practising scientists view them. Do not, by the way, confuse inductive support and the sort of inductive reasoning which issues in judgments of inductive support, with the reasoning by induction which we were using earlier in this book. They are quite distinct things, having in common only – and confusingly – the title 'induction'. The latter is a principle which is used as a premise in deductive metalogical reasoning. About the nature of the former there is still some controversy, though traditionally it has been held that evidence supports a hypothesis if it increases the probability that the hypothesis is true. Further elaboration of this idea is beyond the scope of this book; more information can be gained from a good elementary philosophy of science text and I hope I can be forgiven for recommending one of which I am an author (Howson and Urbach 1993). Note that on this reading of true counterfactuals, as conditional consequences of laws, all the principles (i)–(iii) above, of transitivity, contraposition and strengthening of the premises respectively, are valid.

2   MODAL PROPOSITIONAL LOGIC

Some people dislike any appeal to 'possible worlds' at all; and the strongly realist view of them advocated by Lewis himself is uncongenial to many. However, against this it must be conceded that the apparatus of 'possible worlds' has turned out to be fruitful if only as a conceptual tool and nowhere is this more true than where it was introduced, by Saul Kripke (1963), in the analysis of *modal propositional logic*.

Modal propositional logic is the attempt, initiated by C. I. Lewis, to introduce the two modalities 'necessarily' and 'possibly' *within* suitably expanded propositional languages, as additional one-place operators on sentences. In standard first-order logic the modalities 'necessarily' and 'possibly' are identified with the respective *metalinguistic* predicates is *logically true*, or true in all interpretations, and *is consistent*, or true in some interpretation. By 'bringing down' the modalities into the object-language itself Lewis inaugurated what has since become a branch of formal logic in its own right, within which a whole spectrum of distinct notions of necessity and possibility have been investigated.

In the standard symbolism of modal logic, □A ('box A') is read as 'necessarily A' and ◊A as 'possibly A' and the class of *modal propositional languages* is obtained by simply adding these new logical operators, called the modal operators, to the truth-functional connectives in the standard propositional language (Chapter 3, section 1). Actually, only one need be adjoined, since ◊A can be defined as ¬□¬A and □A can be defined by ¬◊¬A; it is usual to take □ as primitive. An object-language implication operator (which Lewis called 'strict implication') > can even be defined in terms of the operator □ thus: A>B = □(A→B). An alternative way of developing modal propositional logic is to take such an operator > as primitive and define □ and hence ◊, in terms of it as follows: □A = T>A, where **T** is a tautology.

Lewis proposed several inequivalent modal deductive systems, characterised, like **H** in Chapter 10, by sets of logical axioms and rules of inference and classified as S1–S5, but provided little if any independent semantic underpinning for them. The situation was changed dramatically in the fifties and sixties by Kripke, who provided a uniform semantic framework in terms of which it is possible to prove the completeness of various modal systems with respect to different interpretations of the modal operators within that framework. The heuristic motivation for this so-called Kripke semantics was Leibniz's view that this world is merely one among a host of other possible worlds and that a statement is necessary if it is true in all possible worlds. Kripke's innovation was to consider possible worlds as purely formal objects in the domain of a binary relation R called an *accessibility relation*, and he showed that by imposing stronger or weaker constraints placed on R, different classes of interpretation are obtained with respect to which familiar modal deductive systems can be shown to be sound and complete.

We shall limit the discussion to modal propositional logic, since most of the interesting recent work done in modal logic is located there. Where R is an accessibility relation on a set W of worlds and L the modal propositional language generated from some set of sentence letters, the pair (W, R) is called a *frame* for L. An *interpretation* v in a frame F assigns a truth-value, for each world w in W, to every sentence X in L. First v assigns a truth-value to every sentence letter; write this as $v(A, w) = T$ or F as the case may be. The truth-functional connectives are evaluated in the usual way: $v(\neg X, w) = T$ if and only if $v(X, w) = F$; $v(X \lor Y, w) = T$ if and only if $v(X, w) = T$ or $v(Y, w) = T$, etc. For $X = \Box Y$, $v(X, w) = T$ if and only if $v(Y, w') = T$ for all w' such that $R(w, w')$; informally, X is true in w if and only if Y is true in every world w' accessible from w. An interpretation v in F is said to be a *model* in F of X if $v(X, w) = T$ for all w in W. X is said to be *valid* in F if all interpretations in F are models in F of X.

The sentences valid in all frames in which R is reflexive constitute the modal system T. The sentences valid in all interpretations in which R is transitive and reflexive are those of Lewis's S4. The sentences valid in all interpretations in which R is reflexive, transitive and symmetric, i.e. an equivalence relation, are those of S5. Each of these systems has an equivalent syntactical characterisation: as **H**-style formalisations, these various sets of sentences are those derivable from suitably chosen logical axioms by means of two rules of inference, *modus ponens* and *Necessitation*: if A is derivable, so is $\Box A$. T's logical axioms are all instances of $\Box(A \rightarrow B) \rightarrow (\Box A \rightarrow \Box B)$ and $\Box A \rightarrow A$. S4's are those of R plus $\Box A \rightarrow \Box\Box A$. S5's are those of S4 plus $\Diamond A \rightarrow \Box\Diamond A$. For further information about traditional modal logic the reader should consult a good introductory text, like that of Chellas 1980, or Hughes and Cresswell 1972 (who also discuss so-called *quantified modal logic*, the extension of the modal operators to predicate languages).

Anyone wishing to keep logic metaphysics-free might cast a wary eye on Kripke's semantics for modal logic. One response is that sets of possible worlds with weaker and stronger accessibility relations on them are probably best looked on as algebraical structures which furnish a useful mathematical tool for investigating the relation between different modal systems. If this were the end of the story modal logic might by now have ceased to be of much interest to logicians. In fact, interest in it has never been keener, inspired by the fact that various interesting formal deductive systems can be interpreted in an illuminating way in a suitable modal system and vice versa (an *interpretation of one formal system in another* is a translation-function f which maps sentences of the language of the first system into the sentences of that of the second, in such a way that the theorems of the first system are translated into sentences of the second).

For example, Intuitionistic logic is interpretable in S4, the translation exploiting the fact that Kripke models for Intuitionistic logic are closely related to S4 frames. Now Intuitionistic logic is allegedly a logic of constructive provability, which suggests that one way of regarding necessity is as provability from principles themselves regarded as a priori necessary. A fruitful way of exploring this idea is suggested by the following facts (in what follows, 'A' will be the numeral in PA for the Gödel number of A): (i) the provability predicate for the first-order Peano Axioms is definable in the language $\mathbf{L}_{PA}$ of first-order Peano Arithmetic by a formula $Pr(x)$ (Chapter 11, section 5); (ii) first-order Peano Arithmetic seems to be a prime candidate for the status of an a priori necessary body of knowledge; (iii) if A is provable (from PA) so is $Pr('A')$, mimicking the modal rule of Necessitation; and (iv) if $Pr('A{\rightarrow}B')$ and $Pr('A')$ are provable so is $Pr('B')$, mimicking the fact that if $\square(A{\rightarrow}B)$ and $\square A$ are modal theorems so is $\square B$. (i)–(iv) suggest that a substantial part of basic modal logic is interpretable in PA, with the formula $Pr(x)$ in $\mathbf{L}_{PA}$ interpreting the modal box. Some of the very deep results about the structure of provability obtained from the study of this interpretation are collected and clearly explained in Boolos (1993; this work also contains an excellent and very lucid account of the Gödel Incompleteness Theorems).

But there are theorems of all the standard modal systems that do not translate into theorems of PA, for there are sentences A such that $Pr('A'){\rightarrow}A$ is not a theorem of PA. It is not difficult to show why this is so (the result is originally due to Montague (1963)). First, some background. A famous earlier result of Gödel (known as *Gödel's Diagonal Lemma*) is that for any formula $F(x)$ of $\mathbf{L}_{PA}$ there is a sentence B such that $Pr('B'){\leftrightarrow}B$ is provable from PA (we take $\leftrightarrow$ to be defined in the usual way). In particular, $\neg Pr('G'){\leftrightarrow}G$ is a consequence of PA where G is the 'undecidable' sentence of Chapter 11, section 5. A theorem of Löb (Boolos 1993: 56) says that if $Pr('A'){\rightarrow}A$ is a consequence of PA, for any sentence A, then so is A. Löb's Theorem and Gödel's First Incompleteness Theorem jointly imply that if PA is consistent then $Pr('G'){\rightarrow}G$ is not provable from PA. Suppose, however, we add that sentence and indeed all instances of $Pr('A'){\rightarrow}A$ to PA, since for every sentence letter A, $\square A{\rightarrow}A$ is a valid sentence in every traditional modal system and rightly so if necessity means anything familiar at all. Call the result of making all these additions the system M. M is now easily shown to be inconsistent. For by truth-functional logic $\neg Pr('G')$ is a consequence of $Pr('G'){\rightarrow}G$ and $\neg Pr('G'){\leftrightarrow}G$. So is G. Hence G is provable in M and so by (iii) above $Pr('G')$ is provable in M. Hence M is inconsistent.

This startling result shows that for any language $\mathbf{L}$ for which necessity is a predicate of sentences of $\mathbf{L}$, it cannot be one in which (a) is defined by a formula of **L**, (b) renders all the consequences of first-order Peano Arithmetic necessary truths and (c) satisfies all the most basic modal principles. It is tempting to regard this result as showing that assigning necessity the role of object-language operator, as traditional modal logic does, simply obscures the fact that it is essentially metalinguistic, like truth according to the Metalinguistic Theory. But this conclusion would be premature. Montague's result does not demonstrate that there is not some sense or senses of necessity which can be expressed in a suitable object-language. Kripke's semantics shows that there is. There are also more intuitive senses of necessity, like the sort of physical necessity which laws of nature are alleged to possess, for example, in which it is not true that the laws of arithmetic, even if true, are necessary and there have been explicitly modal accounts of physical necessity. There have even been modal interpretations of counterfactuals (Lowe 1983).

3   INDICATIVE CONDITIONALS AND →

It has been conceded that the truth-functional → does not in general provide a good interpretation of counterfactual conditionals (at the same time, however, it seems at least open to doubt whether any definite truth-claims are made by counterfactuals, except when they can be interpreted as the conditional predictions made by scientific laws). A more radical objection to the truth-functional → is that it does not adequately represent even the non-subjunctive, or *indicative*, conditionals used in ordinary speech.

Those who believe it does not employ a battery of informal examples which, they claim, are counterexamples to any formalisation using →. The following are a representative sample from the literature. I hope that by the end of their discussion it will be apparent that they are not counter-examples to →.

(i) Suppose A is the sentence 'I add sugar to my coffee', B is 'It [my coffee] will taste sweet' and C is 'I add diesel to my coffee.' Here we seem to have a counterexample to the inference 'If A then B.' Therefore, if (A and C) then B', which is deductively valid if the conditional is represented by the truth-functional →. Hence, we are asked to conclude, → does not represent the ordinary English conditional.

Answer   It is quite extraordinary that this could ever have been regarded as a serious objection, yet it certainly has been. At any rate, it is no counterexample, merely a failure to be explicit. 'If I add sugar to my coffee it will taste sweet' is accepted as true only because 'and I add nothing else' is tacitly added to the antecedent. What is really being asserted is a statement of the form 'If A and D then B.' The inference is therefore one of the form 'If A and D then B. Therefore if A and not-D then B', which is truth-functionally invalid ('I add diesel' we can represent, at least for the purposes of the discussion, as being the negation of D).

(ii) 'If it rains then it won't rain heavily. Therefore if it rains heavily then it won't rain.' The premise may be true, but the conclusion seems rather obviously false, contradicting the claim that all inferences of the form 'If A then B. Therefore if not-B then not-A' are deductively valid – as they are, of course, when formalised using the truth-functional arrow →.

Answer   This is slightly, but only slightly, an advance on the previous example. 'If it doesn't rain then it won't rain heavily' is something we will presumably accept as a necessary truth (the discussion of adverbial constructions, in Chapter 5, shows that when formalised in first-order logic it is a logical truth). From this and the original premise, 'If it rains then it won't rain heavily', we can infer unconditionally, by a step that seems valid enough (the Rule of Dilemma: 'If A implies B and the negation of A also implies B, then B'), that it won't rain heavily. From 'It won't rain heavily' we infer 'If it rains heavily then it won't rain' by Absurdity (Chapter 10, section 3) and →-introduction (Chapter 10, section 3).

There are people who will reject the answer to (ii) because they reject the Rule of Absurdity. Yet Absurdity seems completely justified by the provisional definition of deductive validity in the first chapter: clearly, if a premise cannot be true then a fortiori it cannot be true and any conclusion false.

However, the inference 'Not-A, therefore if A then B' which it supports has been questioned for the following reason:

(iii) Suppose A is 'A Democrat will be the next US President', and B is 'The next US President will permit racial segregation' (this is similar to an example in Edgington 1991: 180). The problem here is that it seems that we can rationally accept 'Not-A' as true (depending on the state of the opinion polls) and no less rationally reject 'If A then B.' However, a basic principle of probability theory asserts that the probability of the conclusion of a deductively valid inference is at least as great as that of the conjunction of the premises (Howson and Urbach 1993: 25). As we know, A→B is a truth-functional consequence of ¬A, so if we model the English conditional by →, then, if we accept 'Not-A' as more probable than not, we are bound to accept 'If A then B' as more probable than not. But, in this example, 'If A then B' *seems* almost certainly false, quite independently of the probability of 'Not-A', which in the appropriate circumstances might be regarded as probably true. Surely these judgments are not really inconsistent? But if they are not, then it follows that we cannot model the English conditional by →.

Answer We shall argue that while 'If a Democrat will be the next US President then they will permit racial segregation' *seems* obviously false, the grounds for judging that it is false do not on analysis support that conclusion. Further discussion will be postponed until after consideration of the next, related, example.

(iv) Here is a well-known but too-easy proof of God's existence. The sole premise is 'It isn't true that if God exists then we are free to do as we like', which seems to be true. But 'God exists' is a truth-functional consequence of that premise if the latter is formalised as a negated truth-functional conditional $\neg(A{\rightarrow}B)$. Yet nobody in their right mind would believe this inference to God's existence to be really valid.

Answer to (iii) and (iv) The crucial issue in both these last two examples is whether the relevant factual data are properly expressed by asserting the falsity of an English conditional (or equivalently the truth of its negation): in the first example, of the conditional 'If a Democrat will be the next US President then they will permit racial segregation' and in the second, 'If God exists then we are free to do as we like.'

Consider the second first. We presumably feel that our available evidence, as presented in sacred literature and/or the theologians' interpretation of it, indicates that God's existing would be *incompatible* with our freedom to do as we please; i.e. in conjunction with that evidence, 'God exists' implies the falsity of 'We are free to do as we please.' But then what we have grounds for believing true is not the negated conditional 'It is not the case that if God exists we are free to do as we please', but the very different *conditional* 'If God exists we are not free to do as we please'; only from the latter is there a clear implication that we are not free to do as we please if God really does exist. Similarly, in (iii), what our evidence directly supports is not the negated conditional 'It is not the case that if a Democrat will be the next US President then the next US President will reintroduce racial segregation', but the conditional 'If a Democrat is the next US President then the next US President will *not* permit racial segregation.'

In other words, what the evidence directly supports in each case is a conditional of the form 'If A then not-B.' Nor do there seem to be any further grounds for asserting 'It is not the case that if A then B.' 'It is not the case that if A then B' certainly does not follow deductively from 'If A then not-B' when 'If ... then –' is rendered by the truth-functional arrow, nor is there any compelling reason to think it should on any wider consideration. One reading which does make that inference valid is a Lewis–Stalnaker one, in which the conditional is parsed in the same way as either of their counterfactuals. However, even were the Lewis–Stalnaker approach acceptable (and there is one counterfactual that resists their treatment), which it is not if the earlier discussion of it is sound, the conditionals in these examples are not counterfactuals, nor does there seem any good reason why they should be treated as such.

It might be objected that in ordinary English we readily make the inference from 'If A then not-B' to 'It is not the case that if A then B.' The objection to accepting this, even if it were true, which is doubtful, is not only that there appears to be no justification for such an inference, but that to adopt it as a rule would lead to incoherence, as the following example shows. Let $A = B = \neg(0 = 0)$. 'If $\neg(0 = 0)$ then $0 = 0$' seems to be something which, when thought through, is acceptable to anybody who accepts the ordinary theory of identity and the Absurdity Rule. If they also accept contraposition then they should accept 'If $\neg(0 = 0)$ then $\neg\neg(0 = 0)$', i.e. 'If A then $\neg$B.' But they would almost certainly not accept as true 'It is not the case that if A then B', since that is the same sentence as 'It is not the case that if A then A.'

The lesson from this is, I believe, that what we accept and reject in the way of rules should not be based on consideration of an isolated example, but should instead be a decision constrained by more global considerations of how well it contributes to an overall consistent and acceptable *theory*. But this is to acknowledge the authority of *methodological* criteria and in particular two widely accepted as constraints on scientific theorising of any sort, *generality* and *coherence*. The earlier chapters have shown that many intuitively valid inferences involving conditionals can be successfully analysed using the purely truth-functional →. In the light of this and the previous discussion, it may well be (I actually believe it to be) that the truth-functional conditional is overall the best coherent model of inferences involving indicative conditionals and that where our intuitions conflict with its deliverances those intuitions may simply not offer the best, or even good, guidance. There is nothing bizarre about this suggestion: intuitions are frequently, if reluctantly, ignored in the face of a coherent theory which says that they are wrong. Intuitions about probability, for example, can be notoriously at odds with the *theory* of probability (a wealth of empirical studies shows just how divergent intuitions are from the theory), yet the broad consensus is that the latter is the sounder judge of what is correct. I suggest, tentatively, that the same is true in the present case and that the advantages which flow from the truth-functional account will eventually be seen to outweigh contrary intuitions.

It should be said that the foregoing discussion of the relation between ordinary-language conditionals and the truth-functional → is heavily coloured by the author's own views (though these have a certain amount in common with the theory of assertibility conditions for conditionals due to Grice and Jackson (Jackson 1991). There has been much debate of this topic and the reader is strongly encouraged to examine alternative accounts. Fortunately, there are two excellent anthologies, by Harper, Stalnaker and Pearce (1981) and by Jackson (1991), as well as a recent survey article by Edgington (1995). Sainsbury (1991) contains a thorough and clear discussion, as does Read (1994).

4   CONCLUSION

First-order logic has, I believe, a good claim to be regarded as the formal model for an invariant and substantial core of informal deductive reasoning. Its fit is not everywhere perfect, but considering the largely unregulated manner in which human language and reasoning have developed and the variety of purposes to which they are put, a perfect fit is hardly to be expected.

Almost every year, however, brings further claims that first-order logic is 'dead'. One of the most recent is Devlin's (1991), as a preamble to presenting his own theory of logic as a sort of very general theory of information-processing. One of the alleged deficiencies is the familiar problem of conditionals and I have argued that on inspection this does *not* issue in a general condemnation of the truth-functional →. Devlin's second objection is more fundamental: it is to show that the whole idea of necessary *truth-preservation* from premises to conclusion is misconceived. His example is the inference

(*)   Jon walked into the restaurant.
        He saw that the waitress had dirty hands.
        So Jon left immediately.

This, he claims, would be declared valid by any ordinary person untutored in classical logic, because it is an example of a type of reasoning that ordinary people habitually engage in. Clearly, it is not valid in first-order logic.

Indeed, it is not deductively valid according to a much less formal criterion. Nobody who thought for more than a few seconds would say it was a *deduction*, for the simple and obvious reason that it is possible for Jon to enter the restaurant and see what he saw and *yet not leave*. He might know that the restaurant possessed an outstanding chef and regard the state of the waitress's hands as a price worth paying for a superior cuisine. He might have an assignation with the waitress. He might not even like cleanliness. The possibilities consistent with his not leaving are endless.

So Devlin's objection amounts to saying that there are types of reasoning that are not deductive. But we know this; we have already mentioned inductive reasoning, which is the reasoning that we perform when we predict what will happen on the basis of evidence that seems to make such predictions highly likely but not certain. And (*) is a typical example of such reasoning: it is *probable reasoning*, as the eighteenth-century British empiricist philosophers classified it. But to admit that there is probable, or inductive, reasoning is no reason to deny that there is also deductive, demonstrative reasoning. Which, of course, there is. Nor is there any need to construct a theory of general reasoning which blurs the distinction between those two types. As we have suggested above, there is already a general theory of inductive and deductive reasoning which nevertheless maintains the distinction.

Indeed, expounding first-order logic in isolation from the theory of probability is really only telling half the story, for the model of deductive reasoning provided by first-order logic interlocks with probability theory to provide a general account of both inductive and deductive reasoning. Probabilities are a natural and indeed indispensable tool in the theory of non-deductive inference, where evidence supports to a greater or lesser extent some explanatory theory, but does not entail its truth (Howson and Urbach (1993) is an introductory text for a well-known probabilistic account, called the Bayesian theory of uncertain inference). As we have seen in discussion of these examples, probabilistic considerations can be relevant in discussing the adequacy or otherwise of a deductive model and the dovetailing of the theory of probability with that model lends support to both – unfortunately, to an extent we can merely catch glimpses of in this book.

Notation

Chapter 1

¬, ∧, ∨, →, ↔, |, ↓
A, B, C, . . .
X, Y, Z, . . .
T, F
⇔

Chapter 2

$$X \wedge Y \qquad \neg(X \wedge Y) \qquad \text{etc.}$$
$$\begin{array}{ccc} | & \diagup & \diagdown \\ X & \neg X & \neg Y \end{array}$$

Chapter 3

L[S; Π], L[A, B, C, . . . ; ∧], L[A_1, . . ., A_n; ∧] etc.

Chapter 4

α, β, (α), (β), $α_1$, $α_2$, $β_1$, $β_2$

Chapter 5

∀, ∃
a, b, c
x, y, z; x_1, x_2, . . .
P, Q

Chapter 6

L
P_1, P_2
R, S; R_1, R_2, . . .
A, B, C, . . .
$A(x)$, $A(t/x)$
γ, δ, (γ), (δ), $\gamma(a)$, $\delta(a)$

Chapter 7

$\{0, 1\}$, $(0, 1)$ etc.
$\Im$
$D_\Im$, $a_\Im$, $P_\Im$, $R_\Im$

Chapter 9

$=$
R_1, R_2
f, g, h, . . .

Chapter 10

H
ND
$\perp$
$\neg$I, $\neg$E; $\wedge$I, $\wedge$E; $\rightarrow$I, $\rightarrow$E; $\vee$I, $\vee$E; $\forall$I, $\forall$E; $\exists$I, $\exists$E
AX

Chapter 11

$P(A)$
$|A|$
$\aleph_0$
X_i, Y_i, Z_i, . . .
$Pr(x)$
A^*
'A'
Tr

Chapter 12

□→
□
◊
(W, R)

Answers to selected exercises

Chapter 1

Section 4 1 False. 2 False. No.

Section 5 True.

Section 6 1

	(i)				(ii)	(iii)
B C	(B∨C)∧(C∨B)		A B C	¬(A∧¬C)∨B	¬A∧(¬C∨B)
T T	T		T T T	T	F
T F	T		T T F	T	F
F T	T		T F T	T	F
F F	F		F T T	T	T
			T F F	F	F
			F T F	T	T
			F F T	T	F
			F F F	T	T

Section 7 2 B→A

Section 8 1 If you want the answer to be 'yes' if and only if B is true, the question is 'Is ¬(A↔B) true?'
2 ↔
3 (i)　　((A∨B)∧C)→(D∧E).
　　　　　　　　C→E

　　(ii)　　(¬B→A)∧(¬C→¬B)
　　　　　　　D∧(D→¬C)
　　　　　　　　E→¬A
　　　　　　　　　¬E

4 ∧
5 A∧B; A = Untidy work will cost you marks, B = Inaccurate work will cost you marks.
6 No.

7 $(A \land B) \rightarrow (\neg C \rightarrow D)$ A = You are over 18.

B = You are married.

C = You have already received benefit.

D = Your name will go on the register.

Chapter 2

Section 2   1   (a)

X	Y	Z
T	T	F
T	F	T
F	T	T
F	F	P

$Z \Leftrightarrow (X \land \neg Y) \lor (\neg X \land Y)$

(b)

X	Y	Z
T	T	F
T	F	T
F	T	T
F	F	T

$Z \Leftrightarrow (X \land Y)$

2

X	Y	Z
T	T	F
T	F	F
F	T	F
F	F	T

$Z \Leftrightarrow \neg (X \lor Y)$

```
  /  \
 X    Y
```

Section 3   1   (i)

AvB

¬B

∴A

Tree: AvB

¬B

¬A

```
    / \
   A   B
```

(ii)   AvB

∴¬A→B

Tree: AvB

¬(¬A→B)

|

¬A

¬B

```
  / \
 A   B
```

(iii)   ¬A→B
          ∴A∨B

Tree: ¬A→B
          ¬(A∨B)
          |
          ¬A
          ¬B

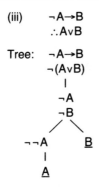

2   (i) The premise is redundant; (ii) the premises are unsatisfiable.

Section 4   3   (i)   Tautology.
          (ii)   Tautology.
          (iii) Contradiction.
          (iv)   Neither.
          (v)   Tautology.
          (vi)   Neither.
          (vii) Neither.
          (viii) Contradiction.
          (ix)   Contradiction.

Chapter 3

Section 1   1   (i)   Two: A, B.
          (ii)   Infinitely many.
          (iii) Infinitely many.
          2   No. No, it does not mean that there is no biconditional sentence in L[A, B; ∧, ∨, ¬, →], since there are sentences in L truth-functionally equivalent to A↔B.
          3   ¬A∨B⇔A→B;   ¬(A∧A)∨B⇔A→B;   ¬((A∧A)∧A)   ⇔ A→B; etc.

Section 3   (a)   A∨¬(A→(B∨C))
                    /   ╲
                  A   ¬(A→(B∨C))
                              |
                         A→(B∨C)
                          /   ╲
                        A   B∨C
                              /   ╲
                             B   C

(b)   ¬(C∨D)∧(D∧¬C)
        /   \
   ¬(C∨D)   D∧¬C
      | / \
     C∨D   D   ¬C
     / \ |
    C   D   C

(c)   A→B→¬(C→¬D))
      /   \
     A   B→¬(C→¬D)
          /   \
         B   ¬(C→¬D)
                    |
                  C→¬D
                  / \
                 C   ¬D
                       |
                       D

Section 4 1 (a)   A∧B, B∧A
                  (b)   A∧B, ¬B
                  (c)   None
                  (d)   A, B→C
                  (e)   A→(B→C)

Section 6 1 2^k
               2 (i)   (A∧B)∨(¬A∧B)∨(¬A∧¬B)
                  (ii)   (A∧B)∨(¬A∧B)∨(A∧¬B)
                  (iii) (A∧B)
                  (iv)   (A∧B)∨(¬A∧¬B)
                  (v)   (A∧B∨(¬A∧B)∨(A∧¬B)∨(¬A∧¬B)
                  (vi)   A∧B∧C
                  (vii) ¬A∧¬B

Section 7 1   A|B   ¬(A|B)
                     /   \ |
                   ¬A   ¬B   A
                                          B

                      A↓B   ¬(A↓B)
                       | /   \
                      ¬A   A   B
                      ¬B

2 The shortest are (A|A)|(B|B); (A↓A)↓(B↓B).

3 The shortest X is A|(B|B). The shortest Y is (A↓A)↓B)↓((A↓A)↓B).

4 (i)   Neither.
   (ii) Tautology.
   (iii) Contradiction.
   (iv) Neither.

5 (i)   A∨B
   (ii) (¬A∧B∧C)∨(¬A∧ ¬B∧C)∨(¬A∧B∧¬C)

6 Because | and ↓ are binary connectives and (A|B)|C is not truth-functionally equivalent to A|(B|C), and (A↓B)↓C is not truth-functionally equivalent to A↓(B↓C).

Section 9* 1 ¬A∨B.
              2 (¬A∨B)∧(A∨¬B)∧(A∨B).
              3 ¬A∨B∨C.
              4 A∨¬A.

Chapter 4

Section 2 1 (i)   β
              (ii) Neither.
              (iii) β
              (iv) Literal.
              (v)   α
              (vi) α

           2 (i)   Closed.
              (ii) Open.
              (iii) Closed.
              (iv) Open.

Section 3   1
$$A \to B$$
$$B \to C$$
$$\neg(A \to C)$$
$$|$$
$$A$$
$$\neg C$$

```
      / \
   ¬B    C̲
   / \
  ¬A̲   B̲
```

$$A \to (B \to C)$$
$$\neg((A \land B) \to C)$$
$$|$$
$$A \land B$$
$$\neg C$$
$$|$$
$$A$$
$$B$$

```
   /        \
 ¬A̲          B→C
            / \
          ¬B̲   C̲
```

2   (i)   A   (ii)   B
          ¬A   ¬(A∨¬A)
          B̲ |
                             ¬A
                             ¬¬A̲

3   (a) $(A \to B) \land (\neg C \to \neg B)$
          $\neg(\neg C \to \neg A)$
          $$|$$
          $$\neg C$$
          $$\neg\neg A$$
          $$|$$
          $$A$$
          $$|$$
          $$A \to B$$
          $$\neg C \to \neg B$$

```
        /    \
      ¬A̲       B
             /  \
          ¬¬C̲    ¬B̲
```

Hence truth-functionally valid

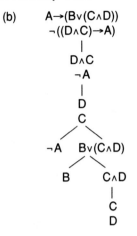

(b)　　A→(B∨(C∧D))
　　　　¬((D∧C)→A)
　　　　　　|
　　　　　D∧C
　　　　　¬A
　　　　　　|
　　　　　　D
　　　　　　C
　　　　　╱　╲
　　　¬A　　B∨(C∧D)
　　　　　　╱　╲
　　　　　B　　C∧D
　　　　　　　　|
　　　　　　　　C
　　　　　　　　D

Truth-functionally invalid. Two counterexamples:

A–F, B–T, C–T, D–T
A–F, B–F, C–T, D–T

(c)　　　　　(A∧B)→C
　　　　　(E→¬F)∧(C→(E∨F))
　　　　　¬((A∧D)→(F∨¬B))
　　　　　　　　|
　　　　　　　A∧B
　　　　　　¬(F∨¬B)
　　　　　　　　|
　　　　　　　　A
　　　　　　　　D
　　　　　　　　|
　　　　　　　¬F
　　　　　　　¬¬B
　　　　　　　　|
　　　　　　E→¬D
　　　　　　C→(E∨F)
　　　　　　╱　╲
　　　　　¬E　　¬D
　　　　　╱
　　　　¬C　　　E∨F
　　　　╱　╲　　╱　╲
　¬(A→B)　C　E　　F
　╱　╲
¬A　　¬B

4 (a) $\underline{ABC}$
       TTT
       TFT
       FTT
       TFF
       FFT
       FTF
       FFF

Chapter 5

Section 2 1 (i)   Everyone is tall.
           (ii)   Someone is broad.
           (iii) Someone is tall and broad.
           (iv)   Someone is tall and everyone is broad.
        No.

Section 3 1 (i)   True: it says that there is a pair of positive integers one of which is less than or equal to the other.
           (ii)   True: it makes the same statement as (i).
           (iii) True: it says that every positive integer is less than or equal to itself.
           (iv)   True: it says that for every positive integer there is one at least as large.
           (v)   True: it says that for every positive integer there is one no greater than it.
           (vi)   True: it says that there is a positive integer less than or equal to every positive integer.
        2 Only (i) and (ii) remain true; the remainder are false.

Section 4
        2 (i) $\exists xB(x, a)$ (or $\exists yB(y, a)$, $\exists zB(z, a)$, etc.)
           (ii $\forall x\neg S(x, a)$
           (iii) $\exists x\forall yL(x, y)$
           (iv) $\exists x\forall y\neg L(y, x)$
           (v) $\neg\exists x(B(x, x)\lor S(x, x))$
           (vi) $\exists x\forall y\neg B(y, x)$
           (vii) $\exists x\forall y(S(y, x)\rightarrow\neg O(y, x))$
           (viii) $\exists x\exists y(O(y, x)\land L(x, y))$
           (ix) $[\exists x\forall y(\exists zB(y, z)\rightarrow\neg L(x, y))]$
                  $\rightarrow [\exists x\exists y(S(x, y)\land\forall z\ L(z, x))]$
           (x) $\exists x(\forall yL(y, y)\rightarrow\neg L(x, y))$
           (xi) $\forall x\forall y(\exists zL(y, z)\rightarrow L(x, y))$

Note: There are sentences equivalent but not identical to each of (i)–(x), and if your answer to any of these is not as given above you should try to see whether it is equivalent to it.

3 (i) $\exists x(M(x) \land D(x))$

(ii) $S(a, b)$

(iii) $\exists x(R(x, b) \land T(a, x) \land \forall y(S(y, b) \rightarrow \neg T(a, y)))$

Chapter 6

Section 1 1 $\forall x \forall y(\exists z R(x, z) \rightarrow R(x, y))$, $(\exists z R(x, z) \rightarrow R(x,y))$, $(\exists z R(x, z), R(x, z))$, $R(x, y)$

2 (a) $P(x)$

(b) $P(x) \land Q(x)$

(c) $P(x) \rightarrow \exists y R(x, y)$

(d) $\exists y R(x, y)$

(e) $\exists y \forall z S(x, y, z)$

3 (i) (a) $P(a)$

(b) $P(a) \land Q(a)$

(c) $P(a) \rightarrow \exists y R(a, y)$

(d) $\exists y R(a, y)$

(e) $\exists y \forall z S(a, y, z)$

6 Closed.

Section 2 1 (a) δ

(b) δ

(c) Neither.

(d) Neither.

(e) δ

(f) Neither.

(g) Neither.

2 (a) $P(a) \land \forall y(Q(y) \rightarrow R(a, y))$

(b) $\neg(Q(a) \rightarrow R(a, a))$

(c) $\neg(Q(a) \land P(a))$

3 (δ) is misapplied at lines 5 and 6: b cannot be used to instantiate line 5, since it already appears at line 4.

4 One such domain is N, the set of natural numbers, with $R(x, y)$ interpreted as $x < y$.

Section 3

    1 (v)   ∀x∀yR(x, y)

            ¬∀y∀xR(x, y)
                  |

             ¬∀xR(a, x)
                  |

              ¬R(a, b)
                  |

              ∀yR(a, y)
                  |

               R(a, b)

    3   ¬∃xA(x)

          ¬∀x(A(x)→B(x))
                  |

           ¬(A(a)→B(a))
                  |

               A(a)
               ¬B(a)
                  |

               ¬A(a)

Chapter 7

Section 1 1 $P_3 = \varnothing$

             2 $P_3 = \varnothing$

             3 $Q_3 = D_3$

             4 (0, 0, 0), (0, 0, 1), (0, 1, 0), (1, 0, 0), (1, 1, 0), (1, 0, 1),
                (0, 1, 1), (1, 1, 1)

Section 2 1 (a) $\varnothing$

                (b) D_3

                (c) $\varnothing$

                (d) D_3

             2 (a) x; all values.

                (b) y; all values.

                (c) x; no values.

                (d) y; no values.

                (e) x and y; no joint values.

                (f) No free variable.

                (g) x and y; those joint values x', y' such that x'< y'.

                (h) x and y; all joint values.

                (i) x and y; all joint values.

Chapter 8

Section 2   4   Because some sentences with finite models generate infinite trees, for example $\forall x \exists y R(x,y)$.

Chapter 9

Section 2   1

$$\neg\forall x\forall y\forall z((x = z \land y = z)\to x = y)$$
$$|$$
$$\neg\forall y\forall z((a = z \land y = z)\to a = y)$$
$$|$$
$$\neg\forall z((a = z \land b = z)\to a = b)$$
$$|$$
$$\neg(a = c \land b = c)\to a = b)$$
$$|$$
$$a = c \land b = c$$
$$\neg(a = b)$$
$$|$$
$$a = c$$
$$b = c$$
$$|$$
$$\underline{a = b}$$

2

$$P(a) \qquad\qquad \neg P(a)$$
$$\neg\forall x(x = a\to P(x)) \qquad \forall x(x = a\to P(x))$$
$$| \qquad\qquad\qquad |$$
$$\neg(b = a\to P(b)) \qquad a = a\to P(a)$$
$$| \qquad\qquad \diagup\qquad\diagdown$$
$$b = a \qquad \neg(a = a) \qquad P(a)$$
$$\neg P(b) \qquad\qquad |$$
$$| \qquad\qquad \underline{a = a}$$
$$\underline{\neg P(a)}$$

Section 5   1 $\{1, 2, 3, 4, 5, \ldots\}$

Chapter 10

Section 2   2   (i)

$$\cfrac{A\land\neg A \qquad A\land\neg A}{\cfrac{A \qquad\qquad \neg A}{\bot}}$$

(ii)

$$\cfrac{\cfrac{\cfrac{\neg A \qquad A^X}{\bot}}{B}}{A\to B}$$

References

Barwise, J. and Etchemendy, J. 1987: *The Liar: an Essay on Truth and Circularity*, New York: Oxford University Press.

Bell, J. L. and Slomson, A. B. 1969: *Models and Ultraproducts*, Amsterdam: North Holland.

Boolos, G. 1993: *The Logic of Provability*, Cambridge: Cambridge University Press.

Chellas, B. F. 1980: *Modal Logic: an Introduction*, Cambridge: Cambridge University Press.

Church, A. 1950: 'Completeness in the Theory of Types', *Journal of Symbolic Logic*, vol. 15: 81–91.

Devlin, K. 1991: *Logic and Information*, Cambridge: Cambridge University Press.

Edgington, D. 1991: 'Do Conditionals Have Truth-Conditions?', in *Conditionals*, ed. F. Jackson, Oxford: Oxford university Press, 176–202.

— 1995 'On Conditionals', *Mind* 104: 235–329.

Etchemendy, J. 1990: *The Concept of Logical Consequence*, Cambridge, Mass.: Harvard University Press.

Fraenkel, A. A., Bar-Hillel, Y. and Levy, A. 1973: *Foundations of Set Theory*, Amsterdam: North Holland.

Galton, A. 1990: *Logic for Information Technology*, Chichester: Wiley.

Grandy, R. E. 1977: *Advanced Logic for Applications*, Dordrecht: Reidel.

Harper, W. L., Stalnaker, R. and Pearce, G. 1981: *Ifs*, Dordrecht: Reidel.

Hofstadter, D. R. 1979: *Gödel, Escher, Bach: an Eternal Golden Braid*, Hassocks: Harvester Press.

Howson, C. and Urbach, P. M. 1993: *Scientific Reasoning: the Bayesian Approach* (second edition), Chicago: Open Court.

Hughes, G. E. and Cresswell, M. J. 1972: *An Introduction to Modal Logic*, London: Routledge.

Jackson, F. 1991: *Conditionals*, Oxford: Oxford University Press.

Jeffrey, R. C. 1994: *Formal Logic: its Scope and Limits* (third edition): McGraw-Hill.

Kleene, S. C. 1952: *Introduction to Metamathematics*, Amsterdam: North Holland.

Kneale, W. C. and Kneale, M. 1962: *The Development of Logic*. Oxford: Oxford University Press.

Kripke, S. 1963: 'Semantical Analysis of Modal Logic I. Normal Modal Propositional Calculi', *Zeitschrift für mathematische Logik und Grundlagen der Mathematik* 9: 67–96.

— 1975: 'Outline of a Theory of Truth', *Journal of Philosophy* 72: 690–716.

Lewis, D. 1973: *Counterfactuals*, Cambridge: Cambridge University Press.

Lindström, P. 1966: 'First Order Logic with Generalised Quantifiers', *Theoria* 32: 187–195.

Lowe, E. J. 1983: 'A Simplification of the Logic of Conditionals', *Notre Dame Journal of Formal Logic* 24: 357–66.

McGee, V. 1990: *Truth, Vagueness and Paradox*, Indianapolis: Hackett.

Martin, R. L. 1984: *Recent Essays on Truth and the Liar Paradox*, Oxford: Oxford University Press.

Martin, R. L. and Woodruff, P. W. 1975: 'On Representing "True-in-L" in L', *Philosophia*, 5: 213–217.

Mendelson, E. 1987: *Introduction to Mathematical Logic* (third edition), Belmont: Wadsworth.

Montague, R. 1963: 'Syntactic Treatments of Modality, with Corollaries on Reflexion Principles and Finite Axiomatizability', *Acta Philosophica Fennica* 16: 153–167.

Read, S. 1994: *Thinking about Logic*, Oxford: Oxford University Press.

Reeves, S. and Clarke, M. 1990: *Logic for Computer Science*: Addison-Wesley.

Sainsbury, M. 1991: *Logical Forms*, Oxford: Blackwell.

Smullyan, R. 1968: *First Order Logic*, Berlin: Springer.

Stalnaker, R. 1968: 'A Theory of Conditionals', *Studies in Logical Theory*, ed. N. Rescher, Oxford: Blackwell.

Tarski, A. 1956: 'The Concept of Truth in Formalised Languages', *Logic, Semantics, Metamathematics*, Oxford: Oxford University Press, 152–269.

Tennant, N. W. 1978: *Natural Logic*, Edinburgh: Edinburgh University Press.

Name index

Aristotle 63, 154

Bach, J.S. xi, 189
Bar-Hillel, Y. 146, 189
Barwise, J. 156, 160, 189
Bell, J.L. 131, 189
Bernstein, F. 145
Beth, E. xi
Boolos, G. 189
Brouwer, L.E.J. 140

Cantor, G. 144
Chellas, B.F. 167, 189
Chomsky, N. 3
Church, A. i, 130, 149, 189
Clarke, M. 141, 189
Cohen, P. 145
Cressell, M.J. 167, 189

Dale, A.J. x
de Morgan, A. 40
Devlin, K. 173, 189

Edgington, D. 170, 173, 189
Escher, M. xi, 189
Etchemendy, J. 154, 156, 160, 189
Euclid 151
Euler, L. 64

Fernandez Diz-Picazo, G. x
Fraenkel, A.A. 143, 146, 189

Galton, A. 189
Gentzen, G. 139
Gibson, R. x
Gödel, K. i, xi, 142, 143, 150, 151, 152, 153, 155, 168
Grandy, R.E. 154, 189

Grice, P. 172

Harper, W.L. 172, 189
Heyting, A. 140
Hilbert, D. 132
Hintikka, J.K. 110
Hofstadter, D. xi, 189
Howson, C. 165, 170, 174, 189
Hughes, G.E. 167, 189
Hughes, R.I.G. x

Jackson, F. 172, 189
Jeffrey, R.C. xi, 189

Kleene, S.C. 152, 157, 189
Kneale, M. and W.C. 64, 189
König, J. 113
Kripké, S. i, 141, 157, 158, 159, 166, 168, 189

Leibniz, G.W. 166
Levy, A. 146, 189
Lewis, C.I. 166
Lewis, D. 161, 162, 163, 171, 189
Lindström, P. 113, 189
Lowe, E.J. 164, 169
Löwenheim, L. i, 112, 146

McGee, V. 156, 189
Martin, R.L. 156, 157, 158, 189
Mendelson, E. 139, 150, 151, 156, 189
Milne, P.M. x
Montague, R. 168, 169, 189
Morrison, M. x

Occam, William of 91

Peano, G. 128, 142, 143, 150, 151, 152

Subject index